W9-DGF-501

Blowing Up

Recent Titles in
The Psychology of Everyday Life

BLOWING UP

The Psychology of Conflict

Randi Minetor

The Psychology of Everyday Life

GREENWOOD™

An Imprint of ABC-CLIO, LLC
Santa Barbara, California • Denver, Colorado

Library of Congress Cataloging-in-Publication Data

Names: Minetor, Randi, author.
Title: Blowing up : the psychology of conflict / Randi Minetor.
Description: Santa Barbara, California : Greenwood, [2017] | Series: The psychology of everyday life | Includes bibliographical references and index.
Identifiers: LCCN 2017022678 (print) | LCCN 2017036183 (ebook) | ISBN 9781440844683 (ebook) | ISBN 9781440844676 (hardcopy : alk. paper)
Subjects: LCSH: Interpersonal conflict. | Social conflict.
Classification: LCC BF637.I48 (ebook) | LCC BF637.I48 .M565 2017 (print) | DDC 303.6—dc23
LC record available at https://lccn.loc.gov/2017022678

ISBN: 978–1–4408–4467–6
EISBN: 978–1–4408–4468–3

21 20 19 18 17   1 2 3 4 5

This book is also available as an eBook.

Greenwood
An Imprint of ABC-CLIO, LLC

ABC-CLIO, LLC
130 Cremona Drive, P.O. Box 1911
Santa Barbara, California 93116-1911
www.abc-clio.com

This book is printed on acid-free paper (∞)

Manufactured in the United States of America

For their many demonstrations of conflict in everyday life, the wide variety of examples they provided, and the wealth of experience of these that drew me to a lifelong examination of conflict at the amateur and professional levels, I dedicate this book to my late parents—who, I have no doubt, are bickering in heaven (good-naturedly, I hope) as I write this.

Contents

Series Foreword

Psychology is the science of behavior; it is the field that examines how and why people do, feel, and think the things that they do. However, in a very real way, everyone is a psychologist. Each of us observes and tries to understand the thoughts, feelings, and behaviors of people we are around, as well as trying to understand ourselves. Have you ever thought, "I wonder why she did that?" Or perhaps, "Why did I do that; it makes no sense." If you have, then you are asking psychological questions. Most people enjoy being "students of human behavior" and observing and thinking about people, human nature, and all of the variants of the human condition. The difference between "most people" and psychologists is that the psychologist has spent many years in school studying and learning about people.

In addition to studying and doing research, psychologists also work directly with people in many settings. For example, clinical and counseling psychologists work with people who are dealing with psychological disorders or are having problems in their lives that require professional assistance, but there are many other branches of psychology as well. Sport psychologists work with athletes and teams to improve performance and team functioning. Industrial/organizational psychologists help workers, managers, and organizations function more effectively and efficiently. Military psychologists deal with military personnel and organizations. Forensic psychologists work with police and other law enforcement organizations to help solve crimes and assist law enforcement personnel. In addition to all of the things that psychologists know about people, for any person, understanding psychology can help take advantage of what psychologists have learned to help all people live better and healthier lives and to deal more effectively with others.

The Psychology of Everyday Life is a series of books that will address many different and important psychological issues and areas, the goal being to provide information and examples of how psychology touches all of our lives on a daily basis. The series will also show ways in which psychological knowledge can help us. These books will address psychological concerns with the most up-to-date and relevant knowledge from the field of psychology. Information from the laboratories, classrooms, clinics, hospitals, and other settings will be brought together to help make sense out of some important and often complex ideas. However, these books will be directed toward readers who are not psychologists, but are interested in learning more about the field and what it has to offer. Thus, the language is not technical but is common language addressing "regular" people. There will be times when professional and technical language may be used, but only if thoroughly explained and related to the issues being discussed.

This series of books will focus on specific facets of our daily lives and show how psychology can help us understand and deal with these issues. A wide range of topics will be covered, from eating to exercising to relaxing to interpersonal conflict. Each book will consist of three distinct parts. Part I will answer the "who/what/where/when/why/how" questions related to the topic. These chapters will examine everything from how the subject manifests in our day-to-day lives and how it impacts our psychological well-being to differences across the lifespan and cultures to what famous psychologists have to say on the subject.

Part II in each book will focus on "real-life" examples and will address many of the issues that were introduced in each book in Part I, but will do so with examples and explanations that will make the issues even clearer. It is one thing to have knowledge, but it is an entirely different thing to be able to apply and use that knowledge, and this is what will be covered by the scenarios and interpretative analyses in Part II. When people read Part II they will begin to see many of the ways in which our daily lives are touched by psychology, and the many ways that psychology can be used to support and help people.

Part III in each book will address the controversial issues related to the book's subject. Like any academic and professional discipline, psychology has many areas where there are spirited disagreements among academics, practitioners, and researchers about important issues in the field. It will be very instructive for people to understand these issues and to see the careful and systematic ways that scholars think about and conceptualize various topics, and to see how they debate, discuss, and resolve some of their differences of opinion. For non-psychologists these controversial issues and how they are addressed will lead to a greater understanding of psychological matters, but also a better grasp of how scientists and professionals deal with differences and controversies and how these disagreements are addressed.

Psychology is a broad and diverse field with many different approaches, theories, methods, and ideas, and to capture this field in its breadth and depth would be impossible in a single book. This series of books, however, will serve as an introductory journey through psychology as it relates to the daily lives of ordinary people. I have been teaching, studying, and practicing psychology for many decades and I can hardly wait to read each of the books in this very exciting series, and I welcome readers to take this journey with me.

—Rudy Nydegger, PhD, ABPP

Preface

I think what makes people fascinating is conflict. It's drama; it's the human condition.
Nobody wants to watch perfection.

—Nicholas Cage

It has been said that the only things in life that are inevitable are death and taxes, but I would add one more thing to this short list: conflict. Hardly a day goes by when we do not find ourselves in conflict with someone or something—whether it is a parent insisting that we fulfill a family obligation, a friend who openly disagrees with us in Facebook comments, or Congress taking a stand that we vehemently oppose. Conflict is everywhere—a natural part of our days and often a necessary method of solving problems and making progress.

That being said, people go out of their way to avoid conflict at all costs, even to the point of placing themselves in uncomfortable or unbearable situations. Many people see conflict as an evil thing—evidence that a relationship is on the rocks or that the world is about to crumble around us. The utopian ideal of living in perfect harmony seems attractive, but it is as unobtainable as a trip from Earth to Alpha Centauri. Fear of a raised voice, a contradiction of a personal belief, or an angry outburst drives some to keep their own feelings buried and hidden, lest an exasperated sigh or roll of the eyes betrays their inner feelings of frustration. They may spend hours complaining to a friend about a spouse or to a coworker about another colleague's behavior or attitudes, but they never confront the situation, clear the air, and move on. The conflict perpetuates, and eventually it ruins what might otherwise be a positive and productive relationship.

Why the fear of conflict? It is a difficult question to answer, because each individual may have a different reason for avoiding it at all costs. Some may have grown up in a volatile household in which arguments were an everyday occurrence, making such an environment seem abhorrent to them as adults. Others may have seen an attempt to resolve a conflict go horribly wrong, resulting in the end of a marriage, a termination at work, or a friend who no longer calls. Everyone can tell a story about a time when a conflict turned into a destructive argument that ended badly. The lesson these people take away from this experience is simple: "Trying to resolve a conflict is a losing proposition, so I'll never try again."

Blowing Up: The Psychology of Conflict is more than a book on a specific aspect of everyday life. This book is designed to help you understand what conflict is, how it develops, why it is so integral to our lives, and how it becomes either constructive or destructive. It contains information about the research done to date that reveals aspects of conflict that take place deliberately or automatically, and it provides examples of many different kinds of conflict, from an argument between a father and daughter to the underlying issues that cause international crises.

Throughout this book, you will see the ways in which conflict can be either negative or positive. Conflict serves many important functions in our lives, from pointing out areas in which work needs to be done to giving us an opportunity to relieve tension. It helps us make many positive changes in our personal and professional lives; it moves organizations forward, and it unites kindred spirits on one side or the other of an issue. When conflicts are resolved in a constructive manner, they can lead to strong solutions that change relationships, organizations, and societies for the better.

In addition, this book contains the points of view of a number of experts in the field of conflict analysis and resolution. Part III provides differing perspectives on such topics as gender differences in addressing conflict, methods of conflict resolution, and the challenges of mediating ongoing conflicts in geographic areas that have experienced significant disasters, whether these are natural or man-made.

Conflict not only can be loud, angry, violent, and divisive, but it also can be useful, constructive, and a part of polite, civil discourse. By studying what makes a conflict go from disagreement to argument to fighting (and even war), we can gain insights that can help us prevent most differences of opinion from turning into acts of aggression. I hope this book provides the understanding you need to resolve your next conflict peacefully, with the benefits of compromise for all parties involved.

Acknowledgments

Writing this book has been a remarkable journey, and I have a number of people to thank for the role they played in it. First and foremost, my editor, Maxine Taylor, has been a consistent source of support and guidance as we navigated this project together. I also thank the production team at ABC-CLIO for all of their fine work on this book and for the many hours I know they have spent in creating this volume in The Psychology of Everyday Life series.

Six essayists gave me their best thoughts about various aspects of conflict, and while they are all named within the book, I want to call your attention to them again here. Mike Bassow, adjunct professor of communications at Central New Mexico Community College, and Juliana Birkoff, PhD, at the Center for Collaborative Policy at California State University in Sacramento, tackled the tough question of how men and women approach conflict in different ways. Prabha Sankaranarayan, president and chief executive officer of Mediators Beyond Borders International (MBBI), and her colleague and MBBI board member, ethicist Rose-Anne Moore, looked carefully at the issues mediators must address in countries in crisis; Sandra Marker of the Conflict Information Consortium at the University of Colorado provided a counterpoint. I am indebted as well to Heidi Burgess at the Conflict Information Consortium, who coordinated the use of Ms. Marker's essay.

Cherise Hairston, MA, at the Dayton Mediation Center generously provided her views on the use of transformative mediation as a conflict resolution strategy. She came to me through the Institute for the Study of Conflict Transformation, where Janet Mueller and Lydia VanderKaay were especially helpful in making connections and keeping the project moving. As a counterpoint, Malik Thompson, a counselor and conflict resolution professional at the M. K. Gandhi Center for Nonviolence, provided their essay on the use of restorative justice in working with high school students in challenged areas. I also thank Kit Miller at the Gandhi Center and professional divorce mediator BJ Mann for suggesting that the center would be a fortuitous connection.

Finally, I am eternally grateful to my personal motivational squad, the friends and family who support all of my writing endeavors. My husband, Nic Minetor, sat through dozens of dinner-table discussions about conflict scenarios and global confrontations without objection, though I cannot imagine what effect this had on his blood pressure. My friends Ken Horowitz and Rose-Anne Moore (again), Martha and Peter Schermerhorn, and Ruth Watson and John King are always there for me. Lastly, my brother Mike Bassow, who has taught this topic for decades, gave me terrific guidance to help me start this challenging project. I hope I did you proud, Big Brother.

Part I

Conflict in Everyday Life

1

What: The Many Forms of Conflict

Why should we try to understand the nature of conflict? Whether the conflicts we study are on a scale as small as two people in a room or as large as global war, they all have the potential to change relationships—and often, not for the better. When the conflict is about opposing viewpoints that may be irreconcilable, it can bring progress to a screeching halt while the people involved look for common ground, try to find tolerable solutions, or seek to destroy the relationship.

We see couples arguing in restaurants and supermarkets, children facing bullies on the playground or in the classroom, work groups and companies that cannot seem to accomplish their objectives, religious groups clashing with one another over moral issues, the U.S. Congress locking horns across political party lines, threats over ideologies that rise to the level of international terrorism, and civil wars that end in the ousting of a dictator or the ruler crushing the rebel forces. Everyone faces conflict at some point in their lives, and we all need the skills to find our way past these roadblocks to peace and progress.

When you are in a conflict with another person, you know it. You may have a disagreement with a professor or classmate or a clash with a friend or romantic partner that moves from a casual word to a quarrel in a matter of minutes. How you got there, however, may seem like a complete mystery. It is worth stopping to analyze how you came to be in the conflict and learning the many paths you can take to resolve the conflict to your satisfaction.

Psychologists—especially those who study organizational behavior—have devoted decades of research to the nature and progression of conflicts and to the best ways to resolve them. In this chapter, we will explore a number of the useful models they have developed. While hypotheses took many researchers in different directions, there is one point on which virtually all of them agree: Conflict is a sequential, progressive process. It begins when we perceive a difference that makes us uncomfortable and builds from there until we reach a point that forces the conflict out in the open.

Let us look at some of the most enduring theories of conflict and discover the path along which most conflicts tend to travel.

THE NATURE OF CONFLICT

Psychologists consider any difference of opinion to be a conflict—whether or not it results in anger or hostility. While conflict may lead to arguments, it does not necessarily begin that way.

When two or more people find that they disagree over a matter of fact or opinion, their points of view are in conflict. This difference between them may be resolved quickly with a conversation, a simple decision, or a compromise, or it may become a greater issue, moving from a disagreement over facts to a heated discussion and from there to anger.

Conflict can arise between individuals; between groups in a place of business, a social situation, or at school; between two or more large groups like political parties or religious organizations; or between countries with different ideologies. The conflict can begin as a discussion between two people and then draw in lots of other people as they take one side or the other of an argument. When a conflict starts small and becomes much larger, this sudden growth is called escalation. This book presents many stories of conflicts that began as basic disagreements and grew to involve many people—and some that escalated into war.

We live on a planet with billions of other people, so we can assume that each person may disagree with others on a fairly regular basis. How we recognize conflict can help us manage the escalation process, giving us the tools we need to control the discussion and de-escalate the problem.

HOW WE RECOGNIZE CONFLICT

Our ability to recognize conflict comes from the way we feel. Conflict brings a range of emotions to the surface—most of which we associate with negative situations.

Let us take an example that comes up between people in all kinds of environments. You and two of your friends are planning to have lunch together. When the question arises, "Where shall we eat?" everyone has a different idea or preference. You would like to go to the new sports bar for burgers and wings, but one of your friends wants to go to a vegetarian restaurant. The third person loves Asian food and pushes hard to get the rest of you interested in this. You do not care for Asian food, and you feel that a meal should have meat—or that meat should at least be an option.

Now you have a basic difference of opinion, and the pleasant meetup you and your friends planned becomes strained. You begin to notice what you feel.

- **Discomfort**: You have a strong opinion, and your friends disagree with it and put forth their own strong opinions. You begin to suspect that your suggestion will not be chosen, and you start to feel tense and frustrated. You may feel this manifest physically through tension in your neck and back, or perhaps your shoulders are rising toward your ears.

- **Disagreement**: Perhaps someone in the group has said flat out, "I don't want to go to that loud sports bar." Your friend has made a negative judgment about your suggestion, so you now have an open disagreement—yet you may feel that you still have a chance of convincing the others of the merits of your idea. You speak more forcefully, and you start asking questions like, "Why wouldn't you want to go there? Who told you it was loud?" You can see your friend's jaw muscles clench, and his voice becomes strained.

- **Irritation**: The more your friend says against your suggestion for lunch, the more you hear your voice change, and the smile you had on your face at the beginning of the conversation is gone. Now you are irked that your friend cannot see the merits of the new place, and you are annoyed that your other friend has not joined in with you, opting for a third suggestion instead. You begin to challenge and knock down the points of their objections, using your fingers to count off all the ways they are wrong. When you look at your friends, you see furrowed brows and narrowed eyes, and their voices are louder. You are all quite irritated with one another, and the conversation is moving steadily toward an argument.

- **Anger**: You are all shouting, and you can feel the literal heat of anger as your face grows warm. You feel betrayed by your friends and angry that they have turned a pleasant outing into a volatile situation. It is no longer about the original idea to go to the sports bar—now you feel the need to convince them both of your point of view no matter where you eventually go for lunch. The discussion becomes less about the merits of any restaurant and more about personal character traits that each of you find annoying in the others. You begin to make judgments about your friends' character: "If you weren't so obsessed with staying thin and ate a sandwich once in a while, you'd be better off!" You may decide you do not want to spend any more time with these people today.

- **Inaction (freezing):** Now something strange happens. One of your friends just stops talking. She folds her arms and looks away and does not respond to anything else being said. It may seem that there is no way to know what she is thinking, but it is a good bet that she has decided that she will lose the argument, and perhaps that you and your other friend do not care what she has to say. Her withdrawal from further discussion is known as "freezing," a choice to avoid further conflict by taking no action. This can be infuriating for the other people in the argument, but it is an effective (and not always deliberate) way to end the conflict by doing nothing at all. For the sake of our example, let us say that you have miraculously decided to have lunch together despite everyone's harsh comments, and you end up going to the Asian restaurant.

- **Resentment:** The end of the argument does not necessarily end the conflict. Someone won, but anger can linger, coloring your long-term impression of your friends and their impression of you. Your vegetarian friend may feel that you did not respect her choices, and your friend who wanted Asian food may still have an issue with both of you. You may feel that your friends did not care what you thought, and you may feel hurt and unappreciated. These remaining feelings are a foundation for resentment, holding a grudge against each other beyond the outward resolution of the conflict. Essentially, the conflict has not ended; it's just been set aside for the time being.

- **Flight:** The episode may have ended another way: Instead of all three of you going to lunch, one person may have decided to abandon the other two and not go at all. He or she may have pulled out of the disagreement as soon as it escalated to an argument, choosing to avoid the fight. This urge to flee rather than face the conflict comes from the instinctive "fight-or-flight" reflex documented by psychologists and anthropologists for many generations—the automatic response to the amount of risk a person perceives within the situation. One person's response to conflict might be to double down and see the battle through to the end whatever the cost, while another may seek to avoid the conflict, running from the scene.

You can see how a minor disagreement over a mundane topic can turn into an explosive situation in very little time. Before we even realize that we are in conflict, the emotional states involved take hold and we find ourselves in an escalating situation, getting more and more angry, defensive, hurt, and resentful. When we feel these things, we lash out at the opponent all the harder, and the conflict gets worse.

THE FIVE STAGES OF CONFLICT

In 1967, psychologist Louis R. Pondy, a professor at the University of Illinois at Urbana–Champaign, developed a model of the path conflict takes within organizations. The model easily adapts to interpersonal relationships as well as to larger groups, and it has become one of the most referenced and applied theories of conflict in use today. His original model provided five steps in the path of conflict, but many organizational consultants and psychologists have added a sixth one—conflict resolution.

Pondy examined what he called the "conflict episode," the manner through which a conflict develops.

Latent Conflict

The potential is there for a conflict to develop, but no conflict has come to the surface. He identified four basic kinds of latent conflict:

1. **Competition for scarce resources**: When two or more people or groups know that they will each get a share of a limited resource—whether it is food, money, shelter, or a natural material like oil or water—this awareness places groups or people in a realistic and practical conflict. Here the individuals or groups realize that the strongest, cleverest, or most persuasive will receive the largest share, so each begins to build the case that makes them more deserving than the others. Two people clashing over who gets the last piece of pizza, two work groups at a university trying to get their fair share of supercomputer time, several divisions of a major corporation attempting to get the biggest share of the annual budget, or countries making deals with Middle Eastern powers for their share of X million barrels of oil—all of these are situations in which conflict may or may not develop.
2. **Drive for autonomy**: Individuals and groups often come into direct conflict with the authority that has power over them—whether that

authority is a government, a law enforcement official, an employer, a supervisor, or a parent. Indeed, the desire to get out from under someone else's authority is so common that it is part of the fabric of human existence. When the person or group has reached the limit of its tolerance for the body in power, conflict can erupt in the form of an argument, a demonstration, a strike, or a revolution. Every time a teenager approaches the day when he or she had enough of parental supervision, the potential exists for the situation to become a conflict. It is even part of our nation's history: In the years before the beginning of the Civil War in America, leaders in the Southern states talked a great deal about the importance of states' rights and the possible need to defend themselves against the U.S. government to keep those rights. Once the days of answering to another power show signs of coming to a conclusion, the next steps toward separation have the potential to be either amicable or difficult—and many countries have gone to war over one side's need to retain power and the other's need to sever the tie.

3. **Divergence of goals**: People and groups are very likely to have different goals—in fact, groups often form around the desire to reach a goal shared by their membership. When two or more people or groups have different goals and only one of these goals can be fulfilled, conflict may escalate as they compete to give their goal the higher priority. For example, half the students involved in a theater club at a university may want to produce "A Funny Thing Happened on the Way to the Forum," while the other half want to do "How to Succeed in Business without Really Trying." Their difference of opinion has not yet risen to the level of a conflict, but their faculty advisors see considerable potential for dispute among the students.

4. **Role conflict**: Miscommunications and disagreements about who does what in a relationship can cause friction—and if these differing points of view are not resolved, they will lead to much greater conflicts. Here is a common twenty-first-century role conflict: A married couple is startled to realize that the wife makes more money in her corporate job than her husband does as the executive director of a nonprofit organization. While the man is no longer the primary breadwinner, he continues to assume that his wife will handle all the housework and childcare. She thinks it is time for the husband to split the chores with her. This is the most basic of role conflicts, but it serves as an example of the kind of issue that will certainly become contentious before long.

Perceived Conflict

Even when there is no latent conflict, people involved in a relationship, a work group, an athletic team, or any other kind of association with others may perceive that someone else in this mix would like to undermine or thwart their progress toward a goal. Without a latent conflict, this perception may come from a misunderstanding or a misreading of a person's reaction or comment. For example, employee A may believe that employee B has taken action against him or her, or that B intends to act in a way that will weaken A's position. Simply having a conversation can be enough to straighten out this misunderstanding—but the conversation may not take place in a timely manner, or at all, if A becomes angry with B before clarifying what is really happening.

Felt Conflict

It is not a secret anymore—the parties involved know that there is a conflict between them. At this stage, the people in conflict have not yet taken any action or engaged in behaviors that demonstrate the depth of the conflict. The issue becomes personalized, however, and the people or groups feel anger and frustration. Pondy described two ways in which the conflict moves from latent to felt:

1. At least one of the people involved develops anxiety when the issue reaches a crisis point, or when outside pressure builds. Two people in conflict over a project at work, for example, may come into conflict when one drops the ball on the tasks assigned to him or her, or when he or she makes a decision without consulting the other. In a marriage, one spouse may feel that making the bed every morning is a waste of effort, while the other feels that a clean, organized household must have neatly made beds. Over the course of time, these scenarios and many others can move a conflict from latent to felt.
2. An individual's entire personality and sense of worth become involved in the conflict. One of the two spouses mentioned previously believes that disorder in the house reflects badly on the marriage or on his or her worth as a person, while the other feels that the unmade bed represents his or her relaxed approach to life. At work, one employee becomes afraid that the lax attitude of the other will reflect badly on both of them, diminishing his or her chances for promotion.

Manifest Conflict

The conflict is out in the open, and the person who feels the conflict engages the other in discussion, which may well lead to argument. The outburst requires a response from the other person, which in turn may escalate the conflict further. While most conflicts do not manifest in violence, the result can injure both parties—aggressive language, sabotage, withdrawal (the "flight" condition discussed earlier), and a lack of respect for one another's viewpoints can all turn this conflict into a long-lasting argument—perhaps with consequences that change or even end the relationship. Alternately, the mere expression and acknowledgment of the conflict can sometimes bring it to a close, as the two people—one of whom may not have been aware of the conflict until now—quietly negotiate a settlement or correct what was perceived as a slight.

Conflict Resolution

If everyone feels heard and acknowledged and the parties take steps to correct the situation, they may lay the groundwork for a quicker and less contentious conflict resolution process, allowing them to continue their relationship in a positive way. The expression of this particular conflict may open the door to getting other issues out on the table, allowing the people involved to resolve a number of things in one sitting.

Conflict Aftermath

After the parties express the conflict, it may or may not be resolved to everyone's satisfaction. Resolution is the ideal, of course, but not all people are so reasonable or willing to compromise or even to accept that they have been in the wrong. Some people in conflict may deny that a problem exists or insist on having everything their way, making them incapable of bargaining for an equitable resolution. They may find that admitting to a problem makes them feel that the blame is entirely on them—a condition some people find difficult or even impossible to accept. In these cases, the conflict may be repressed in the face of one person's resistance to its resolution, or it may continue to be a conflict for a much longer term.

PERCEPTION LEADS TO CONFLICT

Pondy's proposed nature of conflict provided a structure on which many social psychologists and researchers could build. In the 1990s, a number of theories pointed to three new classifications for conflict: task, relationship, and process conflict. These three kinds of conflict are based on the way the parties involved perceive one another's viewpoint, making perception a key variable in every conflict.

Task Conflict

People working together in groups usually take on a number of tasks that must be completed for group success. When members of the group perceive that others do not agree with their viewpoints, opinions, or ideas, the beginnings of task conflict develop. The group may engage in lively discussions to determine the course of action that will lead to the goal.

Remarkably, a number of researchers have determined that task conflict actually leads to better decision making, because the group will delve into the issue more deeply than they would if there were no difference of opinion. People or groups in task conflict may do additional research or provide background and detail to prove or disprove a point, leading to a better decision overall—and task conflict engages more members of the group in the final conclusion, so the entire group becomes functionally stronger and more committed to the solution. A wide range of researchers have discovered that task conflict can lead to increased satisfaction with group decisions, boosting the members' desire to be part of that group.

Too much task conflict, however, can tear a group apart. A 1999 study by Randall S. Peterson found that haggling over tasks frustrated team members when the group required consensus decision making. In building consensus, every team member must have a voice in the proceedings so that every decision is unanimous. This means that one dissenting member of the group can hold the entire decision-making process hostage by refusing to go along with the group opinion. This kind of task conflict can signal the end of productive work as a unit and a need to rethink the management strategy.

Relationship Conflict

Whether in a work group, on a team, or in a friendship or marriage between two people, relationship conflict takes place on an emotional level. At least one person involved in the relationship perceives that he or she is incompatible with the others—and small annoyances and tension may blow up into a real argument. Decades of research have revealed that relationship conflict has a negative effect on group interactions, as you might imagine. The group has little choice but to focus on the two (or more) people who are unhappy with each other, limiting the time and energy the other participants have to complete assigned tasks or move toward goals. As team members see their goals become subsumed under relationship issues, the conflict increases stress for everyone—and anxiety may prevent the group from developing solutions. In the worst scenarios, the group members in conflict begin to spread their anger and resentment around to other people in the group, creating an atmosphere of animosity toward everyone. They may even believe, rightly or wrongly, that the other group members have taken sides with or against them—and what seems like paranoia from the outside becomes a seriously dysfunctional group, one that can no longer work toward accomplishing the task.

Researchers have determined that most groups have both task and relationship conflict—but many groups pull through and complete their tasks, often with a high degree of success. The ability to succeed may be linked directly to the ability to resolve relationship conflicts or set them aside long enough to complete the task. Some couples or groups may find ways to do this, whether they work together as a whole to bring the conflict to an end or at least to make it tolerable, while other groups will bog down, becoming unable to move forward as long as the relationship conflicts remain unresolvable.

Process Conflict

When people disagree about assignments, responsibilities, and how to complete the work, they are in process conflict. Some process conflict can help move a project along, because it stimulates discussion and helps bring issues to the surface before they stymie progress altogether. Too much, however, and group members begin to lose motivation. Jealousy, resentment about being passed over for a desired assignment, and dissatisfaction with the group and the job as a whole can happen as a result of process conflict.

Jessica Katz Jameson provided an additional dimension to the classifications of conflict in her work in 1999. She proposed three further definitions of conflict, based on the target issue:

- Content conflict involves a disagreement about an idea, whether it involves an entire religious ideology or something as basic as the way bathroom towels should be folded.
- Relational conflict, like Karen A. Jehn's relationship conflict, refers to issues of personality between people or groups.
- Organizational conflict involves people versus their employer, a corporation, a government entity, or any other group that has authority over them.

These classifications can be useful in advancing our analysis of a specific conflict in progress.

Now that we have an understanding of the basic structures of conflict, we can use these in examining the way conflict develops within a number of kinds of relationships.

INTERPERSONAL CONFLICT

The definitions of interpersonal conflict are as diverse as the people who have them, as each researcher has a specific goal in exploring the topic. The common thread through most of them is this: a situation in which an individual or a group frustrates another person's (or group's) effort to reach a goal is an interpersonal conflict.

This definition seems limiting, as some conflicts are not associated directly with goals but instead involve issues of personality and point of view. Cupach, Canary, and Spitzberg (2009) propose four kinds of conflict between individuals and groups:

- **Interpersonal conflict as pervasive**: Conflict can come to the surface in any situation, and no specific behavior must be present for the conflict to exist. People disagree with one another in all kinds of ways and using all kinds of behaviors, from the most overt (yelling or punching) to the least obvious (refusing to speak or ignoring the other person). Any kind of interaction may produce a conflict—one person may have no idea he or she is in conflict with another, because the other has not revealed his or her frustration. Sillars and Weisberg (1987) noted that conflict can contain an "element of surprise," because one person who had no intention of offending or inconveniencing the other may have done so without his or her own knowledge. Cupach et al. (2009) noted, "Conflicts cannot be separated from the experience of everyday living; they potentially occur in every interaction we have."
- **Interpersonal conflict as explicit disagreement**: When people disagree with each other, they have a conflict, whether or not they have an emotional response to the disagreement. Some linguists have attempted to pin interpersonal conflict to a pattern of speech, and behavioral psychologists and sociologists look at strategies for behavior that appear when people are in conflict. In the end, modern research suggests that conflict can be expressed verbally in many different ways, some of which do not involve words spoken in anger, raised voices, or hurtful slurs. As long as there is a disagreement, there is conflict—and the rest is up to the individuals involved.

- **Interpersonal conflict as a hostile episode**: No one wants a conflict to continue indefinitely, as prolonged conflict can destroy relationships. Viewing the conflict as an episode—an event with a beginning, middle, and end—gives the conflict a place in time and space, usually based on when the individuals involved began to feel the tension and aggravation caused by the conflict and when these feelings came to a head. This perception does not necessarily shorten the conflict, however. Many interpersonal conflicts continue for days, months, years, and even significant parts of a person's lifetime.
- **Interpersonal conflict as disagreement in particular episodes**: This approach combines elements of the three already listed, defining conflict as expressed outwardly, in episodes in which it is clear to all parties involved that the conflict has come to some kind of climax. Such episodes can happen repeatedly over the course of a conflict, but the fact that they occur makes it clear that everyone involved knows there is a conflict and that they are all participants. The disagreement is explicit; the situation involves feelings and expressions of anger and hostility, and the issue becomes part of the consciousness of all the people involved.

A number of researchers, including Cupach et al. (2009), have added the concept of interdependence as a key factor in interpersonal conflict. When two people depend on one another for some aspects of their lives—whether they provide each other with payment for work, basic necessities of life (food, clothing, shelter), companionship, the skills required to meet a goal, partnership in times of war, or any number of other things—they have the power to affect one another's outcomes. Interdependence requires them to work together to achieve their goals.

Braiker and Kelly (1979) looked carefully at conflicts that arise from interdependent relationships and broke them down into three levels:

- Level 1 includes conflicts that result from specific behaviors. People can come into conflict over which way the toilet paper roll should go, how often to walk the dog, or what radio station to play in the office. This level also includes any behavior that one person in the relationship finds annoying, such as how loudly a coworker talks on the phone or how much time a teenager spends texting.
- Level 2 conflict results from the coordination of norms and roles in a relationship. Two people or groups may have differences of opinion over who does what—for example, which spouse does the laundry, which should pay for the groceries, and how the couple handles the family's

money matters. In groups, conflict may arise over which work group does the creative work and which does the mundane office work, or whether the sales force or the research team should have more authority over product decisions. These issues have to do with power, commitment to a relationship or a goal (or both), and mutual respect—some of the most central issues between people who work or live together. When trust is broken through infidelity, betraying a confidence, or lying, for example, the conflict can become irreconcilable.

- Level 3 conflict deals with personal characteristics and attitudes. A clash of personalities, a disagreement over religious or political beliefs, or a difference in work styles can start as an annoyance, but these things can simmer beneath the surface and boil over in an argument. In most cases, a heated discussion or a fight would not change the beliefs or attitudes, so such issues can end relationships.

In many cases, these three levels combine in the course of a conflict. Let us take an example.

Mary and Pete are a recently married couple, and they are finding their roles within the marriage. After dinner one night, they begin to discuss who should do the dishes.

Level 1: Conflict over Specific Behavior

Mary: I cooked dinner, so would you do the dishes? I think when one of us cooks, the other should clean up.

Pete: But you made a big meal with a lot of pots and pans. You made the mess, so you should clean it up. I wouldn't try to stick you with cleaning up after me if I made that big a mess.

Level 2: Coordination of Norms and Roles

Mary: But I do most of the cooking. What do you think—that because I'm a woman, I should do all the cooking and cleaning?

Pete: No, I don't think that, and you know it. I think that if you cook, you should clean up, and if I cook, I should clean up. I would never leave a big mess like that and then expect you to clean it up.

Level 3: Personal Characteristics and Attitudes

Mary: So I made you a nice dinner, and you think I made a mess? That's a lousy thing to say to me after I gave up my Sunday afternoon to work so hard in the kitchen.

Pete: Now you're just being a martyr. That was your choice—I didn't ask you to do that. I don't need you to make big, fancy meals for me. And I really don't need the guilt trip from you, as if I made you spend the day cooking!

If you have ever been in an argument, you know that conflicts between two or more people can be influenced by the way you remember a conversation or situation versus the way the other person remembers it. This difference—often a pronounced one—is known as actual versus perceived conflict. Deutsch (1973) explored this and found that the memory of a conversation deteriorates over time, often becoming vague within an hour of having it. You can see how this natural, normal memory loss can turn a casual conversation into a contentious issue.

For example, let us take two friends having lunch together. Jenny is pregnant, while Donna does not have children and has no plans to have any. Jenny makes an offhanded comment about which car seat to buy for her baby, and Donna agrees with her on the merits of one over the other. Jenny, with a laugh, says, "Oh, I appreciate you trying to understand this, but you really can't unless you have children of your own."

Jenny thought she was making a joke, but the comment jars Donna. Later, the more she thinks about it, the more certain she is that Jenny meant (or even said), "You don't want children, so you can't understand me." Donna believes that Jenny implied that her lack of children makes her a lesser or bad person. Jenny did not mean any offense, but Donna perceives that she did. The next time Donna sees Jenny, she arrives ready to argue about how motherhood does not make Jenny superior or herself inferior and that Jenny had a lot of nerve telling her off the way she did.

Jenny, not expecting this onslaught of anger at all, apologizes immediately for offending Donna. Donna is angry enough that she continues to defend and explain her point of view even though the perceived slight has been resolved. Jenny, becoming defensive, finally finds herself admitting that she does think a little less of Donna because she does not have children. Jenny tells Donna, "I've been worried about how my having a child would affect our friendship, and now I know." Donna's perceived conflict has turned into an actual conflict, because Jenny's casual comment has been revealed as a real issue.

As you can see in this example, knowing what the actual conflict is— the revelation that Jenny really does think that it is odd that Donna does not want children—will not necessarily lead to an effective and amicable resolution. Donna perceived a conflict, perhaps through her defensiveness of her own decision not to have children. When she confronted Jenny, the perceived conflict was resolved with an apology, but Donna's persistence in hammering her point home led to an actual conflict, one that may become a wedge in her continued relationship with Jenny.

In subsequent chapters, we will look at the many forms of interpersonal conflict throughout the life cycle and the ways conflict can affect a person's life both positively and negatively.

INTRAGROUP CONFLICT

When two or more members of the same group or team come into conflict with one another, this is known as intragroup conflict. This is different from intergroup conflict, which takes place between two or more groups.

Just about every organization in the world, from social groups to multinational corporations, requires people to work together in groups—and within these work groups, conflicts often arise between people over work styles, approaches to a problem, methods used to move toward a goal, levels of responsibility for getting the work done, and a wide range of other issues. Some conflicts come from personality issues that do not directly affect work toward the goal, but that become obstacles to the group's ability to work together and depend on one another.

Issues within work groups can affect the growth and success of the entire organization, so the psychology of intragroup conflict has produced an enormous body of research. At the same time, management consultants and organizational behavior specialists outside of the field of psychology have proposed a number of methods for dealing with intragroup conflict.

Earlier in this chapter, we discussed the differences between task conflict and relationship conflict, considered the two leading kinds of conflict in intragroup situations. Further research has shown that intragroup conflict can have a serious effect on the group's ability to achieve its goals. Evans and Crumbaugh (1966) determined that interpersonal attacks limit group-level performance and productivity, and they have a negative effect on personal performance within the group. People within a group can experience uneasiness and frustration when they dislike the others in their group or when they feel the other members dislike them. This can result in people withdrawing from the situation—for example, showing up for group meetings but sitting in silence and not contributing.

Perhaps it seems obvious that when group members have issues with one another and anger develops between them, they work less effectively—but research also proves this point (Argyris 1962; Braiker and Kelley 1979). A person who is angry, or one who is making others angry, can lose perspective about the task at hand, reducing the person's ability to perform well.

Threats and anxiety that come from relationship conflict also inhibit the group member's ability to process complex information, making such conflicts counterproductive on many levels.

As noted earlier, when members of the group have relationship issues, much of the group's work time and energy goes into resolving the interpersonal issue instead of working on the task at hand. Productivity gets stymied, even if the group chooses to ignore the relationship issue—the problem disrupts progress whether or not the group elects to acknowledge or attempt to solve it. In the same vein, anger and frustration between two or more group members can affect communication throughout the entire group (Baron 1991).

Jehn (1995) took this a step further in her research. She hypothesized that the more relationship conflict group members perceive, the lower their satisfaction with the group experience and the less likelihood that they will remain in the group. Her work produced the intragroup conflict scale (ICS), which provides an empirical way to determine how relationship conflict will affect group outcomes. Eight items in this scale measured the presence of conflict:

1. Friction between members of the group
2. Evident personality conflicts
3. Tension among members of the group
4. Emotional conflict among members of the group
5. Frequency of disagreements
6. Conflicts about ideas
7. Conflict about the work the group does
8. Differences of opinion

Jehn had participants in the study provide their opinions of the level of each of these conflicts in their groups, using a scale of 1 to 7 for responses, with 1 being none at all and 7 being extreme. She found that the more relationship conflict group members perceive, the less satisfaction they find in the group experience. Remarkably, her data showed no correlation between the amount of friction between some group members and their performance, even when group members described raised voices and profanity, people crying, slamming doors, or pouting through meetings. While these conflicts cause stress among group members—whether or not they are involved in the actual battles themselves—they continue to perform their work responsibilities at their accustomed level.

What does affect performance, Jehn discovered, is interdependence: when group members must depend on one another to get their individual jobs done. The potential for relationship conflict increases when one group member perceives that another is not doing his or her job. The friction that results can have a negative effect on both members' performance.

Most interesting were Jehn's discoveries about the type of tasks groups perform and the task's effect on the entire group's performance. Groups working on routine tasks found that disagreements hindered their ability to function, as suggestions only frustrated group members who wanted to do "what we've always done." On the other hand, groups performing nonroutine tasks often benefited from disagreements and the new ideas that came from open discussion, even when the discussion became heated. These conflicts led to "critical evaluation of problems and decision options, a process crucial to the performance of non-routine tasks."

INTERGROUP CONFLICT

Groups often have to work with one another to accomplish a common goal, and these working relationships can have negative consequences. When two or more groups clash over tasks, goals, property, ideologies, or a wide range of other issues, they are in intergroup conflict.

Members of a group develop a sense of group identity—the similarities or shared goals that hold a group of people together. This identification with a group can happen on a small scale, such as a sports team, work group, or social club, or on a regional, national, or even global level. For example, the hostilities between police and minority residents in East St. Louis, Missouri, in 2014 are a clear case of intergroup conflict, as is the movement that created Occupy Wall Street in 2011—separating "the ninety-nine percent" of working-class people from the "one percent," the wealthiest people in America.

As far back as 1906, psychologists have observed a phenomenon in which people perceive their own group, whatever it may be, as the ingroup—a group that is somehow superior to all others. The other groups, then, become the out-groups—and therefore inferior to their own group. The in-group then engages in stereotyping of the out-group—attributing undesirable characteristics to the other group while reserving all positive personal characteristics for the in-group.

For example, the members of a school hockey team see themselves as paragons of fair play and sportsmanship, but they may decide that rival hockey teams are bunches of thugs who are looking for a knockdown fight on the ice. Whether this perception holds any truth makes little difference —the stereotype becomes the truth for this group, even if the rival team behaves within all boundaries of good sportsmanship.

Once the conflict between two groups begins, it can intensify even as it strengthens the bonds between group members—and further demonizes the other group. Ronald J. Fisher (2000) notes that "parties are drawn into an escalating spiral wherein past investment justifies increasing risk, and unacceptable losses foreclose a way out." With too much at stake to walk away, and with maximized internal pressures to remain loyal to the group, the group members may continue a conflict far beyond any benefit—often losing sight of the group's original goals.

In Chapter 4, you will read about the elaborate experiment conducted by Sherif et al. (1954), in which the researchers created two groups of 11-year-old boys and placed them in a situation in which they would bond within their groups and then participate in competition against one another. The conflicts between the two groups—the Rattlers and the Eagles—escalated so quickly that the researchers had to take steps to prevent significant violence between them.

What causes this rapid formation of group loyalty and the equally fast willingness to stereotype those outside the group? Fisher attributes this to strong pressures within the group to conform to norms—a situation strengthened by conflict. This cohesiveness within the group also can lead to a phenomenon called "groupthink," in which the members of a group all believe the same thing and act the same way, even when doing so becomes irrational. (A classic case of groupthink has become a fixture in the public consciousness: the famous case of the religious zealots led by Jim Jones, who drank poisoned Kool-Aid and committed suicide in the belief that they would ascend into the afterlife together.)

INTRAPERSONAL CONFLICT

So far, all of the types of conflict discussed are focused outwardly, between individuals, groups, or people within groups. Intrapersonal conflict looks inward, at the conflicts that emerge within ourselves.

Nearly every day, human beings encounter decisions that must be made and ideas that challenge our beliefs, and each of these can trigger an intrapersonal conflict. These conflicts can be short-lived and easy to resolve—such as whether to have high-cholesterol steak or heart-healthy chicken for dinner, a decision that may challenge a person's belief system for a few seconds—or difficult, disturbing, and long-lasting, provoking the individual to question his or her own values and principles.

A college student, for example, may reach a point in his or her major course of study when he or she knows that he or she no longer wishes to pursue that major. The student may consider changing majors or staying with this one because so much money and effort have already been spent in achieving that goal. Before he or she takes this up with his or her parents, possibly causing a conflict with them, he or she spends time evaluating other options. What other major might he choose? What will his or her career trajectory be like if he or she makes the change? What does this mean to the fulfillment of his or her lifelong dreams? Will he or she put those dreams aside, now that he or she knows this course of study is not what he or she hoped it would be? And how will he or she tell his or her parents that he or she may need to stay in school longer to pursue a new major?

All of these questions create an internal struggle—and intrapersonal conflict. The student struggles with the uncomfortable questions of talking with his or her parents and selecting a new career path as well as the mundane issues of the bureaucratic work involved in making the change. If the student has the self-confidence to grapple with these decisions and resolve the issues fairly quickly, he or she can end the conflict and move on toward his or her goals. If, however, the student becomes trapped by his or her own anxieties and misgivings about making any kind of change, this conflict can take over his or her life. Internal conflicts like this one can cause long-term uneasiness, mood swings, sadness, anxiety, and even clinical depression.

When people become mired in intrapersonal conflict and cannot find their own way of resolving the issue, professional help may be required. Clinical psychologists, counselors, life coaches, and guidance counselors all have training in moving people toward the ability to make a decision and end the conflict.

ARMED CONFLICT

Some intergroup conflicts take place on a national, continental, or global scale, pitting one ideology against another. A number of these result in armed conflict—what the Department of Peace and Conflict Research at Uppsala University in Sweden defines as "a contested incompatibility which concerns government and/or territory where the use of armed force between two parties, of which at least one is the government of a state, results in at least 25 battle-related deaths." State, in this case, refers to the governing power—most often at the national level.

Uppsala goes on to define incompatibility with two classifications.

Incompatibility Concerning Government

This disagreement about the type of political system, the replacement of the central government, or a change in its composition can lead to significant conflict. Such incompatibility can include a group's desire to remove a leader from power, throw out a rule of law, or revolt against a regime. The war in Iraq from 2003 to 2011 was an armed conflict over incompatibility concerning government—in this case, the United States' interest in overthrowing the dictator Saddam Hussein and establishing a democracy in the Middle East.

Incompatibility Concerning Territory

This is a desire by one group to change control of an area of land. This can take the form of *interstate* conflict—a demand to change the state controlling the territory—or *intrastate* conflict, in which those protesting the state's control are within the state itself. The ongoing conflict between Israel and Palestine is an interstate conflict, while America's Civil War was an intrastate conflict.

Not all armed conflicts lead to war, though they invariably produce significant loss of life. Demonstrations against governments, including those in the Arab Spring of 2011, have resulted in police or military forces opening fire into crowds of protestors. Riots in major cities in the United States have involved people with weapons—rocks, sticks, clubs, and knives are valid weapons in an armed conflict—attacking people they consider part of the opposing side. We will look closely at such conflicts in Chapter 6, as we explore some of the largest and most contentious conflicts around the world.

In this chapter, we have looked at the many forms of conflict and the characteristics of each, and we have discovered what makes all conflicts similar as well as what makes them different. Conflict can take place between two people, among all of the people in a small group, between two factions in a larger group, or even within a person's own situation and the beliefs he or she brought to this stage in his or her life. Conflicts between groups can be resolved through the systems in place within their government or organization for that purpose, or they can escalate to the point at which the groups take up arms against one another.

In the next chapter, we will examine the purposes conflicts can serve in people's lives, and we will begin to see the ways in which disagreements between individuals, groups, and the perspectives of one's own psyche actually can strengthen us. Conflict plays an important role in helping us define who we are, what we want to accomplish, and how we come together with others—all important components in our way of being in the world, together.

2

❖❖❖

Why: The Importance of
Conflict in Our Lives

"Without conflict, there is no growth," wrote modern philosopher Marcelo Gleiser. "It would be quite naïve to expect a life without conflict, naïve and boring. After all, as we struggle to find solutions, conflict leads to new ways of thinking. Nothing ever changes in a world without discord."

Ask a psychologist, an organizational management specialist, a life coach, or a mediator, and they all will tell you the same thing: conflict is a critically important aspect of any relationship, because it helps set the boundaries within which this relationship will function. When people are in conflict, the resolution often produces new ideas that would not have emerged if the two sides had not clashed. A conflict also can raise unasked questions, bring flaws in a plan to the surface, and open the minds of the people involved. Where there is conflict, change often follows— some of it for the better, and some of it not.

Even with all of these benefits, however, conflict is something most people work very hard to avoid. Family members tiptoe around one another's well-known "hot buttons," doing their best to keep a holiday gathering peaceful despite known issues between individuals. Work groups go well out of their way to appease a single member who is known to be volatile if everything does not go according to his or her plan. Social groups exclude certain people from gatherings, to avoid a confrontation between one low-status person and a more popular person who are at odds.

Workers go so far as to hide from supervisors whom they believe "have it in for them." Rather than addressing the conflict and clearing the air—and perhaps progressing to a better place—people do all they can to dodge any situation that might cause raised voices and discomfort.

Conflict plays a pivotal role in our lives, and embracing the opportunity to present differing viewpoints can move an issue toward constructive resolution. In this chapter, we will explore the various aspects of conflict in everyday life and the importance of allowing it to play out to achieve new levels of understanding and harmony.

CONFLICT ESTABLISHES IDENTITY

Every person must develop a sense of his or her own identity as he or she matures—a unique conception of who he or she is, what he or she believes, and to what groups he or she belongs. For example, a person will understand early in life that he or she is male or female (even if that identification changes later), a child of specific parents, a sibling or cousin, a resident of a specific place, and so on. Later a person will discover that he is a member of a religion, a student in a particular classroom in a certain school, and a member of subgroups within that school—sports teams, cliques, clubs, and so on.

All of these elements help us define who we are in our own minds, in our families, in our communities, and in the world in general. Within all of these contexts, we have opinions about how we fit and what these memberships mean to our lives. These opinions may differ from those of others in the same group (the in-group) or in other groups (the out-groups). When this happens, we have a conflict. How that conflict gets resolved will have an impact on how we perceive ourselves within each group and how strongly we feel about being part of it.

Let us say, for example, that you attend Washington High School, and you go to your school's basketball games against other teams in the area. You become passionate about this team and its performance, and you learn about your school's arch rivalry with Adams High School, a few miles down the road. When you attend home games, students from Adams High come to cheer for their team—and in the heat of play, you suddenly find yourself hollering louder than you ever have before, standing with your classmates to drown out the cheers of the Adams students. You grow even more determined to shout down the other school when the Washington team leads by a narrow margin, and you begin pointing and jeering at the rival students. It does not occur to you that if you met those students at church or at a community event, they might actually become your friends—in this context, they are the enemy, because you identify as a student of Washington High. Sharing school pride becomes more important than treating the Adams High students with respect and courtesy.

Throughout our lives, conflicts create the "us" and "them" situations that help us establish our place in the world and our identity in relation to other people. Our identities may make us feel more powerful than others or victimized by them, or we may see other groups as our allies against a common adversary. We may be in competition with another group for the same goal, strengthening our identity with our in-group while placing the other group in conflict with us. Whenever we achieve a sense of belonging and partnership with one group, that group becomes part of our identity. Others, then, become potential objects of conflict with us.

Kreisberg (2003) looks at the effect of identities on conflict, noting that identities are part of anyone's life in relation to others—but the content of these identities can contribute significantly to lasting, intractable conflicts.

Persistent identities can create long-term conflicts. These very often stem from the ethnic group to which a person belongs. For example, in the United States, conflicts arise between some African Americans and segments of the Caucasian population, resulting in discrimination and exclusion of members of the black population. Each group's enduring identity, made permanent by the color of their skin, is perpetuated by the way members of each group are socialized—how they learn to see others through the influence of their own peer group. African Americans who face discrimination from the white community may be socialized to expect this racism and to rebel against it; some Caucasians may be socialized to see African Americans in ways that lead to subtle discrimination or to aggressive behavior and violence.

Primary identities can contribute to long-term conflict. Here Kreisberg refers not to the first identities we develop (say, as a member of a family) but to the elements of our identity that become most important. Most people have many identities, but only a few of these are truly significant and take precedence over all the others. Native Americans, for example, may identify with the land of their ancestors that was taken from them by the U.S. government in the nineteenth century, while Americans living on this land now identify with it as the home of their families, often for several generations. This dichotomy is central to each group's sense of who they are and what they believe they deserve—creating a long-standing conflict.

Noncompromising identities are those in which the person or group's identity places them at a higher rank than those around them. These may include people in authority (or people who are used to being in authority), royalty, people at the top of their country's social classes, some elected officials, the very wealthy, top-level business executives, and others who have been socialized to expect others to defer to their opinions. The presidential campaign of billionaire Donald Trump, for example, repeatedly illustrated his disinterest in compromise or resolving conflict, because he was socialized from a young age to believe that his wealthy status should make those around him accept and abide by his decisions. Likewise, the owner of a successful small business is likely to feel that his or her employees should take his or her decisions to heart and follow them to the letter, because he or she has built the organization and he or she pays their salaries.

Views of the Other have an enormous impact on the way people resolve conflicts. By identifying with one group, each individual immediately accepts that there are other groups with which he or she now will come into conflict. The way the individual views these others will affect his or her ability to resolve these conflicts. If he or she sees the others as less than him or herself, he or she may opt to ignore them, run roughshod over their ideas, allow them to come to harm, or even attempt to exterminate them. Such was the case in Nazi Germany, when Adolf Hitler determined that Jews, Poles, Jehovah's Witnesses, Roma Gypsies, Catholics, Christian pastors, homosexuals, and the disabled all should be annihilated, in the interest of creating a master Aryan race. In the United States, the enslavement of Africans before the Civil War represents another startling example of one group identifying itself as superior to another and the other group as so inferior as to not require basic human rights.

CONFLICT BRINGS PROBLEMS TO THE SURFACE

Most people see conflict as something to avoid, a path crossed with treacherous tree roots that can trip up anyone who passes through. Conflicts quickly move from disagreements to arguments, escalating until the people involved have said things they wish they could take back. Arguments can end friendships and marriages and create continued friction in the workplace, and in global situations, they can lead to war.

On the other hand, conflict can reveal issues that only one party in the conflict knew were problems. By bringing these problems to the surface, the people involved can find solutions, thus removing the conflict and strengthening the relationship.

Married couples often believe that if they fight, it is a sign that their marriage is in trouble. In his book *Why Marriages Succeed or Fail*, marriage researcher and therapist John Gottman noted, "If there is one lesson I have learned from my years of research, it is that a lasting marriage results from a couple's ability to resolve conflicts that are inevitable in any relationship. Many couples tend to equate a low level of conflict with happiness and believe the claim 'we never fight' is a sign of marital health. But I believe we grow in our relationships by reconciling our differences."

When people live, work, or play together, disagreements will arise—this is a fact of any relationship, because every person is different. Everyone brings their own likes, dislikes, pet peeves, emotional needs, and expectations to every relationship they have, whether it is with their spouse or significant other or the clerk at the supermarket checkout counter. Many people do not accept this basic fact of being in a world full of people, however, because they fear that the least disagreement will tear their relationships apart. These people may find themselves in situations of increasing stress, because they are unwilling to bring a problem out into the open and address it with the other people involved. The problem becomes "the elephant in the room"— the issue that those who see it are afraid to mention.

Ignoring a problem, however, creates the unhealthiest of relationships. If one person is blissfully unaware of the problem, while the other becomes increasingly tense and angry, the conflict eventually will erupt—and at a much more volatile level than it would have if it had not been hidden for so long.

Bringing issues out into the open allows the people involved to examine them and determine how they will move forward from this point. Each new problem provides an opportunity to build communication and conflict resolution skills, negotiate for mutually beneficial solutions, and open minds to new possibilities.

Let us take an example. Four male freshmen sharing a dormitory room find that Ken likes to leave his radio playing near his bed all night, even after he is asleep. This does not bother Jacob and Mark, but Frank, the one whose bunk is nearest to Ken's, cannot get to sleep while the radio plays.

Frank talks privately to Jacob and Mark about the problem, but they shrug it off and tell Frank he needs to talk to Ken. Instead, Frank tries to go to bed earlier than Ken, so he is asleep before the radio goes on. This works on occasion but not every night. Soon Frank is at his wits' end with Ken and his music, but he has said nothing to Ken. Jacob and Mark comment to Frank that he looks tired and frazzled, and he has got to talk to Ken if the issue is really disturbing him. Frank tells them he "hates confrontation," and he "will just have to find a way to deal with it."

This continues for several weeks until mid-term exams, when Frank— who by this time has tried earplugs and other uncomfortable noise-blocking devices—wants to get a good night's sleep before an exam the following day. He goes to bed earlier than usual, hoping to avoid hearing Ken's radio. However, he cannot get to sleep because he is worried about the exam, and when Ken turns on his radio, Frank snaps. He gets out of bed and comes at Ken, shouting, "What is wrong with you? Don't you know that people are trying to sleep? Do you have no consideration for anyone else?"

Ken, taken completely off guard, first responds defensively, "Hey, take it easy," but Frank is wound up and needs to let all his anger fly. Frank tells Ken that the radio has bugged him since the first day they lived together and that if he does not turn it off, "I'll throw the thing out the window."

Now Ken gets angry as well. "This has bothered you all semester, and you never said anything? You want to know what's wrong with me—what the hell is wrong with you?" he shouts. "You know what bothers me? The way you leave empty beer cups and wrappers all over the place and never clean up after yourself!"

The argument escalates into accusations and hurling insults at one another, until Frank grabs a pillow and blanket and leaves the room to sleep on the couch in the dorm lounge. Jacob and Mark, meanwhile, sit dumbfounded on their bunks, feeling totally uncomfortable and at a loss for what to do next.

How could Frank, who says he hates confrontation, have avoided this one? He had the option of talking quietly with Ken at the beginning of the semester about the radio, perhaps asking him to turn it down or use an under-pillow speaker to listen to it until he fell asleep. This would have brought the problem to the surface immediately, and he and Ken could have negotiated an equitable solution. Here is how this could have gone:

Frank: Hey, Ken, you know, your radio at night—that's keeping me awake. Could I ask you to turn it down, or set a timer, maybe, so it goes off once you're asleep?

   Ken: Wow, I've always listened to music until I fall asleep, but I don't want to bug anyone with it. Let me try the timer thing and see if that works.

Frank: Great, thanks. And if it turns out not to be okay, maybe there's a way to use earbuds or something. We'll figure it out.

Bringing a problem to the surface when it arises is one of the most important functions that conflict serves in our lives. Not only is this important in personal relationships, but it also plays a key role in work situations, especially for people who plan to pursue leadership opportunities. Recognizing problems creates opportunities to fix broken processes, improve systems, and build trust with the people who are affected by the issue at hand.

CONFLICT ACTS AS A RELEASE VALVE FOR ANGER AND FRUSTRATION

When we have an expectation about a situation, person, or ourselves, we assume at first that our expectation will be met. When circumstances begin to show us that we may be disappointed, we may react in a number of ways—one of which is anger.

Many kinds of events—both external and internal—make people angry. A classmate's offhanded comment, a coworker who is not keeping up with a project schedule, or a parent who just does not understand why a teenaged child needs to borrow the car can all lead to frustration and eventually to an angry outburst. Romantic relationships often are fraught with unexpected pitfalls as the two people involved learn the limits of one another's tolerance, and cohabitants—including spouses, no matter how long they live together—seem to find new ways to annoy one another on a regular basis. When these issues are not brought to the surface and resolved quickly, they can fester until they finally erupt in a furious outburst. This can lead to words that are more aggressive and hurtful than intended and in some cases, physical aggression. It also can lead to the severing of the relationship.

This being said, anger in itself is neither positive nor negative. It serves as a natural response to a volatile confrontation, an acknowledgment that we are not getting what we expect, want, or need from the situation. It increases heart rate and breathing to boost our ability to respond with physical aggression if necessary. We cannot always respond physically to something or someone that makes us angry—in fact, in most scenarios, lashing out physically can get us into trouble with an employer, a school's principal, or the law—but the increase in blood flow and oxygen also gives us a mental boost, making us temporarily sharper and more focused.

None of these feelings are pleasant, however, so when anger develops, people tend to want to resolve it as quickly as possible. Psychologists who study anger have determined that people deal with their anger in one of three ways: calming, suppression, and expression.

Calming involves taking control of your angry feelings by taking steps to lower your heart rate, slow your breathing, and turn your negative thoughts toward positive things. People use meditation, techniques of positive thinking, and general self-control to make this happen, with varying degrees of success. The calming may be temporary until the person or situation that caused the anger does so again—at which point, the angry person may move into suppressing his or her anger.

Suppression of anger can include the person's attempts to change his or her thoughts, ignoring the feelings of anger and focusing on more positive things. This can be effective in the short term, but if the stimulus that made the person angry continues, suppression becomes more and more difficult until it is no longer possible. Even then, many people redirect their anger away from a potential outburst, instead using it for behaviors that are known as "passive-aggressive."

Here is a common workplace example. Cathy and Ruth share midmanagement responsibilities at a corporation. Cathy announces that she is taking a week's vacation in about a month, at a time that will leave Ruth with a share of work that she feels is excessive. Rather than telling Cathy that her vacation may be poorly timed, however, she keeps her feelings to herself and becomes progressively angrier as Cathy prepares for her time off. On the day Cathy leaves on her vacation, Ruth sends her an e-mail that says, "I really feel that you should have consulted me before leaving me with all of this work. I think we'll have to have a talk about your lack of consideration for me when you get back from vacation."

Ruth could have talked with Cathy about the timing of her vacation or ways to manage the workload at any time before Cathy left. Instead, she chose to be passive-aggressive, waiting passively until Cathy left for her vacation and then making an aggressive move clearly calculated to ruin Cathy's good time by making her worry about the confrontation she and Ruth would have when she returned. Cathy, having no idea that her plans have made Ruth so angry, has no way to resolve the issue except to spend her time off e-mailing back and forth with Ruth to determine what the problem was and what could be done about it now that Cathy was traveling.

Calming and suppressing anger are not effective ways to resolve a conflict. Instead, studies—as well as common sense—have determined that expressing the conflict in a constructive way is a more successful method for resolving it.

Expressing anger does not necessarily require an aggressive confrontation. A person can be assertive, stating the point that made him or her angry in a forthright way, without the need to raise voices or become highly agitated. Looking once again at Cathy and Ruth, we can see how a simple expression of anger would have resolved the conflict in short order:

Cathy: I'm planning to go on vacation starting July 1. I'll be back July 10.

Ruth: Wait, that's right in the middle of my busiest season, because I've got that trade show starting on July 12. I won't be able to cover for you that week. That will really be a problem for me.

Cathy: Well, let me think . . . maybe we can get Jill to help out. I can ask her to handle one part of the workload—that's the bulk of the job. Would you be able to cover what's left, or should we pull Rob and Peter in for that week? My job really winds down over the fourth of July, so it won't be that much.

Ruth: Yes, that would do it. Thank you.

When Ruth told Cathy right away that her plans could cause a problem for her, Cathy had the opportunity to resolve the conflict on the spot. Ruth did not need to stew over the perceived slight for weeks, finally coming up with a way to get revenge by ruining Cathy's good time.

Not every situation can be resolved so easily, however. In the example above, Ruth and Cathy are peers—equals in rank at their place of employment. Often people who are in conflict are at different levels of status in the relationship, and this difference in rank can keep one person from simply expressing anger or frustration to the other. Employers may not be tolerant of such assertiveness from their employees, and teachers and professors may not be open to spirited discussions with students. Parents can be quick to cut off their children's expressions of anger—and children can be just as quick to shut out their parents. Even in relationships between friends, one person may have more power in the relationship than the other, giving one the option of speaking his or her mind while the other feels uncomfortable doing so, in fear that any objection will damage the friendship. Such an imbalance of power can be especially pronounced between romantic partners or spouses, even when the relationship is generally satisfying for both partners.

In virtually all of these cases, conflict can escalate as one person becomes more and more angry at the other's words or behavior. If this anger does not eventually erupt through an outburst, the angry person may become aggressive in other ways. He or she may be irritable, cynical, and grumpy, or withdrawn and sulky, refusing to interact with people who make him or her angry. In some cases, he or she may become angry with him or herself, criticizing his or her own moods and choices and wearing away at his or her self-image. This can lead to clinical depression, a condition many psychologists consider "anger turned inward."

Conflict gives people an opportunity to use anger as a tool for positive change, if they can master assertive self-expression instead of aggressive outbursts.

CONFLICTS BRINGS OPPORTUNITIES AND CHANGE

On December 17, 2010, a street vendor named Mohamed Bouazizi reached the limit of his endurance in his hometown of Sidi Bouzid, Tunisia. Local police officers did something on that day that they had done many times before: they confiscated Bouazizi's little wheelbarrow filled with produce he had purchased on credit, with plans to sell it for enough profit to feed his family and pay their rent. The police expected Bouazizi to bribe them to allow him to do business, but he had no money to do so—and instead, they took the scales he needed to weigh the produce for customers. When Bouazizi went to the governor's office to complain, the governor refused to see him. Later that day, the desperate street vendor managed to obtain a can of gasoline. He poured it over his head and body and burned himself to death in the middle of the street.

Horrified by Bouazizi's despairing act and being painfully aware that the street vendor was just one of thousands of people victimized by the dictatorial regime of President Zine El Abidine Ben Ali, the people of Tunisia took to the streets in protest. They seized the opportunity to use this conflict to end decades of unemployment, corruption, high prices for basic necessities of living, and obstacles to the most fundamental human rights. It took 28 days of protests and demonstrations, but the people were victorious. The president fled to Saudi Arabia for asylum on January 14, 2011, resigning from office. Continued protests led to the dissolution of the president's political party, and Tunisia had its first democratic election in decades the following October.

No one would recommend self-immolation as a means of getting the attention of authorities, but in many situations, the only way to bring about significant change is to escalate an underlying conflict. Once the conflict has reached a level at which the status quo can no longer function—whether it's a nation's government, an unpopular dress code policy at a corporation, or the choice of meal items in the school cafeteria—the system must either change, compromise, or collapse.

In a big-city advertising agency, the "creatives"—the graphic artists who create ads, brochures, and many other kinds of communications tools—always seem to be at odds with the account managers who have direct contact with the clients. One account manager, when trying to relay information to the artists from the client, finds himself in conflict with the creative team. The artists demand information he does not have—the size of the final piece they are to create, the number of pages, and so on—while the account manager believes that the size, shape, and length of the piece should be a design decision, not a verbatim direction from the client.

The account manager suddenly sees an opportunity. "How about if you come along with me to my next meeting with the client," he says to the lead designer, "and see what it's like to try to get all these details from him up front?"

The lead designer agrees. At the meeting, the designer asks all of her pointed questions, and the client tells her that he expects her to sort out all these details as part of the creative strategy she will develop. Now the designer sees that the account manager was telling the truth, and she realizes that she and her team can bring fresh solutions to the client and let him choose the ones that he likes. She's ready to lead her design team into new territory.

Why did this scenario work? When the design team started out being accusatory and criticizing the account manager's work, the account manager chose not to take the bait. Instead, he saw the opportunity to make a change—not in the structure of the organization or the way he runs the account but in the designer's attitude toward her work on this project and in her opinion of him. These attitude changes, brought about by conflict, now have the potential to lead to much bigger changes throughout the ad agency, including the expectations of designers to create new, fresh approaches for every project.

In any situation in which people work together, intragroup conflicts can arise among team members, and intergroup conflicts can develop between teams. These conflicts can reveal flaws in a system, problems with rules and laws, and the need to make changes to move more swiftly toward a goal. The tricky part for many teams, however, is in determining what problems can be solved constructively by using the opportunity to make change and how to keep these problems from escalating into destructive argument.

Often it is up to the team leader to find a way to resolve the conflict. The most effective team leaders can help team members express the conflict, keeping the discussion on a professional level—focused on the problem at hand rather than on the team members and their interpersonal differences. When conflict resolution takes place in this nonjudgmental way, the conflict itself can become a catalyst for positive change. If, however, the team members descend into personal attacks and name-calling, the conflict is likely to extend beyond the team's work and into the personal lives of the members. Left unresolved, such conflicts can become permanent fixtures in a workplace or organization.

CONFLICT CAN LEAD TO STRONG SOLUTIONS AND INNOVATION

New ideas rarely rise from complacency. When people become comfortable with the way things are today, they are unlikely to search for new solutions that will make tomorrow even better. Conflict helps break people out of this comfortable place, by creating tension that demands resolution before the people involved can be comfortable again.

The conflict may come from outside the group—for example, a new boss or leader wants to see procedures done differently and needs a system for doing so. Members of another team may have developed an innovation that now requires your team to keep up and create your own. The conflict also may come from within: perhaps you find yourself waking up in the middle of the night with your mind racing, seeking a solution to a problem you have not been able to solve. The need to change, the knowledge of all the other solutions that have failed, and the energy that comes with ambitious problem solving all come together to turn a conflict into a fascinating challenge.

One of the most vivid examples of innovation rising out of conflict took place throughout the 1960s, beginning on April 12, 1961, when the Soviet Union launched astronaut Yuri Gagarin into space on the Vostok 1. Weeks later, President John F. Kennedy told a joint session of Congress, "I believe that this nation should commit itself to achieving the goal, before this decade is out, of landing a man on the moon and returning him safely to the earth." At that point, the United States did not yet have a space program working on manned space flight, much less a plan to put a man on the moon. The conflict with the Soviets, however, sparked a level of national pride that had not been seen in the United States since World War II. The National Aeronautics and Space Administration (NASA) pooled its scientists and developed rockets that could push a capsule into space—mechanisms for protecting the capsule and the man in it from the cold, g-forces, lack of breathable air, weightlessness, the heat of reentry, and all of the other hazards that manned space flight produced. By 1969, the program had sent a number of men into orbit around the Earth and beyond, including two missions that traveled all the way to the moon and achieved orbit around the planet. In July 1969, the lunar earth module (LEM) on the Apollo 11 mission detached from the main module and carried Neil Armstrong and Edwin "Buzz" Aldrin to the surface of the moon, where they became the first people from Earth ever to walk on another planet.

How did NASA and the U.S. government pull off this eight-year marathon and reach Kennedy's goal? First, the conflict with the Soviets placed a level of urgency on the matter, as the United States and the Soviet Union were bitter ideological rivals mired in the Cold War. When Kennedy issued his call to action, NASA's scientists were already on the case, fresh from their own first manned space flight: Alan Shepard blasted into space on May 5, 1961, in the Freedom 7 capsule—just three weeks after Gagarin. Blistered by the near miss, NASA plunged into the moon challenge and turned out one innovative solution after another, from the battery-powered drill to long-distance telecommunications via satellite. By the time the hatch on Apollo 11's LEM popped open on the moon, NASA had poured out more innovations than in any other time in its history.

Brilliant solutions like the ones that led to the moon landing come from a level of motivation people achieve when they see themselves in serious competition with others. The importance of the situation can spur even greater performance and more original solutions as well. While most of us will not find ourselves working on projects that send people into space, many other kinds of conflict are critical to changing lives for the better. We have seen the extraordinary results of man-against-nature conflicts that have led to pharmaceutical research and finding cures for diseases. While political conflict has slowed the battle against climate change, innovation still emerges in places like New York City, where people battle oncoming storms and flooding by building a new system of water tunnels and barriers below the city's surface. In South Sudan, where sources of fresh surface water dry up for six months of every year, a relief organization teaches people to locate and drill wells to serve thousands of people in impoverished villages. All of these innovations spring from conflict—and while these situations play out on a global scale, the power of conflict to lead to original, effective solutions is just as strong in an office, a place of business, a science lab, a student organization, or within a family unit.

Conflict that leads to innovation and creativity can take a different form from other kinds of conflict. First, creative conflict rarely takes place among isolated individuals. The conflict tends to exist between an in-group and an out-group, and the in-group is eager to work as a unit to achieve innovation. Leadership expert Jagoda Perich-Anderson has observed, "We will need to seek and incorporate multiple perspectives in order to have meaningful dialogue and broaden the array of ideas. We will also increase our chance of long-lasting success if we include stakeholders who don't see things our way. Therefore, it behooves us to actively invite divergent ideas, opinions or experiences into the conversation. To make the most of this diversity, we need to learn to become more comfortable and skillful with conflict."

Cultural and political columnist David Brooks, writing for the *New York Times*, noted that a key feature of creativity is "the joining of the unlike to create harmony. Creativity rarely flows out of an act of complete originality ... It is usually the clash of two value systems or traditions, which, in collision, create a transcendent third thing."

Brooks observes that this kind of dichotomy can exist within one person, someone who thrives on an internal conflict that drives him or her to resolve this through innovation. Such people have the capacity to hold and explore two opposing thoughts at once, and they often place themselves in environments where they can "maximize the creative tensions between different parts of themselves."

CONFLICT CREATES ALLIANCES AND COMMON GOALS

Alliances are relationships between individuals or groups to accomplish a specific goal, purpose, or task. In an alliance, all members of the group will benefit in some way, and they combine their resources—money, influence, skills, power, and others—to achieve the goal.

Most of us have formed alliances at one time or another, selecting friends, family members, or rivals to work with to achieve a specific objective. Siblings who squabble continuously as a matter of course may suddenly come together in perfect harmony if they want their parents to consider getting a dog or taking them to a theme park. Classmates from rival cliques may form a cautious alliance when they walk into a group therapy session and discover that they are all victims of child abuse. People who work in different departments of the same company often become allies in achieving even the simplest changes in the workplace, such as convincing the management to change the drink selection in the vending machines.

People have a number of reasons for forming alliances, but the four most common include the following:

1. **In response to a threat**: Individuals and groups may come together to protect themselves and their interests from a threat outside of the groups.
2. **Similar or shared beliefs**: The people in two or more groups share the same goals, but they may have different resources that could further their shared cause.
3. **Economic interdependence**: The groups already rely on one another financially.
4. **Shared membership**: Some of the members of one group are also members of another group, so alliances are natural.

The outside threat is the most germane to our discussion, but all of these elements come into play when alliances form. While the members of the alliance share a common goal, they may have no other connection with one another—and they may be rivals in all other aspects of their existence. Their interest in surmounting the conflict often is their only similarity.

When psychologists, researchers, and strategic analysts talk about alliances, they almost always refer to relationships between organizations. Shenkar and Reuer (2005) determined that alliances always involve two or more organizational actors with separately defined identities, interests, and power. Each of these actors can make decisions about the behavior within the alliance, so each actor can be sure that his or her organization benefits, regardless of the level of benefit to the others. The alliance exists only to achieve the goals each member has set—and these goals may be different for each member. In other words, one member may participate in the alliance because of the opportunity for his or her own company to profit, while another member may be there for a more altruistic purpose.

Most high-profile strategic alliances take place between major companies, pooling resources and knowledge to make a whole that is greater than each of the parts. One of the most visible and successful examples of this took place between the nation's number-one bookseller chain and the world's most popular coffee shop company. Barnes and Noble bookstores have contained Starbucks coffee shops since 1993, a strategic alliance that came from a conflict: the need for the bookseller to beat the competition by bringing coffee concessions into its stores. Barnes and Noble had the choice of developing an entire business model around running coffee shops or creating an alliance with a company that already had a name in that business. Starbucks gave the bookstores a proven, high-profile brand favored by millions of customers and gained hundreds of additional locations in stores that offer books, creating a reason for people to sit and linger in their shops—drinking more coffee and eating more pastries. The alliance works for everyone, including customers who can order their favorite espresso drinks while relaxing with a good book.

Not all alliances form for the greater good. For example, the formation of alliances in World War I is considered one of the main elements that caused the war to become one of the most destructive in world history. It began when Germany came to the aid of its ally, Austria-Hungary, after a Serbian team assassinated Austro-Hungarian leader Franz Ferdinand, making it inevitable that Austria-Hungary would go to war with Serbia. When Germany joined the war, Russia—on the border with both Germany and Austria-Hungary—saw the oncoming threat to its own security and mobilized in preparation to defend itself against the two countries' combined forces. Germany then confirmed Russia's suspicions by declaring war on Russia, prompting France—a Russian ally—to mobilize in Russia's defense. Germany took this opportunity to declare war on France, invading Belgium so its armies could invade France from the north. Great Britain, a Belgian ally, then declared war against Germany—and eventually, the United States acted on its allied relationship with Britain and entered the war against Germany as well. What began as a localized conflict between two countries grew through alliances on both sides, resulting in casualties that topped 38 million—17 million dead and another 20 million wounded.

On the positive side, alliances against a single conflict can lead to remarkable success. In 1986, the Carter Center—led by former U.S. president Jimmy Carter—allied with the U.S. Centers for Disease Control and Prevention, the World Health Organization (WHO), UNICEF, and a number of smaller agencies to address the spread of a parasitic disease called guinea worm. At that time, 3.5 million people annually contracted the disease by drinking water that contained the parasite. The alliance between these health organizations to reduce contaminated drinking water sources, provide more sources of clean water, and develop a filter that kept the parasites from entering the body has led to 99.99 percent reduction in disease cases. As of 2017, only 5 cases of guinea worm remained in the world, and the disease was on track for total eradication.

CONFLICTS SHIFTS POWER IN A RELATIONSHIP

When two people come into conflict with one another, they can tell almost immediately which of them holds more power. It may take only moments before the disagreement includes a statement like "I'm the supervisor and you're the employee, so you'll do what I tell you," or "I'm the one who brings home the bigger paycheck, so we're going to get the car I say we can afford."

Most conflicts involve some kind of a power struggle. When two children squabble over a toy, the one who actually owns the toy becomes the power player in the relationship. When an argument between two teenagers escalates into a fistfight, the one with more strength and muscle is almost certain to come out the winner. And when two romantic partners disagree, the argument usually reveals that one has more knowledge, money, property, or even love from children than the other, shifting the power to the one with the greater advantages.

Peter T. Coleman and Robert Ferguson note in their book, *Making Conflict Work: Harnessing the Power of Disagreement*, that talking openly about differences in power is taboo in most relationships, workplaces, and organizations, even though most conflicts are actually about the balance of power between individuals or groups. As directors of the International Center for Cooperation and Conflict Resolution at Columbia University, Coleman and Ferguson have conducted training in conflict resolution at global-level organizations, including the United Nations. They describe a training session at the United Nations in which a role-playing exercise involved a conflict between a superior and a subordinate. "Participants playing the boss would quickly leap into command-and-control mode, seeking to protect their authority and reputation and impose their will," they wrote. "They struggled to listen or stopped listening altogether. Empathy fled the scene. Negotiations morphed into competitive power struggles." They observed that the people in subordinate roles reacted with "a strange combination of submissiveness and inflexibility," trying to hold on to their positions without losing power entirely. The more pressure they felt, the more likely they were to dig in their heels, refusing to give in for fear of becoming entirely powerless in the relationship. This resulted in conflicts that could only be resolved by the boss pulling rank, insisting that the others do as he told them or risk losing their jobs.

Beyond authority given by employment, the power in a relationship can come from a diverse array of factors that are relevant to the specific situation: physical strength, attractiveness, intelligence, knowledge, confidence, authority, rank, ownership of property, wealth, or the power of the group each person represents.

These traits are not the only ways that one person in a conflict can gain power over the other. Power can also come from refusal to negotiate: even if one person has more power for other reasons, the subordinate's stonewalling of any solution except his or her own can sometimes result in a shift of power to his or her side. If one person has something the other one wants—regardless of either person's position in the relationship—the person who "has" may enjoy more power than the person who "has not."

Adler and Silverstein (2000), writing in the *Harvard Negotiation Law Review*, discuss the situational character of one person's power over another. "The critical test of one's effectiveness in a negotiation is what one has convinced an opponent that one can do, whether or not one can actually do it," they note. "Unless exposed as bluffers, parties that convince their opponents that they have more power than they really do will generally be able to exercise the power they have asserted."

If one person in a conflict holds a power that he or she is unwilling to actually use, however, this can result in his or her having no real power at all. In a marriage, for example, if one spouse threatens the other with the statement, "If you don't cut this out, the next person you hear from will be my attorney," that spouse must be willing to go through with the threat to maintain the power in the relationship. If, however, this spouse has no intention of contacting an attorney to begin divorce proceedings, the threat is empty—and the other spouse may know it. The first spouse has no real power over the other in this case.

The same is true of a parent who regularly threatens a child with "whip-pings" if the child does not do what he or she is told. If the child knows full well that the parent would never raise a hand against the child, the state-ment becomes meaningless, and the child sees no consequences ahead for his or her actions, whatever they may be.

So power can shift from one person in a conflict to the other in the blink of an eye, based on far more than their official positions in relation to one another. Adler and Silverstein note that power typically arises from the dependence that each party has on the other and that the most suc-cessful negotiations are between people who have a mutual dependence. "For example, one who negotiates the purchase of an automobile depends on the dealer to supply a suitable vehicle, while the dealer relies on the customer to pay money for the car. Each depends on the other for a vital part of the transaction." When the negotiation becomes a conflict, chances are that one side has something that the other considers to be of higher value. In the case of the car sale, the dealer may have the only vehicle in the area with all the features the buyer wants, so the buyer sees no alternative but to pay more than he or she had intended.

Having power is neither good nor bad—it is simply a fact of most rela-tionships on some level. Establishing who has the power in any conflict can help both sides understand what they must do to resolve the issue to their satisfaction and what they may be asking the other side to sacrifice to make this happen. The benefits and consequences to each side will help determine what all parties involved are willing to do to bring the conflict to a conclusion, no matter who eventually benefits.

CONFLICT CREATES RULES AND LAWS

In 1776, as the Second Continental Congress grappled with the text of the Declaration of Independence they would send to King George III, the mem-bers of Congress faced an existential question: What did they actually want the new United States of America to be—and how would they codify this in text? It became critically important that they not only list the many crimes that England committed against the people of America but also that they decide what the rules and laws of the new country would contain. What kinds of actions should the new government be forbidden to take against its people? What rights should every citizen of the United States have and consider unalienable? How would the new government protect its people while giving them the tools to protect themselves against any future tyranny?

The resulting Declaration was developed in direct reaction to the con-flict between the people of colonial America and the leaders in England.

It established that life, liberty, and the pursuit of happiness were rights every person in the world should enjoy without threat of reprisals from a dictatorial government. The document lists a long litany of insults against the colonists, from "rendering the Military independent and superior to the Civil power" to "imposing Taxes on us without our consent" and "depriving us in many cases, of the benefits of Trial by Jury." The document, signed by the 56 members of the Continental Congress, became one of the foundations (along with the Articles of the Confederation) for the Constitution of the United States.

So fresh in the minds of many of the new nation's leaders were the crimes against humanity committed by the British, however, that they insisted on an additional document that spelled out the rights of individual citizens. The resulting Bill of Rights is the ultimate example of rules and laws developed specifically because of the conflict that preceded them. These 10 amendments to the Constitution established freedom of religion, speech, and the press; the right of the people to peaceful assembly and to petition the government for a "redress of grievances"; the right of the people to bear arms, to be protected from unreasonable search and seizure of their property, and to refuse to allow a soldier into their homes in times of peace; and the people's rights should they be accused of a crime and brought to court.

These most basic tenets of the American democracy came out of conflict, establishing laws that are emulated (and envied) by countries around the globe today. Sometimes, however, the rules that result from conflict are not as strong as the laws of the land, and they do not represent the high ideals of the people who create them. A new rule may instead be the result of considerable compromise, if the people involved in the conflict make the misguided attempt to satisfy everyone and offend no one.

Zoe, the owner of a small business, objects to the current fashions that involve visible facial piercings, short skirts, and bare midriffs. Only one employee comes to work this way, so Zoe has the option of taking this employee aside and discussing her appearance with her, asking her quietly to remove her lip ring and to wear blouses that cover her exposed stomach. As the owner, she has the authority to determine any kind of dress code she wishes. Instead, however, she decides to bring all 12 of her employees into the discussion of what they feel is appropriate dress, making this a "conversation among all the stakeholders."

This results in a series of meetings in which all employees have input, and Zoe soon realizes that this is not going to go her way. The young staff members want to wear whatever they like, while older staffers want to see more conventional business dress. Instead of setting her own policy, Zoe now has to reconcile all of these disparate opinions to create a written statement of what is proper and what is unacceptable. The final document is so vague that it accomplishes nothing, except that the employee with the piercings and the bare midriff continues to dress this way. The conflict led to a new rule, but the person who wanted it now must live with a rule that satisfies none of her goals.

You can see the same kind of rulemaking play out in conflicts between individuals or in organizations in which you are involved, whether they regulate the length of time children in a household can play video games every day or the way grievances are addressed in your school or on your sports team. Every organization needs rules, but it can be instructive to consider how these rules were made, what they were meant to accomplish, and what conflict they resolved on the day they took effect.

CONFLICTS CREATE INSTITUTIONS

Thousands of organizations around the world had their origins in conflicts as well, bringing people together to combat an injustice, a disease, or a threat to some aspect of society. The American Heart Association, for example, began as the Association for the Prevention and Relief of Heart Disease in 1915, when patients who had heart disease were essentially condemned to bed rest until their inevitable death. Seeing the conflict between the lack of information about heart disease and the quality of life for these patients, the physicians and social workers who started the organization conducted research and discovered that many bedridden patients could return to work. Soon other heart health organizations sprang up in cities throughout the United States and Canada, and the American Heart Association was born. Today the organization works to fight heart disease, stroke, and related disorders, raising money for research and distributing information about heart disease to people who may be at risk.

People of similar ideologies seek each other out during times of conflict, uniting in their like-mindedness and forming groups that can become movements. In 2004, a branch of the organization known as Al-Qaeda formed in Iraq, taking advantage of the lack of security in the country in the years after the United States overturned Saddam Hussein's regime. At the time the minority Sunni population, which had held power during Hussein's rule, had become disenfranchised under the democratic governance by Nouri al-Maliki. Al-Qaeda saw the opportunity to use the Sunnis' alienation to mobilize them, waging war against the American and coalition forces in Iraq. When the United States killed Al-Qaeda leader Abu Musab al-Zarqawi in 2006, the move weakened Al-Qaeda, but this new conflict opened the door to an umbrella organization known as ISI. The new organization gained strength over the next five years, moving into the void left when the United States left Iraq in 2011. It lost its relationship with Al-Qaeda during the outbreak of fighting in Syria, however, creating a new conflict of ideologies that was ripe for a merger.

During the U.S. military action in Iraq, a number of inmates of the American prison at Camp Bucca came together in their shared hatred for the United States. The prison, described by former prison commander James Skylar Gerrond as "a pressure cooker for extremism," gave one of the detainees—Abu Bakr al-Baghdadi—the opportunity to radicalize a number of others into the organization that calls itself the Islamic State, or ISIS. By 2012, ISIS had joined with ISI and mobilized to fill the rift between ISI and Al-Qaeda.

Good or bad, right or wrong, conflict brings people together to accomplish a shared objective and defeat a foe—whether they intend to eradicate a disease, make the world a better place, or wipe out a civilization. We will talk more about the ways conflict plays both a positive and negative role in our lives in Chapter 3.

3

---◆❖◆---

How: The Positive and Negative Effects of Conflict

Now that we have a clear idea of the many roles conflict plays in our lives, we can see that the effects of any conflict have the potential to be either positive or negative. Many people see conflict as exclusively negative and something to be avoided at all costs, but each disagreement reveals an opportunity for change—for better or worse.

Rubin, Pruitt, and Kim (1994) identified five ways in which conflict has a positive impact on society as a whole:

1. *Conflict contributes to social change*, so people, organizations, and governments can see issues that reflect the current realities of our time.
2. *Conflict keeps groups from making unilateral decisions* without examining all of the interests at stake.
3. *Conflict allows all of the parties involved to come to an agreement* that benefits everyone's needs.
4. *Conflict provides an opportunity for all of the people within a group to discuss their issues* and negotiate solutions in their best interests—often resulting in a stronger and more unified group.
5. *Conflict between groups produces more unity within the two (or more) conflicting groups*, promoting cooperation within the group as its members work toward a common goal.

Most important, groups need conflict to survive. In-groups often form because their members agree on a common foe, whether the enemy is a tyrannical supervisor, a competitive sports team, or a rival clique. If the in-group has no one to disparage, it loses its cohesiveness and begins to deteriorate. Relationships erode or end; passion dissolves, and the group eventually disintegrates.

Groups also need conflict within their own ranks to help the members determine their own leadership, their social mores, and the way the members will proceed against their common foe. Most of these conflicts are resolved peaceably, giving the group the structure and established norms it needs to go forward.

There is no question, however, that some conflicts escalate until they become destructive. Rubin et al. (1994) note three dire consequences of extended conflicts:

1. **Conflict distracts groups and individuals from their primary purpose**: When the conflict becomes very contentious, it can force the people and groups involved to devote all of their time to attempting to resolve it—or to perpetuating it, as in wartime. Eventually, people and groups outside of the main conflict may be swept into the fray as well, even though this is not their fight.
2. **Conflict can affect the physical, mental, and emotional health of the people involved**: In the worst cases, this can result in post-traumatic stress, an inability to cope with the situation, and even physical injury and death.
3. **Conflict can lead a group to identify itself with the eventual outcome of the battle**: Rubin et al. (1994) call this "collective trauma," a way of taking ownership of a specific event with such passion that this identity gets passed down from one generation to the next. A particularly vivid example of this is the Holocaust during World War II, which Jewish people around the globe consider to be a critical part of their historical identity—and many decades later, generations of young people who had no personal experience with the Holocaust still embrace it as a defining event in their own history.

What turns a conflict toward the positive or the negative? The pivot point often comes very early in the disagreement, when the parties involved identify and define the problem. The people or groups in conflict have the option of looking closely at the issue at hand and deciding how they will work toward a solution—or of increasing the friction between them by making the problem larger, louder, and more public.

Let us see how this turning point plays out in an example.

Stan and Eileen are a married couple who have been together for more than 20 years. They are working parents with two children, and even after all these years together, they avoid any discussion about money for fear that it will lead to an argument. One day when Stan comes home from work, he sees that his son, Tom, has new, expensive running shoes. He turns to Eileen in surprise. "Where did Tom get the money for those shoes?" he asks.

Eileen is matter-of-fact. "I bought them for him."

Stan instantly becomes angry. "With whose money?" he asks. "That brand costs a fortune. Can we afford those?"

Eileen raises her voice as she answers, "It was my money, and I decided he should have them."

Already this conflict has reached the pivot point. Stan is upset because he was not consulted about a purchase. Eileen feels that what she does with the money she earns is her business. In a moment, this conflict can go one of two ways: it can result in a frank discussion about finances and the fact that this married couple considers money a taboo subject, or it can devolve into an argument.

If Stan chooses at this point, he could say to Eileen, "Okay, the new shoes just took me by surprise. I would like to talk about how we handle a big purchase like this in the future. I think we should both be in on the decision." Here Stan states his point of view, suggests a way he would like such an issue to be handled, and asks for a meeting to negotiate. He does not judge Eileen or blame her for doing something without his involvement. The conflict will move toward an equitable solution, making it a positive influence on the family and the marriage.

Or Stan could choose to escalate the problem: "So you think that you can just make any decision you want without talking to me at all? Your money's yours, and my money's mine? Fine then. You just pay all the bills with your money, and I'll go buy a sports car with my money. See how you like that!" Now Stan has elected to turn the conflict into a negative influence. He will use the conflict as an opportunity to insult Eileen, make his children uncomfortable, and nurse his anger and resentment. There may still be an option for negotiation down the road, but first this anger must play out, and the conflict will become more serious in the interim.

Here's the remarkable thing: what goes on in one family's living room demonstrates exactly what happens in conflicts on a national and global scale. The people at the apex of the conflict—community groups, police departments, chiefs of staff, mayors, governors, presidents, and emperors— have the same opportunities as Stan and Eileen to take a conflict to a positive result or to escalate that conflict through aggressive action toward a negative outcome.

NEGOTIATION: CONFLICT RESOLUTION THROUGH COMPROMISE

Ideally, anyone who finds him or herself in a conflict should be ready to negotiate. Negotiating allows all parties in the conflict to collaborate with one another to find a solution that benefits both of them. The person or people on each side will receive some benefits, but everyone will give up some things they wanted in favor of receiving others.

Carsten K. W. De Dreu has written extensively about his research in negotiation with his team at the University of Amsterdam. The team's writings note that in negotiation, the parties involved depend on one another to produce a positive outcome and to avoid any negative outcome, giving them a cooperative incentive to work together for mutual benefit. At the same time, however, they also have an incentive to achieve their own personal gain, so the transaction between parties may be out of balance. Some negotiators may enter the relationship knowing that they have good alternatives to coming to an agreement with the other person, so the incentive to cooperate is fairly low. In other situations, the negotiators want to create or maintain a relationship with each other, so they are more motivated to come to an agreement.

Negotiations by nature tend to take place in what researchers call "fuzzy situations," in which the issues and the goals may be ambiguous and messy. The negotiators may not know all of one another's motivations or what the other may be willing to accept. They may not know what resources the other person or group can access to help them come to an agreement, and they often have little idea of what may be important to the other negotiator. Each only can be sure of his or her own payoff goals—what he or she is willing to take or give up to reach a successful conclusion.

It becomes critical that the negotiators listen to one another's needs and share information—but not all negotiators are ready or willing to do this. "The exchange of honest and accurate information fosters the achievement of high joint gain and, at the same time, makes one vulnerable to exploitation by a (relatively more knowledgeable) partner," De Dreu et al. wrote in 2006. Rather than share information honestly, negotiators may use deception or misrepresent their motivations and resources to achieve a higher value outcome for their side. "Because of the information dilemma, negotiators have a fundamental reason to doubt any information from their partner," the researchers noted.

With this in mind and with decades of research in laboratory settings to help them understand the anatomy of a negotiation, psychologists have defined five basic kinds of negotiations:

- **Contending**: One side works entirely to its own advantage by imposing its will on the other negotiator. Such a negotiation may involve bluffs, lies, threats, and refusal to compromise on any point.
- **Compromising**: The negotiators work to find common ground between sides so that each side comes away with some gains and some losses.
- **Conceding**: One side capitulates, giving over to the other person's side entirely. This results in one side getting most or all of the gain, while the other agrees to a number of losses.
- **Problem solving**: The two sides determine the problem that has led them to this negotiation and take steps to remove the problem and thus regain balance.
- **Inaction**: One side or the other (or both) refuses to come to the table, essentially deciding not to negotiate. While this can be used as a tactic in a contentious negotiation, here it signifies one side's disinterest in working with the other at all.

The key to a successful negotiation is a willingness to exchange information honestly and clearly, but as you can see from this list of potential types, negotiators are often more interested in guarding their information and achieving the greatest possible gain for themselves or their organization.

Let us look at a proven negotiation strategy to see how it works. In their seminal interpersonal communications text *Looking Out, Looking In*, Ronald B. Adler and Russell F. Proctor II define the steps in a successful negotiation.

1. **Identify your problem and unmet needs**: If you are looking to negotiate, you are the one with the problem—you have an objection to the way things are, and you want to seek resolution. If your spouse has spent money without your knowledge, you are the one who is angry about it. If your roommate plays his or her radio all night, you are the one who is kept awake by the noise. The spouse and the roommate are content with the way things are now, so you need to bring your problem to their attention to find a way to get what you need. What do you need from your spouse, for example? Most likely, you need your spouse to involve you in major spending decisions,

because you share the responsibility for the money. What do you need from your roommate? The answer is simple: a good night's uninterrupted sleep.

2. **Make a date to talk**: Negotiations take place at a designated date and time, while arguments happen whenever one person ambushes the other with an angry accusation. Setting a time to discuss an issue— and letting the other person know what the issue is—allows everyone involved in the negotiation to give it their full attention.

3. **Describe your problems and needs**: It can be hard to air your grievance concisely and without judgment, but this is the first step in moving toward a solution. Let us take the case of Stan and Eileen. Stan might begin his negotiation with Eileen by saying "Look, I have a problem. When you go out and buy something expensive without telling me, I don't have the opportunity to budget for it. Then I have to fit it into this month's budget, which means we don't do something else we've planned. When I say later that we can't do that thing, I'm the bad guy. I don't think that's really fair. I'd like to come to some agreement about how we can communicate with one another so I don't get trapped by this." Here Stan speaks about his own problem, without judging Eileen or labeling her actions as irresponsible or selfish. He simply states his point of view and gives her the opportunity to respond.

4. **Consider the other side's point of view**: Eileen has her own feelings about the situation, so it is only fair to hear her out as well—and if Stan understands what Eileen needs, he has information he can use to negotiate. A successful negotiation provides benefits for people on both sides of the issue, so it is important to hear what the other person needs and respond to this. In this case, Eileen may say, "I earn my own money, so I should have discretion about how at least some of it gets spent. I contribute a certain amount to the household budget every month, so I want to use the rest of it the way I see fit."

5. **Come up with a solution**: Look at all sides of the problem, and develop a list of possible solutions. In the business world, this process is known as brainstorming—coming up with a range of possible solutions that you can evaluate to find the most useful and practical way to resolve the problem. Once you feel that you have a number of ways to go forward, stop and consider which of these will provide the most benefits to all parties involved. In the case of Stan and Eileen, they may brainstorm solutions, including a monthly meeting to go over the month's budget, a quick text whenever one of them wants to spend unbudgeted funds on something major (and a

threshold for what "major" means), or a decision about how much discretionary money each spouse can spend each month without consulting the other.

6. **Follow up the solution**: Once you have determined which solution is best, put it in place and try it out for a while. Agree to come together again to discuss whether the solution is effective, whether it needs to be modified to make it work better, or if you need to try something else. Here Stan and Eileen may decide that their monthly budget meeting also will be used to check in with each other about how their new system is working.

When you find yourself in a negotiation, chances are that you would like to come up with a win-win solution that maximizes benefits for all of the parties involved while minimizing sacrifices, but this is usually a fanciful notion. In most cases, each side gets a share of what they hoped to achieve while giving up some of what they had before. This is a natural outcome of even the most successful negotiations, so setting expectations accordingly at the outset makes a difference—for example, if Stan expected that the outcome of his negotiation with Eileen would lead to his achieving full autonomy over the household budget and funds, he would have left the meeting in grave disappointment. Instead, he probably came away with an opportunity to keep peace in the household by creating a quick, effective system in which he and Eileen can make financial decisions together.

COMPETITION: CONFLICT THAT IMPROVES PERFORMANCE

In almost any situation, one person can feel that he or she is in competition with another. Competition can develop at home between siblings before they even begin preschool, and it can influence us in school, in our neighborhoods, in our social groups, in after-school activities, in our places of worship, and in the workplace. We even compete online for the number of "likes" we can gather on social networking sites or the number of connections we amass on LinkedIn.

Not only is competition everywhere, but it also pervades our consciousness. It makes us want to try harder, do better, and achieve more in relation to the objects of our competitive feelings. The need to beat someone else's record or to achieve a goal before someone else does can lead us to greater accomplishments than we might have made without that competitive drive. In the push to be better than another person, we may even put ourselves at risk by spending more money than we can afford or by taking physical chances that place us in dangerous situations. Seeking to be superior to someone else can become an all-consuming need, one that blurs logic and rationality as we focus only on the desire to beat the other guy.

Given the ubiquity of competition in our lives, it seems odd that there is little recent research into the psychological processes that create it. In 1954, Leon Festinger published a paper that has become the basis for modern theories about competition: he proposed the theory of social comparison processes, which examines the ways in which people evaluate their own opinions and abilities against the opinions and abilities of others.

Festinger hypothesized that every human being has a drive to evaluate his or her opinions and abilities and that we make this evaluation by comparing ours with those of others. If there is a physical basis or empirical data for this comparison—for example, if we have test scores that we can compare with classmates, or the time recorded for each of us to run a 500-yard dash—then we can see the difference in our abilities at a glance. If there is no physical data, however, we make a subjective comparison, and this evaluation may be changeable based on whatever new information becomes available.

According to social comparison theory, people evaluate themselves in relation to others who are fairly close to them in opinions or abilities, rather than comparing themselves to people who are at the top or bottom end of the scale. "Thus, a college student, for example, does not compare himself to inmates of an institution for the feeble minded to evaluate his own intelligence," Festinger wrote. "Nor does a person who is just beginning to learn the game of chess compare himself to the recognized masters of the game."

When we narrow the field of people to whom we compare ourselves, we feel the drive to reduce the discrepancies between us—especially between us and the people who are incrementally better or who are just slightly behind us. This triggers competitive behavior. We begin to work to close the gap with the person ahead of us and to widen the gap with the person who is not quite as good.

The desire to compete can be positive, of course, and it can even be fun. Members of the same sports team may compete against one another to improve their skills and then work together to compete against a rival team. Classrooms, summer camps, and Boy and Girl Scout troops or dens often use competition between groups to introduce incentives for students or campers to improve all kinds of skills, from spelling to hitting softballs. The need to triumph can become the glue that holds a group together, as its members use their combined skills to beat another group.

In many cases, however, competition can lead to hostilities between individuals or groups, taking the place of cooperation and compassion in a quest for personal gain. This is the trend first reported in 1899 by Charles H.

Cooley, a pioneer in the field of sociology, when he combined his knowledge of economics with observations of the changes taking place in American society. He noted that as the United States became more industrialized, working people had become more competitive and less inclined to aid one another or reach out to their neighbors in need. Traditional family units became less important as people reaped the benefits of the new society, putting more value on the individual and their personal accomplishments than on the collective power of the extended family. Cooley had hoped to reverse this trend by pointing it out, but instead he codified what became a central and lasting theme in modern society.

Much more recently, Kilduff, Elfenbein, and Staw (2010) looked closely at rivalry between individuals and groups, making a careful distinction between competitors who have no personal relationship and rivals, who have "increased psychological involvement." Rivals are more competitive with one another than they are with other opponents, in part because they have an extended relationship during which the rivalry was established. The stakes between rivals become magnified, driving them to exceed one another's accomplishments or progress toward a potentially unobtainable goal. As the stakes become higher, the rivals become less rational about the outcome, and the outcomes of their rivalry provoke stronger emotional reactions than more regulated competitions.

Rivalries can form between friends, siblings, coworkers, sports competitors, and in virtually any other relationship, even when the people involved have a strongly positive relationship. Here social comparison theory comes into play again, as people compare their own performance with others they know well. When a rivalry forms, two people who are close and who have many similarities can grow to feel threatened by one another—or one of the people may develop this sense of a threat, while the other is blissfully unaware that he or she is in a rivalry with his or her friend or coworker.

The result of this change in the relationship has the potential to remain a cheerful competition, but as the rivals perceive that the stakes are getting higher, the former friendship or comfortable work situation may transform into a conflict. Friends become enemies when they both want one thing, and only one of them can have it.

CONFLICT MANAGEMENT: IMPROVING GROUP OUTCOMES

As we discussed in Chapter 1, conflicts can develop within groups as well as between them. Intragroup conflicts can have a significant impact on the way the group functions—and not always in a negative way.

When problems form between group members, they often reveal flaws in the group's structure, systems, or methods of working. Resolving the conflict can improve the group's work methods, making it a stronger, more effectively functioning unit that can produce better outcomes.

For example, the production crew for a college's student-run theater organization includes people who can build scenery, find and manage props, hang and focus lighting, run the lighting console, and run the rigging. Some of the people on the crew double up on responsibilities because they have more than one skill, so the group develops an expectation that everyone will do more than their one job. Suzanne has just stepped into the role of assistant stage manager. She is very good at running the lighting console, but the responsibilities of her new position make it difficult for her to do both.

Rather than admitting to what she believes the group will see as a shortcoming, however, Suzanne continues to juggle both positions until her stage management work begins to suffer. When other students point out to her that she has forgotten to do things, she gets angry. "What do you want from me? I'm already doing everything I can!" she snaps. The other crew members begin to step lightly around Suzanne, until several of them avoid her altogether. This means that crew members do not receive instructions that should be coming from Suzanne, so set pieces, props, and furniture do not arrive on stage at the right times during rehearsals. This becomes painfully apparent to the director, Thomas, when a rehearsal grinds to a halt because at the climax of the play, the actor who plays the assassin points his finger at the actor he is supposed to kill and yells, "Bang! Bang!" because he does not have his pistol.

Communication breakdowns, missed task assignments, gaps in participation, and fear of a specific group member are all fairly typical signs of intragroup conflict, according to Hadad and Reed (2007). They list the five most common causes of conflict within groups:

- **Faulty communication**: People do not receive task assignments, or they get left out of communication to the group, making them feel devalued.
- **Attribution errors**: Members guess at the causes of others' behavior. For example, one group member has trouble completing a task, and others decide that she is lazy or incompetent, or that she does not care about the group's goals.
- **Mistrust**: Communication gaps and attribution errors make group members feel that others cannot be trusted to do their jobs.
- **Grudges**: Members feel they have been treated unfairly; they have been criticized when they do not deserve it, or they have been left out of the communication loop. They become angry and nurse this

anger until it blocks their ability to do a job well or to get along with others in the group. In the worst cases, one group member actively does something to undermine or harm another one.

- **Personality clashes**: Some members just are not a good fit with others, and this creates friction that becomes a problem for themselves and others.

When issues like this arise within a group, any number of conflict management experts can offer solutions. The best of these demonstrate that the conflict can actually reveal an opportunity to create a better understanding between people, change a flawed process, or find new solutions to recurring problems. Here are the most constructive steps a leader can use to resolve the conflict in a positive way:

1. **Do it now**: Deal with each conflict as it arises. Conflicts that go on for a long time without resolution can tear gaping holes in the team's morale, reducing its members' ability to work together to achieve the common goal.
2. **Be supportive**: Let all of the people involved know that they are valued members of the team and that you want to resolve the issue in as fair a manner as you can.
3. **Start off-line**: Ask each of the team members in the conflict to talk with you privately about their concern or grievance and to do so in a calm and professional manner.
4. **Come together**: Bring the people involved together to talk through the issue.
5. **Avoid blaming, shaming or judging** the people involved, and quell any insulting or provoking statements. Keep the discussion civil and constructive.
6. **Look for common ground**: Try to find areas of agreement among these people. Pinpoint their shared goal(s), and be sure that they know that in the end, they all want the same thing.
7. **Encourage participation**: Ask them for their solutions to the conflict. When you have a list of possible solutions, take each in turn and discuss what is good or bad about that idea. The final solution may use parts of several ideas.
8. **Be the leader**: If the conflict cannot be solved through group solution finding, be prepared to make a unilateral decision that will keep the group on track toward achieving its goal.

Let us go back to our stage crew to see this strategy in action.

At the end of the rehearsal, Thomas calls a production meeting and sits down with the stage crew. "There have been a lot of errors during rehearsals," he says, "and we need to fix these problems. We've all worked together before, so I know that you do a terrific job—and as we all know, every person on the crew has an important job to do during the performance. I'd like to know what's going wrong this time and get us all back on track."

The crew is silent for a moment, as no one wants to be the first to say that Suzanne has not been giving all the notes. Thomas says, "Okay, let's take one example. The gun wasn't in the desk drawer when Scott had to get it out and fire it. Who is in charge of putting it there?"

The crew members look at one another. Finally Linda says, "We aren't sure."

"Okay," says Thomas. "Then that's the problem. Suzanne, let's assign the gun to someone."

Suzanne assigns the placement of the gun to Linda, and Thomas, beginning to realize what the problem is, continues to go down the list of his notes until all the props and set pieces are assigned. At the end of the meeting, he thanks everyone for their patience and their willingness to solve the problem.

Once the crew has dispersed, he quietly takes Suzanne aside and asks if she wants to talk further about what has been happening. Suzanne readily admits that she feels overworked and torn between two crew positions. Thomas assures her that while she is capable of handling either role, the new assistant stage management position has more responsibility and requires a greater time commitment than Suzanne has been asked to take on before. "Let's find someone else to run the lighting console for this show," he said, "and after this production, when you've had the full experience, you can decide which job you prefer."

Suzanne agrees to this, and at the following day's rehearsal, Thomas asks for a volunteer to learn and run the lighting console. A crew member volunteers, and as it must, the show goes on.

By using the basic steps for effective conflict resolution, Thomas brought the matter to a close without causing new rifts between crew members or placing blame on any individual or group. He took the matter in hand immediately when he realized that things were going wrong, brought the entire group together to help solve the problem, and told the crew that he valued all of their skills and contributions to the effort. When he understood the source of the issue, he took Suzanne aside and came to an agreement, rather than blaming or shaming her in front of her colleagues.

The sooner conflicts are addressed, the sooner they can be resolved in ways that benefit as many people as possible—while minimizing the number of people who are hurt, humiliated, or angered by the outcome.

RESOLUTION: STRENGTHENING RELATIONSHIPS BY BREAKING CYCLES

One of the key elements in conflict management is achieving resolution, bringing together all of the parties involved to come to a solution that is agreeable—or at least not injurious—to as many people as possible.

In the stage crew example, Thomas clearly knew that he needed to preserve the sense of teamwork and camaraderie between workers that had begun to erode during the conflict. The more quickly he could bring the matter to a close, the better his chances were of allowing the damage to repair itself in short order. This would permit the crew to work together with the same level of efficiency they had had before the conflict arose.

Breaking the cycle of conflict is not always so easy, however. Nowhere is this more apparent than when a conflict arises between a husband and wife or between other close family members. Families have a special skill for perpetuating a conflict, cycling over and over through the same series of beliefs about one another to refuel their angry feelings.

Professor Jerry Robinson of Iowa State University, in his 1980 paper for the Department of Agricultural Economics, identified the most widely recognized stages in the conflict cycle. Most conflicts move through this or some variation of steps as they begin to perpetuate themselves.

- **Tension development**: The people involved find themselves on opposite sides of a disagreement.
- **Role dilemma**: The people begin to examine the problem and try to determine a course of action. They may come to some independent conclusions about who is right or wrong, and they decide what role they want to play in the conflict, choosing to be on one side or the other.
- **Injustice collecting**: Every infraction on the opposing side's part now becomes a reason to perpetuate the conflict. Small deeds or casually spoken words take on special meaning as proof of the other side's opposition or guilt in causing the conflict. Soon everything the other side does appears to be a direct slam against "our" side—further justification for each side's position against the other. Each side begins to develop strategies for attack, with a plan of proving themselves right and just.

- **Confrontation**: A showdown of some kind takes place. The two sides meet face-to-face, and an argument or battle ensues. If no one wins this direct confrontation, the two sides regroup and rally once again—and the conflict may go on for years.
- **Adjustments**: One side or the other—or both—agrees to adjust their actions or attitudes to lessen the conflict or even to resolve it once and for all. Perhaps both sides agree to abandon their angry feelings in favor of resolving a longtime family rift, or a husband and wife agree to sit down and talk through their differences calmly, to help them see one another's point of view. If the parties cannot find common ground and the period of adjustment goes wrong, however, the tension begins to develop once again, and the cycle starts over.

Breaking this cycle of conflict is the key to happy marriages, harmonious family relationships, and peace in the workplace—but it can be very hard to keep a conflict from perpetuating itself in this manner. Recent observations by psychologists of their own patients have led to the definition of "high conflict people," or HCPs, who actively create problems between themselves and others because of their inability to take responsibility for their own actions or admit to making a mistake. Randi Kreger, who has written extensively about people with borderline personality disorder, describes HCPs as people who "blame you for their own problems, have no empathy, and always seem to be conjuring up trouble." She notes that these people often have borderline personality disorder or narcissistic personality disorder, two mental illnesses that lead them to argue with people who try to give them constructive feedback and to insist on their own rigid points of view as the only correct ones—making everyone around them wrong.

Not all people who perpetuate conflict are suffering from a personality disorder, however. It can be easy to build up negative impressions and long lists of slights about a friend, spouse, parent, sibling, teacher, or other important person in your life and to become so certain that your own point of view is correct that every move the other person makes becomes a deliberate move against you. Breaking such a cycle may come through the assistance of a professional—a counselor, clergy member, or mediator—or through an indirect source that changes the perspective of the conflict.

Miranda and Fred were siblings who had a falling-out when they were both in their 20s, one severe enough that Miranda kept her distance from Fred and his family for more than a decade. Fred, meanwhile, married and had two children. Miranda heard about the children's birth and growth through her parents, but she resented every loving word her parents said about their grandchildren and every reference to Fred and his pleasant life. Over the years, she built a veritable catalog of hurts, slights, and offenses that made it seem impossible that she and Fred could ever repair their relationship.

When Fred and Miranda's parents celebrated their 50th wedding anniversary, Fred and his wife did not attend, but they sent their children—who were now 16 and 18—to celebrate with their grandparents. When the two teens stepped off the plane and discovered that the aunt they had never met was waiting for them, they were so excited to meet "Auntie Miranda" that they both began to cry with happiness. This moved Miranda to tears as well, and in minutes she realized that despite their long feud, her brother had not told his children that they should not love their aunt. Miranda realized that she had perpetuated a conflict for no good reason. That evening, she called her brother for the first time in years, and they began the process of reuniting as a family.

ESCALATION: WHEN CONFLICT GETS OUT OF CONTROL

Why can some conflicts be resolved with a minimum of pain to either side, while others become so volatile that they lead to angry words and deeds, severing of relationships, divorce, job termination, or even war?

For an answer to this question, we can turn to something so common that we have come to expect it. We see conflicts escalating every day in the comments sections of blogs and websites, as one or more commenters stray from the central point of an article or essay and begin to attack one another on an increasingly personal level. Sometimes it seems almost inexplicable that a perfectly reasonable discussion among people who do not know one another turns ugly.

In his seminal 2008 essay, "How to Disagree," business incubator investor Paul Graham suggests, "If we're all going to be disagreeing more, we should be careful to do it well." He cites seven levels of disagreement, each one building on the one before until the argument descends into labels and insults. (Graham actually cited these in reverse order, but others have noted that the sequence below is a solid model for the progression and escalation of most conflicts, especially those online.)

- **Refuting the central point**: One person disagrees with the point the reader/speaker has made and tells him or her so by respectfully presenting an opposing view in a reasonable fashion: "You have said that eating more whole grains will make people healthier, but I think that the accompanying gastric discomfort creates a difficult trade-off."

- **Refutation**: This differs from refuting the central point in that a person actually quotes the author/speaker, using the speaker's own words to make the case that the thinking is wrong: "You said, 'Whole-grain pasta is a smarter choice than regular pasta.' But some pastas now contain both whole grains and processed wheat as well as some nutrients. These also may be viable choices."
- **Counterargument**: Graham defines this as "contradiction plus reasoning and/or evidence." He notes that counterargument can be convincing when it is aimed at what the writer or speaker actually said—but usually, it is aimed at something else: "You said eating whole grains is healthier. I say you should be talking about fruits, vegetables, and low-fat foods as better alternatives." When the writer or speaker responds by saying "These foods are good as well, but my essay was about whole grains—you've brought up an entirely different thing," the commenter most likely will respond again with an angrier tone: "You're so focused on whole grains that you're not seeing the bigger picture. That's misleading to your readers."
- **Contradiction**: The commenter states an opposing case, often with no basis in fact. "You say whole grains are good for us, but I say that they're loaded with hormones and genetic modifications, and no one should eat them."
- **Responding to tone**: Here is where so many comment threads go wrong. People following the comments begin to post their emotional reactions: "Why do you have to be such a jerk? This is about whole grains, not everything you should or shouldn't eat. I don't like your attitude. I'll bet you're stuffing your face with white bread, mayonnaise, and potato chips right now."
- **Ad hominem**: The commenter may point out some useful information but in a confrontational fashion: "She's just writing about whole grains because she works for a big baked goods corporation. That's why she doesn't care about overall healthy eating." The goal of the commenter is to discredit the writer but not to descend to the next level.
- **Name-calling**: Actual disagreement and reasoned discourse fall away, and the commenters simply start calling each other puerile names: "You're a hipster poser and a socialist! I hope you choke on your quinoa."

This hierarchy of disagreements gives us insights about the escalation of a conflict, but it is meant to examine the most basic arguments, particularly the ones that take place online. As we look to larger and more serious conflicts, we need greater levels of evaluation to understand how such a conflict gets out of control.

Salzburg University professor and conflict prevention authority Friedrich Glasl developed what has become the classic model of conflict escalation. Published in 1992, it continues to serve as the most detailed and applicable template for understanding the phenomenon. In developing this model, Glasl meant to encourage the parties involved in the conflict to recognize the stage they have reached and to look for potential action to end the conflict before it gets out of control.

1. **Calcification**: Each side becomes rigid and solid in its conviction that it is right. The people involved know that they are in conflict, but they hope to find an amicable solution by meeting and discussing their differences.
2. **Debate**: Shades of gray begin to disappear as the two (or more) sides of the argument begin to see things in black-and-white terms. Thought, emotion, and will become polarized, and the opponents see themselves in terms of good versus bad, superior versus inferior, and right versus wrong.
3. **Action**: The sides determine that there is no point in continuing the discussion. They no longer wish to find common ground or compromise with the others. Now every move one side takes becomes more evidence of wrongdoing for the other side, and vice versa.
4. **Coalitions**: Each side begins to spread rumors about the other, and stereotypes form as prejudices mount up. The sides begin to search for and round up supporters. Tensions build, and the sides actively look for opportunities for confrontation.
5. **Loss of face**: During acts of aggression, it is inevitable that one side will win, while the other comes out looking weaker.
6. **Threat as a strategy**: The two sides make threats and counterthreats, and the conflict escalates as one side administers an ultimatum to the other.
7. **Limited attempts to overthrow the opponent**: The two sides lose sight of the fact that their opponents are people, seeing them instead as a government, a coalition with a name, an organization, or a level of power (i.e., "management"). One side now tries to overthrow the other by discrediting it, making life very uncomfortable for it or—in the largest conflicts—actively demonstrating and rioting. Any damage done to the opponent's name, reputation, property, or person becomes an incremental victory.

8. **Dissipation:** The side that strives to topple the other one (especially in situations where one has power over the other) pursues this goal of destruction with great zeal.
9. **Together into the abyss:** Massive confrontation takes place, often leading to ongoing war. Both sides accept that in working to destroy the other, they may be destroyed themselves. This truth is not only accepted but also made a badge of honor as people begin to "die for their cause."

While this model gives us some vivid insights into how wars develop, it also shows us how conflicts escalate between entities like employee unions and corporate management, opposing political parties, and religious extremists and their targets for terrorism. We will look more closely at some of these in Chapter 6, but let us examine one prevalent issue that affects people around the world: racial discrimination.

PREJUDICE AND DISCRIMINATION: WHEN ONE GROUP DESPISES ANOTHER

Negative emotions and irrational beliefs about one group are the bases for prejudice, a form of conflict that can lead to hatred and violence between groups. The irrational thoughts often are linked to ignorance, based in the belief that because of the color of a person's skin, the way he or she worships, the sexual preference or gender identity of an individual, or the part of the country in which a person lives, he or she acts, thinks, behaves, or is genetically predestined to be any number of negative things.

We see the results of prejudice every day in the news media and online. One of the most dramatic examples in recent years took place in Missouri in 2014, when police and residents clashed for weeks over the August 9 shooting death of Michael Brown, an unarmed black teenager, by a white policeman. Protestors filled the streets with angry demonstrations, which quickly led to destruction of property and violent acts. When a grand jury concluded that Officer Darren Wilson should not be indicted for the shooting death, protests erupted again as black residents—joined by many demonstrators of other races—decried the decision as an act of bigotry. Chanting "Black Lives Matter," the phrase that would become the motto of a nationwide movement, protestors filled the streets as some vandalized, looted, and burned businesses and buildings throughout Ferguson's commercial district. Missouri governor Jay Nixon called in the National Guard to bring the situation under tenuous control, mobilizing as many as 1,200 armed guards into the city to protect federal buildings and assist local police in quelling the violence.

Amid all of the chaos, however, the U.S. Justice Department stepped in to determine the truth to claims that the predominantly white police force deliberately targeted black citizens. The numbers turned out to be staggering: while the population of Ferguson was 67 percent black and 29 percent white, black people accounted for 86 percent of the vehicle stops made by Ferguson's predominantly white police force in 2013 and for 92 percent of the arrests for disorderly conduct. The Justice Department report also stated that black people "had force used against them at disproportionately high rates, accounting for 88% of all cases from 2010 to August 2014 in which an FPD officer reported using force." The *Washington Post* said when the report came out on March 4, 2015, "The federal investigation produced overwhelming evidence that these disparities are due to bias in the criminal justice system." The Justice Department determined that the city of Ferguson had violated the U.S. Constitution, and it ordered the city to overhaul its criminal justice system.

Prejudices against a specific group are one of the oldest reasons in recorded history for acts of aggression against individuals, gangs, neighborhoods, districts, countries, and entire races. We have seen this in recent years in the wars against people of different nationality backgrounds in Bosnia-Herzegovina; between Sunnis and Shiites in Iraq; among the various terror organizations including ISIS, Al-Qaeda, and the Taliban in their disdain for people of Western cultures; and here in the United States as several southern states attempt to pass and enforce laws that permit discrimination against transgender individuals using public restrooms.

What causes these prejudices between groups? This question has troubled psychologists since the earliest days of the science. Sigmund Freud proposed that prejudice springs from the "narcissism of irrelevant differences," a tendency for some people to magnify the minor differences between themselves and others and view these as intolerable faults. Taking this to the logical extreme, such people believe that only those who are identical to them are good and right, so all others who are different must be avoided.

In 1954, psychologist Gordon Allport hypothesized that prejudice may be reduced by repeated contact between people of equal status from the conflicting groups in pursuit of common goals. "The effect is greatly enhanced if this contact is sanctioned by institutional supports (i.e. by law, custom or local atmosphere), and provided it is of a sort that leads to the perception of common interests and common humanity between members of the two groups." Allport's contact hypothesis has borne out in a great deal of research: in 203 studies involving more than 90,000 participants, prejudice was reduced 94 percent of the time as contact between groups increased.

The theory works in the shelter of a study, but the real world application has proved much more difficult to achieve. The biggest stumbling block is equal status: when competition and conflict fuel prejudice, the groups involved usually are not of equal status. In Ferguson, for example, the police had all the power, while the black citizens were at a significant disadvantage in every encounter.

Today researchers are examining techniques that place people in small, racially diverse groups, in which they must work together to achieve a common goal. The cooperative and interdependent relationship helps break down stereotypes between groups, increasing empathy and decreasing the barriers that form when people "type" one another into categories based on skin color, religion, or sexual preference.

DOMESTIC VIOLENCE: THE PSYCHOLOGY OF DOMINATION

Of all the forms of conflict, one of the most difficult to understand is domestic violence. This aggressive, physically hurtful behavior within the home, usually entailing the abuse of a spouse or partner, involves increasing levels of conflict for the purpose of willful intimidation. The ongoing physical assault, battering, sexual assault, psychological violence, and emotional abuse all stem from one partner's continuous effort to maintain control and power over the other.

The National Coalition against Domestic Violence (NCADV) reports that more than 10 million men and women are victims of physical abuse by a domestic partner each year. It may seem that the potential for such a relationship would be obvious from the very beginning, but the NCADV reports that the pattern of domestic violence intensifies over time, so it can be difficult or even impossible to tell from the outset if a partner will become abusive in the relationship.

Once a person finds him or herself in an abusive relationship, escape can come with its own set of hazards. Abusers may stalk their victims, deny that they abused them, or beg the victim to return because "things will be better." Even when courts issue retraining orders or law enforcement intervenes, the abuser may ignore the orders and come after the victim anyway.

The results of this inability to extricate oneself from an abusive relationship are staggering. The World Health Organization (WHO) has determined that more than 38 percent of all murders of women worldwide involve an intimate partner as the murderer. One in three women around the world has been the victim of physical violence at the hands of an intimate partner.

The perpetrators of domestic violence tend to be people with little education, previous exposure to violence in the family (often as children), and the belief that violence is an acceptable option within the family unit. These people often see women as the lesser gender with fewer rights. Many offenders also abuse alcohol. The victims, according to WHO, accept violence and gender inequality as norms within the family, and they may have been abuse victims as children or witnessed abuse between their parents while growing up. Lack of education is a factor among victims as well.

In terms of conflict management and resolution, relationships involving domestic abuse rarely, if ever, can be transformed into nonviolent relationships in which both partners are on equal ground. Instead, therapy focuses on prevention strategies, including training in gender equality and relationship skills, to keep people who may have grown up in families in which violence was commonplace from carrying this experience into their adult relationships.

In this chapter, we have examined the many roles that conflict can play in our lives and the potential for any conflict to be either positive or negative. Each disagreement reveals an opportunity for change—for better or worse. Some conflicts grow far beyond a heated exchange between two or more people, and they become the basis for years, decades, or centuries of continuous feelings of hostility. Others become the catalyst for improved performance as one side works to prove its superiority to the other.

What turns one conflict into an opportunity for change and another into a destructive force? This question and many others have puzzled researchers since the earliest days of the study of psychology and sociology. We will take a close look at the theories and research in Chapter 4.

4

Who: Psychologists' Theories about Conflict

Theories of the motivations for conflict form an important bridge between the fields of psychology and sociology. Not only do individuals perceive conflict within themselves (psychology), but they also relate that sense of conflict to their environment, the people in all aspects of their lives, and their perception of the place they fill and the role they have within that context (sociology).

While conflict has been a significant part of human life since the very first people walked the earth, the first theories and analyses of these human inter-actions did not emerge in any major way until the nineteenth century—and then in the context of political and social struggle.

MARX AND ENGELS: THE STRUGGLES BETWEEN CLASSES

Karl Marx, the originator of the political theory known as socialism, also served as an economist, sociologist, and philosopher whose work influ-enced the governments of entire countries. He proposed the theory that class struggle is the root of conflict in human societies: the difference in perspective between the ownership class, which owns the businesses and factories that control production, and the laboring class that provides the work that produces goods and services. As long as the ownership class has more power and money than the laboring class, the owners will lord their power over the workers. Social conflict, then, was the struggle between these two groups in society over limited resources.

"The history of all hitherto existing society is the history of class strug-gles," Marx and his collaborator, Frederick Engels, wrote in the first chap-ter of their most famous work, *The Communist Manifesto*. "Freeman and slave, patrician and plebeian, lord and serf, guild-master and journeyman, in a word, oppressor and oppressed, stood in constant opposition to one another, carried on an uninterrupted, now hidden, now open fight, that each time ended, either in a revolutionary reconstitution of society at large, or in the common ruin of the contending classes."

Marx and Engels saw society in terms of just two classes: the *bourgeoisie*—the class that owns the vast majority of the society's wealth and property; and the *proletariat*—the common wage earners who worked for the bourgeoisie. While these terms are associated most closely with the communist view Marx espoused, he actually used them to define the roles in a capitalist soci-ety: the wealthy class and the working class. These two groups could only exist on opposing sides of society—Marx and Engels noted—as "two great hostile camps" whose views and motives could not possibly be reconciled without revolution. Through this paradigm, society became an arena in which inequality served as the catalyst for conflict—and that conflict created social change. Only a few could benefit from such a construct, and those few were the ones with the vast majority of the money.

The bourgeoisie and the proletariat had been in conflict for centuries—these philosophers wrote—taking similar roles during the Middle Ages, when landowners employed serfs to till their land and required these workers to provide a hefty share of their harvest to the landowners. When manufactur-ing replaced the feudal system and the demand for goods from factories grew, the role of a middle class of skilled craftsmen vanished, pushing these people down into the proletariat. Over time, "steam and machinery revolutionized industrial production. The place of manufacture was taken by the giant, Modern Industry; the place of the industrial middle class by industrial mil-lionaires, the leaders of the whole industrial armies, the modern bourgeois."

When the feudal era ended and the Industrial Revolution invited work-ers to leave the fields for all the jobs in manufacturing, free competition changed the way the bourgeoisie saw their role in society—all while expanding their earning power exponentially. Now they not only owned the means of production, but they also faced new challenges to their wealth, one of the most threatening of which was overproduction: the problem of exceeding the demand for products with the supply. This—Marx argued—created the most volatile conflicts in the social construct.

"It is enough to mention the commercial crises that by their periodical return put the existence of the entire bourgeois society on its trial, each time more threateningly. In these crises, a great part not only of the existing products, but also of the previously created productive forces, are periodically destroyed. In these crises, there breaks out an epidemic that, in all earlier epochs, would have seemed an absurdity—the epidemic of over-production. Society suddenly finds itself put back into a state of momentary barbarism; it appears as if a famine, a universal war of devastation, had cut off the supply of every means of subsistence; industry and commerce seem to be destroyed; and why? Because there is too much civilization, too much means of subsistence, too much industry, too much commerce."

And how—Marx and Engels ask—does the bourgeoisie get past such crises? "On the one hand by enforced destruction of a mass of productive forces; on the other, by the conquest of new markets, and by the more thorough exploitation of the old ones. That is to say, by paving the way for more extensive and more destructive crises, and by diminishing the means whereby crises are prevented."

The Communist Manifesto proposed that conflicts within society are not only man-made but also deliberately crafted—vehicles through which the very wealthy find ways to make more money.

This macro view of societal conflict became the first to examine the relationships between groups and the conflicts that can arise through two important catalysts: inequality and competition. When one social group has more power than another one, the basis is already in place for conflict to arise. If one group has something other than power that the other group feels it should have—land, money, resources, or status, for example—the unequal status between the two will inevitably lead to some level of conflict.

WE, OTHER, IN, AND OUT: THE ROOTS OF ETHNOCENTRISM

In 1906, William Graham Sumner, a professor of political and social science at Yale University, presented a somewhat less macro view of conflict between social groups in his book, *Folkways: A Study of the Sociological Importance of Usages, Manners, Customs, Mores, and Morals.* Sumner saw divisions within society that went well beyond the either-or segments of Marx and Engels's theory, noting that people divide into groups he summarized as "we-group" and "other-group." Most people are in a selection of groups based on, according to Sumner, the conditions of their "struggle for existence." Groups may have some relation to one another—perhaps they share a neighborhood or a family, or they are all part of a larger organization like a company or an association. In all cases, however, the group develops characteristics that make its members part of the "we-group" and make those with different characteristics part of those "other-groups."

Sumner took this a step further, describing the connections and divisions with words that imply more deliberate judgment. People who share comradeship are in the "in-group," while those in the other groups may be seen as "out-groups." "The relation of comradeship and peace in the we-group and that of hostility and war towards the other-groups are correlative to each other," he wrote. "The exigencies of war with outsiders are what make peace inside, lest internal discord should weaken the we-group for war. These exigencies also make government and law in the in-group, in order to prevent quarrels and enforce discipline. Thus war and peace have reacted on each other and developed each other, one within the group, the other in the intergroup relation."

Sumner coined the term *ethnocentrism* to describe "this view of things in which one's own group is the center of everything, and all others are scaled and rated with reference to it. . . . Each group nourishes its own pride and vanity, boasts itself superior, exalts its own divinities, and looks with contempt on outsiders. Each group thinks its own folkways the only right ones, and if it observes that other groups have other folkways, these excite its scorn."

Ethnocentrism leads people to exaggerate the characteristics of one group over another or to use a single trait of the out-group as a reason to hate the people within it. For example, differences in the skin color of one group may lead another group to decide the darker-skinned group deserves scorn and hatred. The customs of one religion's worship service may seem grounds for disparaging other groups—so if one group rejects pork products, its members may determine that all who eat pork should be despised. A country's leadership may decide that all people who wish to enter that country must speak the language of that land, immediately making anyone who does not speak that language an outcast.

This decisive, specific anger or hate toward one group by another may seem almost entirely random, but it can perpetuate through generations, Sumner notes. "Men of an others-group are outsides with whose ancestors the ancestors of the we-group waged war. The ghosts of the latter will see with pleasure their descendants keep up the fight, and will help them. Virtue consists in killing, plundering, and enslaving outsiders."

SMALL GROUP DYNAMICS AND CONFLICT

In 1954, a group of scientists from the fields of psychology, sociology, and anthropology came together to do actual field and laboratory work in the area of small group dynamics. Others had attempted studies of social behavior in a lab setting at the beginning of the century, but the group led by Muzafer Sherif designed a new approach. "In the 1930s it became increasingly evident that social behavior (cooperation-competition, ascendance-submission, etc.) could not be properly studied when the individual is considered in isolation," the study points out. "Psychological 'trait' theories or personality typologies fell far short in explaining social relations."

In an effort to bring all the disciplines in the social sciences together for a single study, Sherif and his cohorts chose to study small group dynamics, a field that had gained in popularity among social scientists of the time. The small group offered the opportunity to study the behavior of individuals (psychology) as well as the influence of the group (sociology). It also provided a chance to observe the development of collective actions on the part of the entire group, including customs and mores that would be of interest to anthropologists.

This landmark experiment came to be known as Robbers Cave, because it took place at a state park by that name in the Sans Bois Mountains in southeastern Oklahoma. Here in a 200-acre Boy Scouts of America camp, Sherif's three-week study placed two groups of 11-year-old boys in isolation in a summer camp setting, planning their activities and controlling the times when the two groups would interact.

The scientists selected boys from established Protestant families, choosing only boys who were considered "normal" (no unusual degree of frustration in their homes or schools) and who had a similar level of education. These boys were divided into the two groups, keeping the groups separated for the first several days of the experiment so that no accidental interaction took place. "Step-by-step tracing of group structure and its norms is essential in pin-pointing the factors that enter into the shaping of group behavior now," the researchers wrote. "Groups in actual life do not ordinarily strive toward goals which are furnished by the instructions of an outsider. Group goals exist or arise because group members are situated in a certain place and time, under given circumstances, and because the pattern of interaction is what it is. All of these determinants have specific implications in relation to the state of motivation of group members."

Sherif and his cohorts introduced problem situations "appropriate to the characteristics of the stage in question" and then stayed out of the interactions among the group participants while relationships came to light and situations unfolded. This made the experiment unique among studies of small group dynamics up to that time. In most of the previous studies, a researcher often interrupted the activity to check in with the subjects about their thought processes, feelings, or actions. By keeping a professional distance from the situation and using camp counselors as "participant observers," Sherif et al. (1954) allowed the group to move forward spontaneously, without the intrusive sense of being observed and studied. The participant observers introduced activities and served as "the ultimate authority in setting bounds," but the real purpose of these adults was the running of the experiment itself. They introduced problem situations by "setting appropriate stimulus conditions at appropriate times," keeping quiet as the groups determined their next actions and interfering only when absolutely necessary.

In the first week—what the researchers called Stage 1—the two groups did not interact with one another at all, and they did not even know another group was at the camp until their sixth day at the park. The two groups formed their own structures, with some campers rising to positions of esteem within their groups, while others sank in status and took no leadership roles.

One group, who called themselves the Rattlers, worked together toward common goals with a minimum of internal conflict. Of their own volition, they decided to become proficient in pitching tents and held drills to improve their skills, and they encouraged one another to jump from a diving board at the swimming area "so that we will all be able to swim," providing a supportive environment for boys who were afraid to jump. The Rattlers established roles for each boy in preparing meals and playing baseball and rehearsed and presented group skits at a campfire—all of their own volition. When given problems to solve—such as the number of items they could order from the camp canteen—they worked together to determine which items they would request.

The Eagles, the name selected by the second group, entered into lengthy negotiations over activities like where to swim and whether to ask for window screens for their cabin, which was closer to water than the Rattlers's cabin, making the boys targets for mosquitoes. Two members of the Eagles developed such keen homesickness that they were allowed to leave the experiment at the end of the first week. Even with these challenges, the group coalesced around a leader, just as the Rattlers did, and consistent patterns of communication formed in which the leader (a boy named Craig in the study) had the opportunity to accept or reject any suggestions from other group members.

The researchers observed that both groups formed their own structure and norms of behavior, which were reinforced and standardized by the leaders. Each group discovered places in its half of the park that the group adopted as "ours," including a swimming hole the Rattlers decided was "our hideout" and a campfire circle the Eagles gave a name on their first day in camp. Boys in the Rattlers decided that crying over an injury meant that they were not "tough," and toughness became a norm for the group. The Eagles determined that swimming in the nude was preferable, and many of the boys shed their trunks over the course of the next few days. They also made fun of the two homesick boys, determining that homesickness was not acceptable in their group.

By the time each group realized that there was another group in camp—discovered by overhearing them playing baseball—this new group immediately became an out-group. Suddenly a baseball diamond neither group had claimed previously was "our diamond," and there were comments about "those guys" who had "better not be in our swimming hole." The Rattlers were ready to challenge this new group to a baseball game and started working on their ball-playing skills in anticipation of that opportunity. One member of the Eagles went so far as to refer to the other group using racial slurs, though it took several days before any of the Eagles suggested that they challenge the other group to a game.

By the end of Stage 1, the two groups had met all of the researchers' criteria for the next stage. The boys in each group had formed in-group structures and norms, and they had established a sense of "us" versus "them" when they discovered that a second group existed in camp. Now the researchers could proceed to Stage 2 and introduce friction between the two groups.

Both groups were eager to play competitive games with the other, so the staff members made arrangements for a tournament, introducing the ideas of a trophy, prizes, and medals. The Rattlers had confidence that they would win the tournament, while the Eagles were more reticent, asking if the other group had been practicing their skills. Staff members announced a series of contests and events the experimenters had chosen to keep the balance of winners and losers fairly even, holding all of the boys' interest through the end of the seven-day tournament.

The contests became the main focus of the week for all of the boys, and they produced the conflict the researchers hoped to create, "manifested in actual physical encounters and practice sessions in preparation for them, in group discussion, in self-justifying and self-glorifying words used in relation to themselves, and invectives and derogatory terms hurled at the out-group in actual encounters and in reference to the out-group in the privacy of the in-group circle." The norms of good sportsmanship the boys brought with them to camp gave way by the third day of the tournament "to increased name-calling, hurling invectives, and derogation of the out-group to the point that the groups became more and more reluctant to have anything to do with one another." Since the Eagles had only nine members after two boys had been sent home at the end of the first week, two Rattlers had to sit out each of the baseball and tug-of-war competitions—but the two on the sidelines became the most vocal in yelling insults at the Eagles, as if to make up for their lack of play.

When the Eagles lost both competitions on the first day, they spotted the Rattlers's flag on the ball field, yanked it down, and set fire to it, hanging the charred remains back up where it had flown. "This flag-burning episode started a chain of events which made it unnecessary for the experimenters to introduce special situations of mutual frustration for the two groups," the report said. When the Rattlers discovered their burnt flag, they made a plan for retaliation that included stealing the Eagles's flag and starting a fistfight, both of which took place just as they had intended. Staff members had to step in to stop the fighting.

Throughout the rest of the experiment, conflict escalated to include raids on each other's cabins and threats of more violent retaliation, some of the boys preparing bats, sticks, and socks filled with rocks. The Eagles, however, came to believe that they were starting to win because of the prayer sessions they held at the beginning of each game, and they resolved to be good sports despite the catcalling hurled at them by the Rattlers. When the Eagles won the tournament and all the prizes, the Rattlers responded by raiding their cabin and taking the prizes and medals. The Eagles came after them and shouted insults and accusations across "an invisible line," but once two boys made physical contact, staff members stepped in and broke up the battle, forcing the boys up the trail to their cabin. The camp director rounded up the prizes taken by the Rattlers and returned them to the Eagles.

This fascinating study took the understanding of the psychology of conflict to a new level. Its findings could be applied to all kinds of group conflict, from the behavior of street gangs to warring nations.

- If the interests and goals of the out-group are in harmony with the in-group, the in-group will attribute favorable features to the out-group. If the out-group's interests and goals do not integrate with the in-group's goals, the in-group will ostracize the out-group, attributing negative stereotypes to them and seeing them as the reason for their frustrations.
- Leaders of each in-group will use stereotypes and derogatory terms to manipulate the in-group into escalating conflicts with the out-group.
- During group formation, each group will select physical areas that are "ours" and will defend these areas against what they consider intrusion from the out-group.

- Members of the in-group will judge the overall performance of their group to be higher than the out-group, even in situations in which the actual performance is about the same.
- Members of the in-group will continue to have negative attitudes toward the out-group, even when they have no further interaction with them.

Next, Sherif et al. (1954) implemented a third stage of the experiment: an approach to reducing the friction between the two groups. "It would have been a relatively easy task to bring about positive relations or harmony between groups right after the formation of the two in-groups," Sherif wrote. "We deliberately postponed this positive step in intergroup relations until after the unpleasant task of producing a state of friction, because the vital issue of intergroup relations in the present-day world is the reduction of existing intergroup friction."

Through a series of situations in which the two groups had contact with one another but were not in active competition, the researchers found that putting the two groups in the same room or area was not enough to reduce the animosities between them. When taking meals in the same mess hall, food fights ensued, and the level of catcalling and cursing at one another increased, rather than decreasing as the experimenters had predicted.

Next, the researchers introduced situations in which the two groups had to interact to reach a common goal. They cut off the water supply to the camp and informed both groups at once that vandals had tinkered with the water system—thus making it clear that no campers or counselors had done this. Volunteers from each group, led by their counselors, formed two details to the reservoir to find the problem. By this time, the boys were very thirsty, a condition that apparently overrode their dislike for one another. They discovered a sack stuffed into the faucet on the side of the reservoir and worked cooperatively to remove it, and then one group stepped aside and let the other group—who did not have canteens with them—drink from the faucet before they filled their own canteens. Over the remaining days at camp, researchers set up other "superordinate situations" in which a goal of interest to all the boys would require them to work together to reach it. The boys found cooperative ways to contribute money to secure rental of a movie, worked out which group would enter the mess hall first at each meal, and stopped one another from initiating another food fight once the cook asked them to end their pattern of throwing food and garbage at each other. When the boys took an overnight camping trip and the truck carrying the food would not start (a contrivance by the researchers), the boys decided together to tie ropes to the bumper and use their combined tug-of-war skills to pull the truck until it started. Soon the boys prepared meals together without being directed to do so, and they began to sit together to eat as well. By the last night in camp, the boys held a campfire sing and roasted marshmallows together at the Rattlers's campfire circle and performed skits for one another.

Sherif and his team concluded from this that when groups in conflict with one another are brought together to reach a common goal, they will cooperate with one another to achieve that goal. This cooperation will have a cumulative effect, so the more goals the two groups work together to achieve, the less tension will remain, and the better the relationship will become between the groups.

The Robbers Cave experiment, despite the issues we may have today with the ethics of performing such elaborate experiments on unwitting young boys, broke new ground in our understanding of conflict between groups and the methods that may be effective in reducing such conflict.

RETHINKING REALISTIC CONFLICT THEORY

Perhaps building off of Sherif's work and others in the field, Lewis A. Coser of Brandeis University introduced the idea of two different types of social conflict: the rational and the irrational. Rational conflict is a means to an end, a competitive situation between two groups with different interests or goals. Irrational conflict, then, is an end in itself—it allows a group or individual to release tensions, choose a scapegoat to blame for a bad situation, or build up lasting discrimination against another person or group whether or not group members can remember the reason for these conflicts at a later time.

Henri Tajfel challenged this dichotomy in his 1970 paper, "Experiments in Intergroup Discrimination," published in *Scientific American*. "Often it is difficult, and probably fruitless, to speculate about what were the first causes of real present-day social situations," he wrote. "Once the process is set in motion they reinforce each other in a relentless spiral in which the weight of predominant causes tends to shift continuously. For example, economic or social competition can lead to discriminatory behavior; that behavior can then in a number of ways create attitudes of prejudice; those attitudes can in turn lead to new forms of discriminatory behavior that creates new economic or social disparities, and so the vicious cycle is continued."

Based on Sherif's findings in Robbers Cave and other experiments, Tajfel and John C. Turner proposed an additional hypothesis about intergroup conflict. They observed that Sherif's work created a situation in

which the distribution of resources became somehow legitimized or justified and that this reduced the ethnocentrism between the groups (e.g.,
when the boys of both groups pooled their available funds to buy access
to a movie they all wanted to see). Tajfel and Turner saw this differently,
suggesting that if one group is dominant and the other subordinate, then
"an unequal distribution of objective resources promotes antagonism
between dominant and subordinate groups, provided that the latter group
rejects its previously accepted and consensually negative self-image, and
with it the status quo, and starts working toward the development of a positive group identity. The dominant group may react to these developments
either by doing everything possible to maintain and justify the status quo
or by attempting to find and create new differentiations in its own favor,
or both."

Simply becoming aware that there is an out-group can be enough to
trigger a sense of competition and even discrimination, the researchers
determined. In a series of studies, subjects were assigned to two groups
based on some trivial and inconsequential criteria. The subjects had no
actual contact, so they had no opportunity to form friendships or hostilities
toward their own group or the other group. Each subject was asked to
assign amounts of money to pairs of individuals in two groups—and the
identities of these people were kept anonymous except for a number
assigned to each (i.e., member 51 of the X group or member 33 of the Y
group). The subjects all knew which group—X or Y—they belonged to,
but they knew nothing else about the rest of the subjects.

Remarkably, the "basic and highly reliable finding" of these experiments
revealed that even this trivial association with one group or another created a bias toward that group. The subjects assigned more money to the
group to which they belonged, even though they themselves would see
no benefit from their group receiving more money. Tajfel and Turner
determined that the subjects "seemed to be competing with the out-
group, rather than following a strategy of simple economic gain for members of the in-group." Their data also showed that the subjects gave relatively less money to the out-group even when the amounts of money the
in-group got were not affected—when they could give as much as they
wanted to either group.

Most striking of all was the researchers' work with subjects assigned into
groups that were explicitly random. Even when the subjects knew that
there were no inherent similarities between the people in either group,
they still discriminated against the out-group, as if they believed their
own group to be somehow superior to the other randomly selected group.
This finding received a great deal of testing by other researchers

throughout the 1980s, and they all replicated the results: "Even explicitly arbitrary social categorizations are sufficient for discrimination."

THE CONFLICT MODEL

Throughout the 1960s and 1970s, a number of researchers examined what came to be called the conflict model. "According to this model the group is like an arena in that it is a place where one sees an endless series of conflicts," wrote Yale University professor Theodore M. Mills in his book, *The Sociology of Small Groups*. "Group experience is conflict. It is a response to the reality that there is a shortage of what people need and want." Citing both philosophers and sociologists in his summary of the model, Mills noted, "Change, which occurs at every moment, is determined both in direction and quality by the manner in which conflicts are resolved. Response to conflict determines the new state of the system. And though one conflict may be reduced, its resolution will be accompanied by new strains, so that the course of group history can be described by its endless sequential confrontation of conflict. No group is conflict-free; when one seems so, it is possible that it is in conflict over facing its real conflicts."

The conflict model suggests that groups and individuals "deny, cover over, and project onto others their internal conflicts," assuming that conflict exists even when the members of the group are not aware of it. By admonishing groups to focus entirely on the conflicts in relationships, the model asserts that it will counteract "the contagious beliefs of strong and satisfied members that everyone else in the group is satisfied."

This model has its limits, Mills noted, in that it does not explain how groups in continuous conflict can manage to hold together as a cohesive unit. Nor does it take into account mutual respect between group members, real admiration for the group's leaders, or the eventual need for consensus within the group to resolve an issue. "One may imagine the leader who takes the conflict model as his only serious guide for action, e.g., a mother frantically quelling one squabble after the other among her children, instead of getting on with the work of the day; or the manager of the firm who is distracted into keeping the peace instead of leading the company. By-and-large, both mothers and managers have a broader perspective on conflict."

Vamik D. Volkan, in presenting his presidential address at the 1984 meeting of the Society of Political Psychology, took on some of the questions of group cohesion and personal identity and the role of conflict in keeping these things sound. He proposed that people need enemies as much as they need allies as well as "stubborn adherence to identification with a group when undergoing hardship and danger." He cited this need as the basis for political psychology, "connecting the public arena of political action with individual psychological development."

Coming from the perspective of psychoanalysis, Volkan defined what he called "suitable targets of externalization" that play a role in linking each person's already internalized values—most often from their parents—with groups outside of him or herself. These not only help the individual define his or her ethnicity, nationality, and other places in the world, but they also become the foundation for choosing allies and enemies. "It is through identification, an unconscious mechanism of the ego, that one assimilates the images of the other into one's own self, becoming like the other in many ways," he explained. "Although identification, with disruptive images of others, may lead to problems, through adaptive identifications one is enriched and enabled to increase his repertoire of psychic functions, including those useful in the protection and regulation of the sense of self."

Volkan suggested that while ethnicity and nationality are environmental rather than biologically related, there seems to be some psychological and biological development that requires us to form some external connection with people of the same background and culture. "Ethnicity, nationality, and similar abstractions are creation of our own psyche and thus it is reasonable to regard the psyche as the creation of the concept of the enemy," Volkan said. "We cannot reasonably assert that the enemy may not be in fact a dangerous force, but it is still true that the 'enemy' is a creation of that developmental process in which perception is complicated by higher-level thought, internalization, and oedipal issues."

The enemy actually resembles us, Volkan noted, but we apply what Sigmund Freud called "the narcissism of minor differences," allowing small dissimilarities to alter our view, regarding the perceived enemy with hostility.

"I believe that the need to have enemies and allies is the basis of political psychology and that it connects politics, not only to the psychology apparent in surface behavior and evident processes, but also with depth psychology which deals with the dynamics of human development," Volkan concluded.

THE CONTACT HYPOTHESIS

While University of Essex professor Michael Nicholson published several books in the 1980s and 1990s on the use of quantitative analysis and statistical methods to study conflict on a global scale, many other researchers focused on the relatively new field of social psychology, examining conflict on the interpersonal or small group level. Quite a number of researchers tested the conclusions of the 1950s that interaction among members of groups in conflict can reduce prejudices and defuse hostilities between the groups.

This theory, known as the *contact hypothesis*, suggests that if people from two groups in conflict came together in one place and got to know one another as individuals, the conflict born of stereotypes and prejudice would gradually disappear. Brewer and Miller proposed the model of decategorization, contact in which the people involved are not painted with one brush—that is, the members of an out-group are not categorized as if they all have identical traits the in-group finds distasteful. If group memberships are made less important when they interact, and if social relations between the groups are more interpersonal, rather than as two separate teams or two sides of a conflict, prejudices should be reduced as the group members see the people of the other group as individuals. The more personalized the interactions among people from both groups, the less stereotyping and prejudice there will be.

Later studies showed that personalized contact by itself does not guarantee an improvement of relationships between groups, because the positive experiences individuals have with members of the out-group do not generalize to the entire group. Hewstone and Brown took another hard look at the contact hypothesis and found that maintaining the importance of the group as a whole strengthens the new, positive attitudes between members of two groups. "Intergroup contact works, if and when it does, because it changes the nature and structure of the intergroup relationship—not because it permits and encourages interpersonal friendships between members of different groups," they noted in their 1986 book, *Contact and Conflict in Intergroup Encounters*. Reducing the perception that every person in the group has the same characteristics—good or bad—prevents the in-group from categorizing the out-group as all one thing or another.

Brewer returned to this issue later to examine it more closely. She noted that stereotypes are a natural consequence of categorization, or forming a simple concept about an object, place, or person—a way to make sense of that person with a few basic characteristics. When a person perceives this person as part of an out-group, this basic concept may take on negative characteristics.

"What makes social categorization different from nonsocial categorization systems, however, is the potential for self-involvement in that social perceivers are themselves members of some social categories (ingroups) and not others," Brewer wrote. "Thus, an additional categorical distinction between ingroup and outgroups may be superimposed onto particular social classifications."

At the same time, members of each group incorporate some of their in-group's traits into their own sense of self—a process Brewer called social identification. "With high levels of social identification, the group's outcomes and welfare become closely connected to one's own sense of well-being," she wrote. "It is this engagement of the self that accounts for the positive valuation of the ingroup and positive orientations toward fellow ingroup members. Self-worth is both projected onto and derived from positive ingroup evaluation."

Brewer proposes what she calls optimal distinctiveness theory: ". . . Human beings have two powerful social motives: a need for inclusion that motivates assimilation of the self into large, impersonal social collectives, and an opposing need for differentiation that is satisfied by distinguishing the self from others." This differentiation does not necessarily lead to conflict with the others, but "positive attitudes and expectations about ingroup members, perceived similarity, and cooperative orientation are all limited to those who share membership in the common ingroup. The extension of positive self-regard to others stops at the boundary between ingroup and outgroups; attitudes toward those outside the boundary are, at best, characterized by indifference. Differential indifference is not without its consequences."

One of these consequences is what came to be called social competition principle—the need for the in-group to perceive itself as better than the out-group. "We cannot improve our position or sense of wellbeing unless the outgroup is doing less well than we are," Brewer wrote. When resources such as wealth, status, and power are involved, "ingroup bias motivated by a desire to establish or maintain positive distinctiveness of the ingroup relative to the outgroup is a second form of intergroup discrimination that can be differentiated, at least conceptually, from simple ingroup favoritism."

CONFLICT WITHIN GROUPS

Beyond the focus on in-groups and out-groups, some researchers turned to the question of work groups and teams—people who are in the same group working toward the same goal. Anyone who has ever participated in a group activity, from a scout troop to a sports team, knows that groups can have enough internal conflict to keep them from reaching a common achievement, winning a game, or agreeing on even the simplest issues.

In 2001, Karen A. Jehn of the University of Pennsylvania and Elizabeth A. Mannix of Cornell University published the results of a longitudinal study that brought new insights to the study of conflict within groups—and its potentially positive effects. They used 51 three-person work teams of college students earning master's degrees in business administration at three U.S. business schools, each performing comparable tasks over the course of the semester. The students all were full-time employees of corporations, attending graduate school part-time.

The study produced what Jehn and Mannix considered a specific pattern of conflict within groups that led a group to higher performance. They found that the highest performing teams began with low levels of process conflict—determining how the group will proceed in accomplishing a task—that gradually increased, while they maintained low levels of relationship conflict or personality issues. During completion of the task, the groups with the strongest performance had a moderate level of conflict over process and operations but not about personal issues. As project deadlines approached, the level of conflict rose to its highest point. Overall, however, these high-performing teams began with high levels of trust and respect among their members, and they were comfortable with openly discussing any conflicts that arose and resolving them as quickly and efficiently as possible.

Groups with lower levels of respect and esteem among the three members generally produced less successful results, Jehn and Mannix noted. "Developing respect and cohesiveness among the group members may aid in the reduction of relationship and process conflict," they wrote. "This suggests that it may only be possible to harness the benefits of task conflict (and even process conflict) if members are not taking these conflicts personally and do not engage in relationship conflict."

INTERPERSONAL CONFLICT APPLIED TO GLOBAL POLITICS

With September 11, 2001, a recent memory, much research and many papers explored the nature of conflict between groups defined by religion or ethnicity. Roy J. Eidelson and Judy I. Eidelson distilled five belief domains that trigger conflict:

- **Superiority**: A person's conviction that he or she is actually better than other people. Individuals may feel that they are special, deserving, and entitled or that the rules of society do not apply to them. These perceptions can make a person unwilling to compromise, because "settling" is an unacceptable condition. On the global level, groups that believe themselves superior to others believe they have the one true set of morals or that they have a special destiny. This view, naturally, makes all out-groups inferior or even contemptible.

- **Injustice**: The perceived mistreatment by others or by the world at large. People or groups who see themselves as treated unjustly may engage in retaliation, whether or not the injustice truly comes from the target of this retaliation. ". . . For all too many, this mindset can lead the individual to identify as unfair that which is merely unfortunate," the researchers noted. When a group feels that it has "significant and legitimate grievances against another group," this belief gives the group the power to mobilize powerful action against the other. This becomes especially problematic between groups from different cultures, because their definitions of justice may be markedly different from one another.

- **Vulnerability**: A person's belief that he or she lives in a dangerous situation over which he or she has no control. Such a situation leads to high anxiety levels—and people who are living in fear may bring about exactly the scenario that frightens them. When an entire group feels threatened, the group likely will lash out at the source of the threat while feeling fully and collectively justified in doing so.

- **Distrust**: The certainty that others are hostile and mean harm to the individual or group. Beyond injustice and even vulnerability, distrust causes people and groups to expect the worst of their foes, believing that members of the out-group mean to hurt, manipulate, cheat, lie, or otherwise take advantage of them. In its most extreme form, this lack of trust advances into paranoia, leading the group to believe that others are actively causing them harm. This results in defensive behavior or a need to strike first to beat the foe to the punch.

- **Helplessness**: The belief that nothing the individual or group can do will produce the desired result. Members of a group who feel helpless may feel that no action they take will make a difference, so they do not try as hard to succeed, and they may give up after one attempt —or not make any attempt at all. On the group level, helplessness creates a sense of inevitability as well as a belief that the group is powerless to change its situation. The group may focus on its own weaknesses in the shared perception that their failures "are attributed to the presumed lasting and pervasive internal limitations of the group itself."

As these five belief domains have credence in both individual and group situations, they can be useful in understanding the sources of conflict on many levels.

Plenty of studies explore the sources and development of conflict, but fewer psychological theories forecast an individual or group's willingness to move toward resolution. I. William Zartman took on the question of determining when the parties on both sides of the conflict may be ready to resolve their differences through mediation and negotiation. Zartman's ripeness theory, in its original form in 1985, suggests two conditions that must be in place before the sides in an argument—led by rational policy makers—are ready to negotiate:

1. **Deadlock**: If both sides realize that they are in a stalemate that causes both of them harm, they may look toward the negotiating table. This is particularly true if the conflict has caused a recent catastrophe or if such a cataclysm looks to be on the horizon.
2. **A way out**: If both sides see that the way to a negotiated solution is "just and satisfactory to both parties," they may be willing to take the next step toward resolution.

In more recent times, we have seen many conflicts between countries or global ideologies that involved leaders that may not be entirely rational policy makers. " 'Objective elements of ripeness' can be defined as circumstances under which a well-informed, dispassionate, and rational decision maker would conclude that negotiation is appropriate," wrote Dean G. Pruitt of the Institute for Conflict Analysis and Resolution at George Mason University in his review of ripeness theory in 2005. Pruitt cited anger, revenge, and a sense that defeating the enemy will bring spiritual redemption as impediments to ripeness, keeping the groups involved from moving toward a negotiated settlement. Militant leaders also look to perpetuate conflicts rather than end them, for their own sense of purpose and competence as long as the conflict continues. The need for leaders to hide their own mistakes, the emotional commitment of an administration or a country to a cause, and the realization that too much money has been invested to quit without a win—all of these are "resistant reactions" in Zartman's ripeness theory.

A number of researchers offer three main theories for overcoming these areas of resistance and moving into negotiations:

1. **Shock theory**: When a sudden major event shocks one or both sides of the conflict into rethinking their position—such as a major battle or bombing with significant loss of life—the disaster (or the need to avoid one) can bring both sides to the negotiating table. The Tet Offensive during the Vietnam War caused substantial loss of life, making the Americans look seriously at leaving the war; the dropping of an atom bomb on Hiroshima in 1945 caused an almost

immediate about-face in Japan's policy of fighting until no man was left standing.

2. **New leader theory**: A change in leadership can give either side of a conflict the opportunity to alter the way one side deals with the other. When Barack Obama was elected president of the United States, he and his secretary of state, Hillary Clinton, took the initiative to "reset" the country's relationship with Russia, reversing the policies the United States established under former president George W. Bush. Pruitt points out that a new leader on just one side of the conflict provides the impetus for the policy change and negotiation.

3. **Third-party intervention**: The insertion of a neutral third party—the entire purpose of the lives of mediators and arbitrators—can help bring an ongoing conflict to an end, even when neither side's leader seems ready to negotiate. The many attempts by the United States to broker a peace between Israel and Palestine are examples of this, though they ended with varying degrees of success.

Pruitt takes ripeness theory to a new level—one that looks at the perceptions and motives of each side's view of the conflict. He calls this readiness theory, an application that looks at the two sides separately to determine which may be ready to move to negotiations, even if the other is not. "Readiness theory—in parallel to core ripeness theory—holds that two psychological variables encourage a party to be ready for negotiation: motivation to end conflict and optimism about the success of negotiation," he wrote. When one leader perceives that his or her side is losing the conflict, the cost is too great, or continuing the conflict creates too much risk to the existence of his or her side, he or she may be ready to negotiate an end. To be ready, the leader needs to see that a mutually acceptable agreement is possible and that the negotiator on the opposite side is empowered to make decisions and commit to terms.

THE STEREOTYPE CONTENT MODEL

Most in-groups see their members as sincere, friendly, and generally good people. It could be said that they perceive *warmth* from their fellow in-group members, while they expect an unfriendly or even angry chill from members of other groups—or they have no reaction to them at all. This perception of warmth is one of the two general qualities that make up the stereotype content model, a linking of emotions to expectations about the "us" versus "them" construct of group relationships.

In addition to warmth, members of a group may see their own members as smart, capable, and trustworthy—all elements of *competence*, the second perception within this model. Members of the in-group may see people of an out-group as foolish, stupid, or incompetent, or they may form no opinion of their capabilities at all.

If these perceptions feel like little more than a starting point to you, you are not alone. Researchers including Donelson Forsyth, author of the 2009 book *Group Dynamics*, fifth edition, acknowledge that "people do not just categorize and judge the out-group. They also respond emotionally to the out-group, usually leaning in a negative direction." This negative reaction may only be a sense of wanting to spend time with people from the in-group instead of others, but it can escalate as intergroup emotions develop. These emotions change based on the relationship status between the in-group and the out-group. For example, if this in-group sees itself in a lower position of status than the out-group, its members may feel jealousy or even fear when members of the out-group are nearby. In-group members may feel contempt for the out-group, especially if members have decided that the out-group has low competence. If the out-group ranks low in competence but has some endearing qualities (and is therefore average to high in warmth), the in-group members may feel pity for the out-group. In rare situations, the in-group may actually feel admiration or other positive emotions toward the out-group, but for this to happen, the out-group must be perceived as high in both warmth and competence—not the way one group normally perceives a rival group.

CONFLICT MANAGEMENT AND RESOLUTION

Much research has explored the nature of conflict, the ways that conflict affects an organization, group or interpersonal relationship, and the points at which conflict resolution may begin. So many of these conflicts take place in the workplace, however, that an entire industry of corporate and organizational psychology has developed, working to determine how workplace conflicts can be reduced ("de-escalated").

M. Afzalur Rahim proposed in 2002 that the level of conflict within the work group or organization has an effect on the styles of handling interpersonal conflict. He classified conflicts as either within a single organization (intraorganizational) or between two or more groups or organizations (interorganizational). Within these categories, he added further divisions: a conflict between two people is, of course, interpersonal; intragroup conflict involves a number of people within the work group; and intergroup conflict involves people from a number of different work groups or departments.

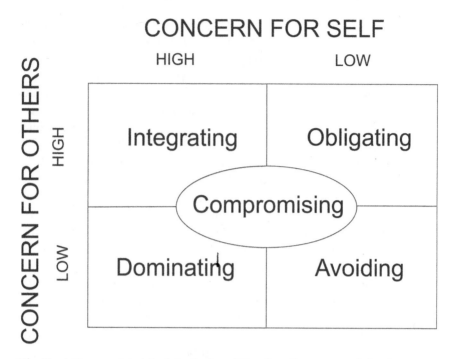

The Dual Concern Model of the Styles of Handling Interpersonal Conflict

From the 1970s through the 1990s, most management consultants and theorists recommended one style or another of managing conflict in virtually all situations. Rahim and his team, like a handful of researchers before him, determined that one style of conflict management might be more appropriate than another in specific circumstances. He based his assertions on what he called the Dual Concern Model of the Styles of Handling Interpersonal Conflict.

The proper conflict management style to use in various situations depends on the junction point between the manager's interest in satisfying his or her own concerns and the concerns of the others involved.

- **Integration style:** If the manager has a high concern for him or herself as well as a high concern for others, this problem-solving approach allows the manager to engage employees with openness, exchanging information and considering alternatives with the group. Participating employees will be involved in finding a solution to the conflict, so their commitment must be secured at the beginning of the resolution process.
- **Obliging style:** When the manager's interest in others' concerns outweighs his or her own, this style allows him or her to minimize the

differences between the group members involved and to emphasize what they have in common. The manager puts aside his or her own role in the decision-making process to facilitate the problem solving with the members of the group. This style is useful if one of the goals is to preserve relationships with the others or if giving up something in compromise now will result in something gained in the future.

- **Dominating style**: When the manager must place his or her own concerns as his or her top priority—to meet a deadline, finish the last steps toward a goal, or override a troublesome employee—an immediate decision will move the group forward toward completion of the task. Sometimes a manager must take control of the situation to overcome subordinates who are standing in the way of progress or when someone needs to make an unfavorable decision. At this point, a unilateral command may be the best (and sometimes the only) effective course of action.
- **Avoiding style**: Some issues are barely important enough to require conflict resolution, and some are so volatile that the people involved need to step back before they attempt to resolve it. When the manager has little concern either for him or herself or others, avoiding the issue—at least for a time—can be the most effective course of action.
- **Compromising style**: In the middle of the chart, the compromising style becomes the fallback position when the conflict cannot be settled without someone giving up something important to them. Consensus may be impossible, especially if the people involved share power or are at the same level within the organization, so one's decision does not necessarily override the other.

Rahim and his team go on to emphasize the importance of diagnosing the problem before beginning conflict resolution, to be sure the intervention style the manager chooses is the right one for that situation. "Problem finding or recognition requires appropriate diagnosis of the problems, a step which is neglected in many contemporary organizations," Rahim wrote. "As a result, very often interventions are recommended without proper understanding of the nature of the problems. This can lead to ineffective outcomes."

Research continues today in all aspects of conflict and its resolution, and the people and institutions studying conflict are far too numerous and varied to detail here. While social psychologists continue to explore our understanding of conflict and the motivations behind it, sociologists examine the effects of conflict on our society as a whole, from the local to the global level. Organizational psychologists delve into the dynamics of corporations, sports teams, military units, and many other forms of large group, while political strategists look for the most effective ways to bring international conflicts to a close in the hope of reducing loss of life.

One of the most fascinating things about the study of conflict is that the insights that lead to resolution between two people in their own living room often form the basis for conflict resolution on a much larger scale. In other chapters in this book, you will find that the concepts in this chronology of the study of conflict come to life in practice—and you will see how the most complicated and volatile situations are resolved, perhaps with solutions that can apply to relationships with your family, friends, and coworkers.

5

When: Conflict throughout
the Life Cycle

Conflict has no age limit. Newborn babies find themselves in conflict with the world around them, and the very old may fight for their last shred of independence as the end of life approaches. While there may be times in anyone's life in which there seems to be a lot more conflict than at other times, people of every age, race, and background experience conflict and search for ways to solve and move past it. In this chapter, we examine the ages at which conflicts come to light and the kinds of coping mechanisms and problem-solving skills we gain as we resolve issues within our many relationships.

CHILDREN AND CONFLICT: ESTABLISHING IDENTITY AND INDEPENDENCE

Imagine opening your eyes and discovering that everything around you is brand new. You see objects, but you do not know what they are. Faces that you have never seen before appear in your field of vision, and you have no idea how to respond to them or if they are important to you. All you know is that you are comfortable or uncomfortable, hungry or thirsty, and that you have other strange and novel sensations inside your own body. You cannot even form a thought, because you do not know what thinking is.

This is most likely what the first moments of any baby's life are like. The world is wondrous, filled with sights, sounds, smells, and sensations with no explanation or frame of reference. Babies spend most of their first few months taking in information and finding ways to process it while discovering methods for alerting the people around them to their need to be fed, changed, burped, held, relieved of pain, or made warmer or cooler. Life is fairly simple and straightforward, based on clear-cut issues that can be resolved immediately.

Gradually, however, babies begin to see the world in terms of what is theirs and what is not, or what they do or do not want to happen to them in a given moment. They begin to establish their own environment and start to assemble an identity of their own. When this happens, the baby—now a toddler—finds itself in conflict at times with siblings, playmates, or others in its home.

In most households, children learn what conflict is through their relationships with one another. Dunn and Munn (1985) studied second-born children at ages 14, 16, 18, 21, and 24 months, observing children unobtrusively in their own homes as they interacted with an older sibling. They discovered that conflict between siblings occurred more frequently once the child reached 18 months and that children came into more conflict with their mothers (the father was not included in the study) as they reached 21 and 24 months. By 18 months old, children had the capacity to deliberately tease a sibling, showing "pragmatic understanding of how to annoy the sibling in family disputes. They not only perceived what would upset the sibling, but also acted upon this understanding."

Daycare workers and preschool teachers can say from experience that conflict between young children is natural and that it is one of many ways children learn about boundaries. Children younger than five years old often come into conflict with their playmates and classmates over the use of a toy, crayons, or a book or over simple issues like one child standing too close to another. Young children squabble over whose friends are whose, over ideas during creative play, or over which child gets to pretend to be Spiderman. Misunderstandings quickly escalate into raised voices and tearful outbursts as children determine their roles with siblings, friends, and classmates.

While all of these moments of conflict may seem chaotic, they are important tools in every child's learning experience. Let us take an example, one that happens daily in living rooms and daycare centers around the world.

Jimmy is two years old, and his neighbor, Teddy, is just about the same age. They are busy playing with a set of farm animal toys. Jimmy reaches for the plastic pig, but Teddy beats him to it, grabbing it and holding it out of Jimmy's reach. Jimmy shrieks in anger.

Mom quickly intervenes. "Jimmy, what's wrong?" she asks.

"I want pig!" Jimmy cries.

"Teddy, give Jimmy the pig," says Mom.

Now Teddy's eyes start to well up. "I'm playing with pig!" he says.

Mom sees a teachable moment and turns back to Jimmy. "Teddy is play-ing with the pig right now," she says to Jimmy. "When he's done, you can play with the pig. Why don't you play with the cow and the horse?"

"Want pig!" Jimmy declares again and starts to whimper.

"Okay, I know you want the pig, but Teddy has it now," Mom repeats. She picks up the cow and the horse and puts one in each of Jimmy's hands. "There are lots of other things to play with. What sound does the cow make?"

Jimmy continues to insist that only the pig will do, escalating the conflict until Mom has no choice but to remove him from play and give him a "time out." At two years old—an age known among parents as the "terrible twos"— children can be particularly stubborn as they try to get what they want.

In her writing for the Scholastic.com website, Carla Poole notes, "Two-year-olds are known to dig in their heels during conflict. This is because they are starting to feel powerful while simultaneously realizing how little control they have over their own lives."

By the time they turn three or four years old, however, children acquire better language skills and begin to understand the power that words have to help them get their way or to dismiss others who cross them. Susan A. Miller, EdD, observed that children at this age will "use such tactics as yell-ing at each other, name calling, and making threats" to defend their own positions or to try to get something they want, like inclusion in play. "Although these verbal strategies may make those using them feel power-ful, the recipient frequently ends up with bruised feelings," she wrote. "This situation is due, of course, to the preschoolers' egocentrism, which may not allow them to completely understand the others' hurt feelings."

Children at this age have usually learned that they can appeal to an adult in authority to help them settle the dispute, an important step in their understanding of conflict resolution. Let us look at a similar conflict to the one we examined between two-year-olds previously and see how it differs when the children are a little older.

Ramanda and Louisa are sisters who are four and three years old, respec-tively. The girls are playing dress-up, and both of them want to be Elsa, the princess in Disney's *Frozen*. There is only one Elsa dress available in the house, so only one of them can be this particular princess.

Ramanda attempts to dominate the situation. "I'm older, so I'm Elsa," she says. "You can be Anna, Elsa's sister."

"You were Elsa last time!" Louisa declares. "It's my turn!"

"That doesn't matter. You're being a poop," Ramanda claims.

"No, I'm not! You can't be Elsa all the time!" Louisa says. "I don't want to be Anna. You be Anna!"

"I don't want to be Anna either," replies Ramanda. "I have to be Elsa!"

Louisa begins to cry and runs to find her mother. "Mom! Ramanda's not playing fair. She won't let me be Elsa!"

Mother comes into the playroom. "Louisa, what's the problem?"

"It's my turn to be Elsa, and Ramanda won't let me!"

Mother looks at Ramanda. "Why won't you let your sister be Elsa?"

"Because I want to be Elsa!" Ramanda replies matter-of-factly.

"All right," says Mother, "let's set a timer. Ramanda can be Elsa for thirty minutes, and then Louisa gets to be Elsa."

The girls consider this novel solution and agree to it. They play co-operatively while they both get a chance to be Elsa.

These two girls had the kind of disagreement many children of this age will have. Such arguments allow three- and four-year-olds to develop social skills, finding ways to play with others that do not always have to lead to harsh words and name-calling. In this instance, while Ramanda is convinced that she is right, she does not yet have the reasoning ability to come up with a response that would actually justify her desire to be Elsa. Louisa, meanwhile, has grasped the concept of fairness but has not learned how to reason her way past her sister's refusal to recognize that it's Louisa's turn to play the more beloved character.

Mother's clever solution opens both children's eyes, resolving the conflict in a way that would not have occurred to either of them. This gives them a new tool for resolving their own conflict the next time a situation arises, one that satisfies Louisa's sense of fairness while giving them both a turn at playing Elsa.

Naturally, conflicts faced by three- and four-year-olds can involve many situations that are not so simply resolved. By four years old, children have begun to wish for more control of their own environment and activities, and they may become quite aggressive with younger or smaller children at home, in the neighborhood, or at preschool. A four-year-old may push his or her way to the front of the line, shove a child out of the way on the playground, or engage in a tug-of-war with another child over a toy. With improving but limited ability to express themselves verbally, pre-school children are more likely to resort to pushing, hitting, or other physical aggression to attempt to get their way.

By the time they turn five or six, however, language becomes the chief method children use to resolve their conflicts. Stronger in verbal skills and more developed in their understanding of the consequences of physical aggression, they are more likely to organize simple facts and attempt to state an argument. They also have a clearer sense of justice and are willing to battle for what they believe is fair. While they may not enjoy sharing, they know that they are supposed to do so and that it is the right thing to do.

Some children are more verbally advanced than others, and they are not necessarily rewarded for their ability to argue their way into and out of a conflict. Parents may be quick to label their own child as "bossy" when the child begins telling other children where to stand or what to do in class or in a playgroup, especially if the other kids do not want to take this direction. Children who show such leadership qualities at this age may believe their way to be right and absolute, and they are not eager to listen to the ideas of others. This can result in new kinds of conflict, through which children learn how to work their way through disagreements without necessarily running to a parent or teacher to arbitrate the discussion.

Many children become more competitive as they reach the ages of seven, eight, and nine, but they do not yet have the emotional maturity to deal with losing or not always performing at their best level. This can mean quarrels and irritation after a team loss or a lackluster spelling bee performance or when a child does not get the part he or she wanted in a school play. Conflicts can arise if other siblings needle them, if parents do not give them the space to have their initial emotional reactions, or if their friends become easy targets of their anger. This is a time when children begin to develop the coping mechanisms and conflict resolution skills that will take them throughout their lives—but they apply these in the context of the slights and hurts that they perceive are directed at them. They have not yet learned to recognize the feelings of others or to take them into account.

As children move toward puberty and adolescence, they learn one of the most important skills they will need to recognize and resolve their own conflicts: listening. Young children do not yet see the value in listening to others, but by the time the child becomes eight or nine years old, hearing what others have to say becomes a useful tool. Children at this age are still the centers of their own existence, focused on their own lives and on the world's opinion of them—but as they move into their early teens, they begin to break away from this inward focus and develop a broader sense of the world and people around them.

ADOLESCENTS AND CONFLICT: ESTABLISHING A PLACE IN THE WORLD

When a child enters adolescence, his or her view of the world and each person's place in it changes dramatically. The son who cuddled with his parents suddenly avoids physical contact; the daughter who told her parents everything becomes secretive and demands privacy; the child who loved doing things with the family now wants nothing more than to be left alone. The transformation not only shocks and baffles many parents and siblings, but it also sets the stage for one emotional conflict after another.

What is happening? Psychologist Carl E. Pickhardt, PhD, defines five psychological "engines" that take hold when children reach their teens and begin to grow away from their families:

- **Separation**: The process of letting go of the things the early adolescent associates with childhood creates a break with the youth of the past. This may include tangible things—discarding toys, redecorating the bedroom in a more mature manner, wearing makeup and more revealing or mature clothes—as well as spending more time with friends and forsaking the parents' affections. The new teenager may talk less with parents or siblings about activities at school or during leisure time and may spend much more time communicating with friends—that is, texting, using Snapchat and Instagram, and making private jokes instead of participating in family conversation.
- **Expansion**: Widening the scope of life experiences can be a great adventure for the young teen, though it may cause significant anxiety for parents. This can include experimenting with things that are taboo for a young child, like drugs, alcohol, or sex; staying out late with friends; and trying more daring or risky behaviors because of peer pressure. Pickhardt suggests that some adolescents will expand their territory at home by keeping a messy room, neglecting to clean up after themselves in common areas, or setting up an extended project in the garage—essentially taking over a larger portion of the house.
- **Differentiation**: Virtually every adolescent searches for a new identity as he or she approaches adulthood. Developing their own interests apart from their families, choosing their own music, taking great pains with their personal appearance and manner of dress, and acknowledging (and becoming embarrassed about) bodily changes are all part of this step in their development.
- **Opposition**: Few things are more associated with adolescence than regular tests of the parents' authority in the child's life. The young teen works to establish his or her individuality by throwing off the yolk of parental supervision and rules, pushing to have more say in his or her own appearance—demanding a tattoo or a piercing, for example—or arguing for a later curfew time or the ability to go out

with friends the parents may not like. Testing of authority and pushing the envelope on rules can become daily occurrences, causing regular conflicts between the child and the parents.

- **Responsibility**: As Pickhardt notes, "Freedom of choice is never free because it always comes with a string attached—the consequence that follows." Teens learn to link their choices with these consequences, sometimes with painful and even disastrous results. As they acquire more freedom—perhaps when they receive a driver's license or they can stay home alone without supervision—they take more chances and break more rules. If they then turn to parents to help them clean up the mess they have created, parents may refuse in order to "teach them a lesson." This, of course, results in some of the most volatile conflicts between parent and child.

Within each of these five drivers of adolescent growth are multiple opportunities for significant conflict. Teens learn hard lessons during these years, sometimes through relatively small incidents between the child and friends and sometimes in nuclear-style meltdowns that involve the entire family.

Here is an example that may have a familiar ring to readers of this book.

Diane and several of her friends take over the family garage to use it for band practice. The five-piece band includes a guitar, bass guitar, keyboard, drums, and a singer. The teens are not superior musicians, but they are all plugged into amplifiers, and the music is uncomfortably loud for the rest of the family. When neighbors start to call to complain, Dad marches out to the garage to put a stop to the noise. He has to stride to the front of the garage and wave his arms to get the band's attention.

"Diane," he says when the music stops, "we're getting complaints from the neighbors. It's too late in the day to practice now. Time for everyone to pack up and go home."

Diane is instantly angry. "We have to practice! We're playing at Marian's party tomorrow."

Dad shakes his head. "You'll have to practice another time. It's enough for today."

"How are we supposed to be good tomorrow if we don't keep practicing now?" Diane insists. "I don't care about the damned neighbors."

"Watch your language, missy," Dad responds, his voice tightening. "You live in a neighborhood with other people, and you have to be considerate."

"Why don't they have to be considerate of me?" Diane lashes out. "It's none of their business what we do in our own house. You don't care about anything that's important to me! All you care about is what the stupid neighbors think."

One of the other musicians says, "It's okay, Diane, we'll pack up."

"No! It's not okay, and we can't just roll over every time someone doesn't understand what we're doing," says Diane. Turning back to her father, she adds, "You can't tell us what to do. You have no authority over my friends."

"This is my house, and I pay for the roof over your head," Dad shouts. "Do you want to live on the street? Because that's where you'll end up if you keep this attitude!"

"Do you have to embarrass me in front of my friends?" Diane yells back. "You're so selfish! I didn't ask you to support me! I can go live with Marian any time I want. Just say the word!"

Nothing good comes of such an argument, in which a reasonable request quickly escalates into a shouting match, parent and teen say things they do not mean, friends are made uncomfortable, and no one gets what they wanted. At the same time, however, we can see how Diane works to establish her independence from the family and her individuality, while her father attempts to counter by reaffirming her place within a larger society—a family and a neighborhood—and her obligations within that construct.

Also apparent are the tensions involved in Dad's identification with Diane as the child she was versus his acknowledgment of the adult she is attempting to become. Dad is quick to correct her use of a mild expletive as if she were still too young to understand such language, even calling her *missy*, a term that defines her as a submissive little girl. This, of course, only infuriates Diane, making her try even harder to establish her autonomy by threatening to move out and room with a friend.

In the end, the substance of the argument hardly matters—the more important points come from the tone and inference of the language used. The teenager struggles to be taken seriously and to be appreciated as a mature individual, while the parent attempts to balance the need to require his daughter to conform to societal norms, obey him as head of the household, and still allow Diane to grow and pursue her own interests. He has not asked her to break up the band—only to stop practicing because the neighbors have complained. His request is for common courtesy, but under the magnifying influence of adolescent stresses, it becomes a statement on Diane's worth as a person.

Relationships within the family are not the only source of conflict in teenagers' lives, nor does the family cause all adolescents' frustration and hostility toward the world around them. In their book *Being Adolescent: Conflict and Growth in the Teenage Years*, authors Mihaly Csikszentmihalyi and Reed Larson look at every aspect of teenagers' experience and find that the rigors of the academic environment are just as powerful as family relationships. "They just want to be kids, but the weight of an unknown future rides on their shoulders," they wrote. "They bear the load of mastering an enormous amount of cultural information, information which is necessary, whether they like it or not, for their survival as adults and for the survival of society ... The tension, frustration, anger, and disorganization these adolescents report in school, is in part terror of the vast amount they need to learn to become adults. No matter how much they acquire, there will always be more; no matter how well they do on a test, there will always be another test that is harder and more challenging."

In response, many adolescents choose to retreat into solitude when they have much-needed downtime, shutting the door against the tumult of home, friends, and others who influence their lives and happiness. "When adolescents are alone, nobody tries to force them to do things they dislike," Csikszentmihalyi and Larson continued. "They do not have to load the dishwasher or study for exams. Yet, surprisingly, solitude brings more emotional entropy than school or the family; loneliness and passivity are an almost inevitable part of the experience. This is a clear indication that teenagers' problems do not all result from conflicts with adults."

Indeed, conflicts in teens' lives are just as likely to come from their interactions with one another. These can range from basic disagreements or misunderstandings between friends to the alarming increase in bullying, particularly among young people between the ages of 12 and 18. The U.S. government only began collecting data on school bullying in 2005, when about 28 percent of students reported that they had been bullied or had bullied others, according to statistics from the U.S. Department of Education. In 2016, more than one out of every five students reported being bullied, as recorded by the National Center for Educational Statistics.

Why do so many students become the victims of bullying, and what kinds of bullying do they experience? The Youth Voice Research Project at Pennsylvania State University delved into this question in 2010, creating an online survey to assess the experiences of students across the country. They discovered that 55 percent of students who were bullied were told by the bully that their looks made them targets, while another 37 percent said that their body shape was the deciding factor. Race, sexual orientation, family income, religion, and disabilities attracted bullies as well, but not with the prevalence that physical appearance had. Girls were more likely than boys to experience mistreatment by their peers over the way they looked or their body shape. The study also determined that students in the lesbian, gay, bisexual, transgender, and queer (LGBTQ) community were likely to experience more severe bullying and trauma at the hands of their peers than heterosexual male and female students.

Students who were victims of bullying most often attempted to handle the bullying situation without assistance from friends, teachers, or other adults. Seventy-five percent of students reported that they pretended that the bullying did not bother them, and 66 percent walked away—while 46 percent said they did nothing at all. Only 58 percent told an adult at home about what was happening to them, and just 42 percent told an adult at school. Only 20 percent lashed out at the bully, hitting them or fighting back.

The Penn State study discovered that the most effective response to bullying—the one that actually made things better—was to tell an adult at home or in school. In most cases, the adult listened to the student, gave advice, and checked in with the student later to see if the bullying had stopped. In cases in which the educator (a teacher, coach, or principal) intervened with the bully in some way, the students reported that the level of bullying either stayed the same or got worse more often than it improved—especially if the bully was punished in some way.

Remarkably, the survey discovered that a number of adults told the students who were victims of bullying that if they had acted differently, they would not be bullied. Some adults told the student to solve the problem him or herself, while others scolded the student for tattling. In these cases, the "advice" had significant negative impact, often resulting in an increase in bullying.

Teens who experience bullying are not likely to shrug it off and go on with their daily lives. Parents may observe that their children's grades are affected as they develop anxiety, depression, and difficulty sleeping. They may have headaches, chronic stomach issues, and other stress-related ailments. In addition, the physical or psychological bullying that may go on at school can carry over into the evening as teens go online to interact with their friends.

Cyberbullying on sites, including Facebook, Snapchat, and Instagram, and through texting and instant messaging apps can pervade a student's waking hours, causing humiliation in front of all of the teen's friends and acquaintances. The Centers for Disease Control reports that 15.5 percent of high school students are cyberbullied, almost as many (20.2%) as those who are bullied on school property. These figures increase significantly for middle school students, 45 percent of whom are bullied on school property, while 24 percent are bullied online.

Researchers Sameer Hinduja and Justin W. Patchin of the Cyberbullying Research Center determined in 2015 that bullying online includes the spreading of rumors; making mean or hurtful statements, texts, or online comments in which the sender threatens to hurt the recipient; posting a mean or hurtful picture of the targeted teen; or even hacking a target's account and pretending to be him or her while posting. Girls are much more likely to be the targets of cyberbullying than boys, according to the Cyberbullying Research Center.

Some of these cases become significant tragedies. In 2003, 13-year-old Ryan Halligan of Vermont took his own life after discovering that a female classmate he had corresponded with in IM exchanges had pretended to like him to get him to share embarrassing things about himself. She then posted these things online to her friends and later told him in person that she thought he was "just a loser." This incident came on the heels of another prank, in which a bully in his class used an amusing story Ryan had told him to start a rumor online that Ryan was gay. The rumor held on throughout the summer, perhaps encouraging the girl to further the joke with her own painful ruse. Ryan committed suicide in October 2003.

In 2006, Megan Meier, who was 14, befriended a boy named Josh on MySpace. Josh seemed to like her a great deal, even though he never asked for her phone number and showed no interest in meeting her in person. One day in October, he turned on her and said they could not be friends anymore. Minutes later, he started sharing Megan's private messages to him with others, and suddenly these others posted "bulletins," surveys that said terrible things about her. Despite her mother's insistence that she sign off and not read all the things people said, Megan stayed online until she was in tears. She ran to her room and hanged herself in her closet. She died the following day.

Despite these and a number of other disturbing cases, cyberbullying is increasing in frequency and prevalence. In 2016, the Cyberbullying Research Center reported nearly twice the number of online victimization rates in the nine years since the center began tracking the trend, from 18.8 percent of students in 2007 to 33.8 percent in 2016.

Most cyberbullying takes place after school hours and off school property, but this does not mean that schools must refrain from taking action. "This is particularly the case in incidents involving serious threats toward another student, if the target no longer feels comfortable coming to school, or if the cyber-bullying behaviors continue after informal attempts to stop it have failed," note Hinduja and Patchin. "In these cases, [we] suggest that detention, suspension, changes of placement, or even expulsion may be necessary."

ADULTS AND CONFLICT: RELATIONSHIPS AT HOME AND AT WORK

When two or more adults interact in any area of life—at work, at home with family, within a marriage or romantic relationship, in face-to-face social situations or online—there is a potential for conflict. The same can be said for interactions between children or adolescents, of course, but adult conflict comes with a higher level of expectation that the people involved can handle their disagreement with maturity and restraint.

Often, however, this is not the case, and the resulting argument can escalate to a point at which the relationship cannot survive. Adult conflicts can lead to catastrophic fissures between people: divorce, termination from employment, selling a home to move away from a contentious neighbor, the end of a friendship, or even violence.

At the same time, conflicts in adulthood can lead to innovative solutions to shared problems or group activism to defeat a common enemy. The question is whether the people involved see the conflict as constructive or destructive—that is, whether they share a common goal or are truly at odds with one another.

Constructive conflict results in a decision shared by the people who have engaged in the disagreement. Let us see what that looks like in this example, in which two groups come together to solve a problem that affects them both.

Company X produces the sample-sized bottles of shampoo, lotion, and other products placed in hotel rooms for guests. There are two major production lines: one (Group A) that mixes the products and the other (Group B) that bottles the products and packs them for shipping. In recent months, Group B has found itself waiting a long time for the big vats of shampoo and lotion to come out of the mixing room. This has reduced Group B's productivity, so Group B is not meeting its production goals. Not surprisingly, this has made Group B's workers very angry.

The leaders of Groups A and B decide to have a meeting to see what can be done about this problem. Jeffrey, who leads Group B, arrives expecting to discover that Group A's people are lazy and perhaps even stupid or that they are holding up production just to spite Group B. Group A's leader, Nicole, expects to be blamed for all of the company's problems, and she arrives defensive and worried about what this meeting will be like.

Jeffrey and Nicole share the same goal: to increase productivity. Coming into the meeting, however, they do not realize that they want the same thing. So the meeting begins on a hostile note. Jeffrey says, "Nicole, I asked to meet with you because my people are standing around waiting for product to come out of your room. This happens just about every day. We're not meeting our goals, so we look bad to the upper management and to the customers. What is going on in there? What's holding things up?"

Nicole starts by lashing out, trying to fend off the attack she assumes is coming. "Well, we're not goofing off, if that's what you think. We're trying as hard as we can to get the shampoo and lotion mixed, but there are all kinds of problems. You don't understand what we're trying to accomplish."

"So tell me what the problems are," said Jeffrey, "and maybe we can help."

Nicole shakes her head. "They're not the kinds of problems you can help with. First, the customers keep changing the products they want— one day the hotel chain wants to put Wonder Lotion in the bottles, and the next they decide they want Miracle Lotion. So we have to throw away the whole batch we just mixed and start over."

Jeffrey, surprised at this news, simply nods. "That's a big issue."

Nicole goes on, "And we're using mixers that are more than forty years old. They're slow, and they break down a lot. When they break down, we can't get parts for them anymore, so we have to tinker with them like they're vintage cars. We can get them moving for a few days, and then they break down again, and we end up mixing the products by hand, using a big stick! No one can do that for very long, so we're all taking turns."

Jeffrey is aghast. "That's crazy! Haven't you told management?"

"Of course, I have," says Nicole. "But they won't listen. They say it's too expensive to buy new equipment, and they don't have the money because we're not meeting our production goals, so we have to make do."

"Okay," Jeffrey says, "I think I have a solution. Every day that you can't mix the products, we lose out in sales and delivery. We have to rush deliveries to the customer, so that costs more in shipping costs. Let's put together a budget that shows that if management replaces the old mixers, the company will save on overnight shipping and will sell more products. When they see that they will make more money, they will see the benefit of buying new machines."

Nicole is pleased. "You'll help with this, then?"

"Yes," says Jeffrey. "We'll work together on it."

Jeffrey and Nicole met because of a conflict, but they left with an innovative solution that neither of them would have found on his or her own. In their meeting, they learned what kinds of problems the other group faced, and they determined a way to move forward that would benefit them both. This is a constructive conflict, one in which both parties want to improve the situation and increase productivity for the company.

Imagine what this conflict could have looked like if it were a destructive conflict—one in which each side only wants what it can get for itself. In a destructive conflict, the people involved do not share a goal. One may seek power over the other, or one side may already have more power and simply chooses to wield it to improve its own group's situation, even if this means that the other group—the one with less power—will suffer as a result.

When Jeffrey and Nicole meet, Jeffrey has his issues lined up in his mind, and he has already decided that Nicole's group is at fault for all of them. "Nicole," he says, "my people are standing around waiting for product to come out of your room. What's the problem? Is everyone in there incompetent, or just lazy?"

Nicole springs to anger instantly. "What a way to talk to me!" she cries. "We have all kinds of problems with the customers and with our equipment."

"So no one in there can handle the job, is that what you're saying?" Jeff says.

"That's not what I'm saying at all! The customers keep changing their minds about which product they want to offer, so we have to break everything down, throw away whole batches, and start over with new formulas."

"Well, if you'd mixed it right in the first place, maybe they wouldn't feel that they had to change!" said Jeffrey, with a triumphant smile.

"There's nothing wrong with our mix! But besides that, the mixing equipment keeps breaking down."

"You're probably using it wrong, then," says Jeffrey. "I've been putting off reporting to management about your group's incompetence, but now I see I don't have a choice. We'll see what they have to say when I tell them that you're holding up productivity for the whole company."

Nothing gets solved; Nicole is devastated when she has legitimate concerns to address, and Jeffrey has enjoyed a "power trip" but has not achieved any kind of remedy for the barriers to productivity. This is why a conflict like this one is called a destructive conflict—someone in this battle has truly been destroyed, and no one gets a lasting benefit.

What happens to each group after such a meeting? Jeffrey reports to management that Nicole is prohibiting productivity. Management investigates and discovers the problems Nicole had described to Jeffrey—but they now begin to question Nicole's leadership, wanting to know why she let the problems fester for so long without coming to them. Nicole may be demoted or replaced as a result. Worse, the problems she cited may not be fixed at all, because no one has made a compelling case that the expenditures required will make a difference to the bottom line.

These are the kinds of conflicts adults face in the workplace, but they can also take place at home and in their activities in the community. Marriages can serve as ground zero for conflict, often causing disruption throughout the entire family.

If every adult had training in conflict resolution, home life might be a more harmonious place all the way around. This, however, generally is not the case. Each individual can have his or her own style of handling a conflict:

- **Silence**: A spouse may internalize his or her feelings, keeping quiet about the conflict and hoping it will go away. This often leads to a furious outburst at another time.
- **Withdrawal**: Some people leave the room the moment a voice is raised in anger, making it virtually impossible to resolve a conflict with them.
- **Aggression**: A spouse may get angry, call the other person names, bring up every slight that ever took place in the relationship, criticize every aspect of the other spouse, or use sarcasm instead of saying what he or she means.
- **Denial**: Some pretend that there is no conflict, believing if they never mention it or bring it out into the open, it will somehow resolve itself.
- **Submission**: Rather than argue or even discuss an issue, the person just gives in to the other, saying, "Yes, you are right, of course." Such a person may never bring his or her own feelings out into the open.
- **Constructive discussion**: Some spouses actually do sit down and work out their differences in a calm and open manner. These people do not attack one another, and they keep their discussion on the conflict at hand, rather than bringing in old slights or criticizing the other's habits.

Two spouses may have different styles for handling conflict. This can turn the attempt to reconcile the conflict into a conflict of its own. Many arguments escalate with the words "I've been trying to talk to you about this, but you keep walking away!" or "Why are you trying to avoid this discussion?"

Why, indeed? Throughout our lifetimes, we develop conceptions about conflict that feed into the way we deal with conflict as adults. We may believe that everyone should live in perfect accord and that conflict is always the sign that a relationship is coming apart. Or we may see our parents fight and make up on many occasions and believe that people who love each other should be able to work out their differences—when this is not always the case.

One of the messages we bring into our adult lives may be that some personalities can get along with one another, while others simply cannot. We may assume that when people are not "compatible," they will never find the common ground required to build a long-term relationship.

All of these conceptions are actually myths. As this book makes clear, conflict is a natural part of everyday life, and many conflicts lead to improved circumstances for the people involved. People who have nothing in common and whose lifestyles are very different can work together professionally with a minimum of conflict, perhaps applying their personal strengths while making up for one another's weaknesses. Such people can also marry and spend their lives together as long as they are willing to work out disagreements in a cooperative manner.

Other conflicts, however, do lead to the end of both professional and personal relationships—and sometimes this is for the best. No one wants to spend his or her entire adult lives in a state of perpetual conflict. If conflicts dominate the relationship on a daily basis and attempts to resolve the issues do not work, it could well be time to move on. This, too, can be a useful application for conflict, alerting a spouse or coworker that it is time for the relationship to end.

One relationship cannot be severed, however: the bond between a parent and a child. As we discussed earlier in this chapter, parents and children have complicated relationships from the child's very first day on earth, as the parent moves to protect, nurture, teach, and encourage the child to grow, and the child pulls away to explore with blissful ignorance of the dangers that may be in store. As the baby becomes a toddler, a school-aged child, and a teenager, conflicts become more frequent as the growing child struggles for independence long before the parent is willing to relinquish control.

"Every parent wants to hold their child close to protect them and keep them safe," wrote Nancy S. Buck, PhD, developmental psychologist and author of *Peaceful Parenting*. "And every child wants to break free of their parents' hold, going out into the world to discover, explore and learn. Each is pulling the other in the opposite direction."

This tug-of-war culminates in adolescence, when teenagers are most likely to battle their parents over issues of responsibility, identity, and independence. For adults, this tumultuous time of development in the lives of their children can seem utterly inexplicable. Why does the child who used to love to cuddle now recoil in horror at his or her parent's touch? Why is everything the parent says taken as an insult? Does a teenage daughter truly hate her parents—and if so, how did this happen?

Neuroscientists have discovered physiological changes in the brain during the teenage years that may cloud judgment and decision making, but this information does not provide parents with much more than something to blame. Parents find that their instinctive need to protect their children from harm makes it especially difficult to step back and allow their teenage son or daughter to make mistakes that could affect his or her well-being or happiness. They are likely to continue to ask a 15-year-old boy if he has his lunch money or recommend that he take a jacket with him, even when the son's response is sharp words and a withering look. Demanding that a teenage daughter be home by a certain hour may lead the girl to insist that she hates her parents and that they do not understand her—but not insisting on a curfew time can leave her feeling that she has permission to participate in potentially dangerous late-night activities. Parents walk a fine line between avoiding conflict and giving the impression that anything a child does is acceptable.

With this in mind, parent-child conflict becomes a necessary element of the maturation process. Without it, children would not have the opportunity to establish their own identity, test their limits, and push the edge of the envelope in a relatively safe environment. It may be wearing for parents, but they have little choice but to participate and hope that when the worst is over, their children will wish to continue their relationship on less volatile terms, even inviting the parents to visit when they have children of their own.

OLDER ADULTS AND CONFLICT: LETTING GO AND LOSING GROUND

As adults reach their later years, many changes take place that can become sources of confrontation and conflict. They see their children replace them with a spouse or life partner and have children of their own, setting up boundaries for their parents' access to grandchildren and to the new homes they have created. Their roles in the workplace may change as new management arrives, some of whom see their older workers as less valuable than younger employees who understand current technology and trends. As they age, older adults feel themselves losing both physical and mental agility, limiting the activities in which they can continue to participate. All of these changes take place while most older adults feel no different emotionally than they ever have—so the implication that they are now less effective, intelligent, useful, or interested in the world around them only serves to demean and insult them.

It is no wonder, then, that the "crotchety old man" stereotype has become such a staple of human expectation. We believe that people become grumpier as they age, without much understanding of why this should be so. Young adults and people of middle age often find themselves at odds with parents and grandparents, certain that these older adults should not have a say in the way their children run their lives. Older adults, meanwhile, struggle to remain relevant as their children no longer require their supervision or counsel.

In their qualitative analysis of the University of Southern California Longitudinal Study of Generations survey in 1999, Edward J. Clarke, PhD, and his team found that conflicts between older parents and their adult children fell into six categories, listed here in descending order:

1. **Communication and interaction style**: A simple basis for communication led the list of conflicts between older parents and their adult children, with 34 percent of respondents noting it. This involves "the way family members engage in their relationships across generations"—that is, criticizing the way mother talks to father or the way a son treats his wife.
2. **Habits and lifestyle choices**: Parents criticize the son or daughter's hairstyle or manner of dress, sexual activity or orientation, the things the adult child does for fun, cleanliness or lack of attention to health, and other personal choices. Thirty percent of respondents described conflicts like these.
3. **Child-rearing practices and values**: Older adults have specific ideas about child raising that are not congruent with the adult child's ideas. When to have children, how many to have, what children are allowed to do, how permissive the adult children are with their offspring, and every other aspect of parenting are all points of contention between 16 percent of older adults and their grown children.
4. **Politics, religion, and ideology**: Disagreements about political parties or ideology, religion, morals, and ethics all arise between parents and their adult children. Parents expect their children to follow in their footsteps in terms of what they believe, but children develop their own ideas and take these into adulthood. Fifteen percent mentioned this kind of conflict.
5. **Work habits and orientations**: Differences in point of view about how much or how little priority an adult child gives to work performance can result in conflict. The older parent may feel the adult child works too much, not enough, too hard, or not hard enough. About 4 percent of respondents described this kind of conflict.
6. **Household standards and maintenance**: Attention to the home can become a point of contention, especially if the older adult feels the adult child does not take care of his or her property, does not keep it clean enough, or does not provide a safe enough environment for the children. Only 1 percent of respondents to the longitudinal survey cited this kind of conflict as an issue.

Why do these conflicts persist so far into the parent-child relationship? Bengtson and Kuypers (1971) referred to this tendency for parents to continue to attempt to instruct their grown children as the *developmental stake*, the psychological investment parents maintain in their children long after the child develops independence. Fingerman (1996) took this concept another step by introducing the idea of a developmental schism between parent and child, an emotional gap created by the two generations' differing concerns.

"Tension or divisions between parents and children may also arise from a related phenomenon, the tendency of parents to see their grown children as reflections of the quality of their parenting," note Susan Krauss Whitbourne and Joshua R. Bringle in the fourth edition of the *Encyclopedia of Aging,* and this may bring us the most telling insight into this lifelong conflict. Ryff et al. (1994) broaden our understanding of this by stating that parents see their children's accomplishments as proof of the quality of their own parenting—so when children perform below their parents' standards or outside of their expectations, they feel the need to continue to encourage (or berate or lecture) their children in hopes of changing their behavior to match the parenting they received.

All of these hypotheses relate to a single truth about growing older, one that creates additional conflict between the aging adult and others in his or her environment. As an adult approaches the end of life—whether the actual end is a month, a year, or a decade away—he or she gradually loses control over what his or her children do, where he or she lives and with whom, when and how his or her money is used, and whether he or she can take care of him or herself or must rely on others.

For most people, the first change comes with the decision to stop working—and this may be one reason that older people are remaining in the workforce longer today than throughout the twentieth century. The Bureau of Labor Statistics reports that in 2012, more than 60 percent of people between ages 55 and 64 were still in the workforce, and nearly 30 percent of people between 65 and 74 were still working as well. The bureau predicts that in 2022, 31.9 percent of Americans ages 65–74 will still be working. This is a dramatic departure from the long-held view that people over the age 65 are retired and enjoying their "golden years" with leisure pursuits. The economic trend tracker DShort reported in February 2017 that the labor force participation rate of people over age 75 has increased by 64 percent since 2000, outpacing people ages 70–74 (46%) and ages 65–69 (39%). This gives testimony to the fact that older adults are not moving quietly out of the working world and into retirement communities and nursing homes with the regularity we may expect.

What does this mean for the kinds of conflict older adults experience today? Still earning money and doing meaningful work well into their 70s, older adults expect to be taken seriously and to have an influence on the world around them. At some point, however, they reach a point at which they can no longer work—and many come to a crossroads when their health fails and they cannot care for themselves effectively.

This can result in one of the most complex conflicts between parent and child: when the parent has no choice but to take on the submissive role while the child becomes dominant. The idea that "the parent becomes the child" is anathema to just about every older adult, but it may be a necessary step when a parent becomes infirm or develops a terminal illness.

When it comes to giving up independence and self-sufficiency, elderly parents often find themselves in conflict with their adult children. The children hope to come to agreement with their parents that the time has come for them to leave their longtime residence and move into an eldercare situation, but nothing could be more horrifying to the parent. This book is not the place to discuss the very real issues with modern eldercare; instead, let us accept that fear of moving into a traditional nursing home is one of the reasons that many elderly adults fight against it until such a move becomes unavoidable.

What is this fear about? Again, loss of control becomes a significant issue. The sacrifice of privacy and dignity and the ability to make even the most basic decisions are all part of the experience of receiving around-the-clock skilled nursing care. It can be hard for adult children to realize how intrusive this kind of care can be, especially when they are overwhelmingly relieved to know that their parent is receiving this kind of close supervision. The children may be surprised to discover that their parent is more angry than happy to see them when they visit. The parent feels robbed of the independence and self-sufficiency he or she enjoyed throughout his or her life, while the child feels that he or she has done the best he or she could in a bad situation, so the parent's resentment is unjustified.

When conflict between parents and children continues until the last days of the parents' life, there may be no opportunity for reconciliation and forgiveness. This can mean that the impact of an unresolved issue may be felt throughout the adult child's life, even beyond the death of the parent. As we have seen throughout this examination of conflict, the end of harsh words and confrontation does not mean that the conflict ceases to exist. Parents and children need to take the opportunity to resolve their issues and find peace before time runs out and the conflict gets passed down from one generation to the next.

6

❖

Where: Conflict around the World

No matter what sources you use to get your news—newspapers, radio, 24-hour news channels, major news sites, Reddit, Facebook, or Twitter—you cannot escape the barrage of stories about conflicts throughout the world. Some of these may be right outside your door: differences between politicians, protest marches, and issues between people of different races, religions, and social classes. Others may be an ocean away, but their repercussions can come close to home as well.

In this chapter, we will examine some of the most dramatic and far-reaching intergroup conflicts taking place all over the world. We will try to understand how these conflicts began, how they became massive and often deadly, and why they have been difficult to impossible to resolve. We will see how these conflicts escalate, how the groups develop their sense of the in-group and the out-group, and how the bonds between members become stronger even as the attitudes toward those in the out-group turn from irritation to anger and then to loathing.

ISRAEL AND PALESTINE: ANCIENT HATRED

Who should have the right to a patch of land roughly 8,000 square miles wide—slightly larger than the state of Massachusetts—in the Middle East? This question of interstate conflict arose first in the late 1800s, when Jews emigrated from eastern Europe to Palestine to escape persecution by the Polish, Russian, and Romanian governments. Over the course of the twentieth century, the conflict over this land grew until it reached the point of war, involving countries beyond the borders of Palestine and Israel. Some of the countries have entered into truces with the Israelis, but issues continue to boil as the Israeli and Palestinian governments attempt to determine the factors required to obtain a lasting peace.

Jews chose this specific land mass because of a scripture in the Bible's Old Testament: "On that day the Lord made a covenant with Abram and said, 'To your descendants I give this land, from the Wadi of Egypt to the great river, the Euphrates—the land of the Kenites, Kenizzites, Kadmonites, Hittites, Perizzites, Rephaites, Amorites, Canaanites, Girgashites and Jebusites' " (Genesis 15:18–21).

The thing about using scripture as literal fact, however, is that people who do not follow this religion are not likely to accept the Bible passage as a divine right. The Arabs had their own plans for the land before the Jews began to arrive in the late 1800s. Arab leaders had begun work to create a unified Arab state from Syria to Yemen, including the land the Jews called Israel and the Arabs called Palestine.

To complicate the issue further, the Jews were not the only ones with their eyes on this land. It was actually part of the Ottoman Empire under Turkish rule, but in 1917, the British Empire arrived and won control of the land in battle. The Jews had begun the process of purchasing this land from Turkey, so the sudden British interest seemed likely to become a conflict in itself. The British, however, determined that they could do the Jews a generous service by creating "a National Home for the Jewish people" while securing their own interests in the Suez Canal, an important shipping hub. They worked with U.S. president Woodrow Wilson to draft the Balfour Declaration in 1917—a document supporting the Jewish state but going against earlier commitments to support the Arab state in the region.

This angered the Arab nations, because the British (and hence the Jews) disregarded the fact that Palestinians already lived on the land the agreement designated for the Jewish people. More than 500 Palestinian settlements existed at the time of the Balfour Declaration.

As World War I ended, the League of Nations placed Palestine under a British mandate, giving the British power over the land and its people—and taking that power away from the Arabs. This did nothing to quell the growing unrest between the Jews, the resident Palestinians, and the ruling British. The mandate essentially established Britain as sympathetic to the Jews, creating an in-group of Jews and British and pushing Arabs into the out-group.

It is little wonder, then, that clashes rose to the level of armed conflict not long after the British took control. A fistfight between Jews in 1921 escalated into Arabs breaking into Jewish homes, killing the inhabitants, and looting their belongings. An uneasy truce followed, but in 1929, a dispute over the famous Western Wall, a key holy site to Muslims and Jews, drew both groups into a deadly confrontation in which nearly 250 people were killed.

In 1935, Sheikh Izz al-Din al-Qassam called for a *jihad* (holy war) against the Jews and the British in Palestine. This formalized the conflict between Arabs and Jews for the first time and led to the creation of the first Palestinian guerrilla groups, which managed a campaign of rioting and confrontations with the Jews. Britain finally had no choice but to splinter its own in-group and distance itself from its ally; it banned further land sales to the Jews, which put an end to the violence between Jews and Palestinians through World War II.

When World War II ended in 1945 and the atrocities and genocide perpetrated by the Nazis became common knowledge, however, displaced Jews fled Europe and arrived in Palestine by the thousands. Not only did Britain lift its ban on land sales, but it worked with the United Nations on a resolution partitioning Palestine into an Arab state, a Jewish state, and the city of Jerusalem, a holy city to people of Muslim, Jewish, and Christian faiths. In 1948, when the British mandate expired, the Jewish People's Council declared the establishment of the state of Israel.

Literally four hours after this declaration, Egypt bombed the Israeli capital of Tel Aviv. More than 700,000 Palestinians fled their homes for other lands—and as the Palestinians evacuated, Israel took control of the 500 Palestinian settlements and began to annex them, building homes for Jews on these abandoned properties. The Jews were in the region to stay, much to the chagrin of those who had just forfeited their land to them.

Fighting for this land continued, including the Six-Day War in 1967 that resulted in Israel gaining high-ground land on the West Bank and the Gaza Strip. This land, beyond what was designated part of the Jewish state in 1948, remains a bone of contention between Israel and Palestine today, as it offers whoever holds it the strategic advantage of high ground above disputed territory. As of this writing, Israel does not intend to relinquish this land, so battles in one form or another continue—and the conflict has led Israel to close its border to Palestinians still living in the region, limiting the potential for violence but compromising their ability to live, work, and access medical care in areas where these activities were historically available.

More than a century after it started, the conflict between Israel and Palestine continues. What began first as a business transaction—Jews buying land from Turkey—became a humanitarian gesture on the part of

Britain and the United Nations, but without the consent or participation of the Palestinians, who would be significantly affected. The Palestinians and their allies in the region escalated the conflict with confrontation and violence, and the Israelis answered with matching violence, closed borders, and further action that assured that the Palestinians would remain the out-group. Today, peace between Israel and Palestine may be the most unobtainable goal on the planet, in which every small, incremental accomplishment garners a Nobel Peace Prize, and leaders maintain an adversarial relationship in which threats and violence prevent any effort toward peaceful coexistence.

SYRIA: REBELLION TURNS TO WAR

One of the most dramatic intragroup conflicts of our lifetimes has played out in the Middle East since 2011, as the president of Syria victimizes his own citizens to retain his power. As of December 2016, more than 470,000 Syrians have died in the civil war, according to the Syrian Centre for Policy Research, and the news bureau Al Jazeera reports that another 12 million citizens have been forced to evacuate their homes and move to refugee camps or flee the country. Despite the swell of rebel forces and the comparative minority fighting on behalf of the government in power, the Syrian civil war shows no signs of abating in the near future. The most daunting challenge to peace, however, is not only the president's determination to remain in power but also the fractured nature of the free-dom forces and the lack of a single, central decision-making body to re-present them all.

How did this conflict begin? In March 2011, in the midst of what would become known as the Arab Spring, law enforcement in the Syrian city of Deraa arrested and tortured a group of 15 teenage boys who had painted slo-gans against the government on a school wall. When news emerged that the police had tortured one of the boys to death, protestors took to the streets in a call for justice, free speech, and democracy. Syria's president, Bashar al-Assad, had no interest in dissent, however, and his security forces opened fire on the protestors. Several of them died in the altercation.

Few things escalate a conflict more quickly than the death of innocent people. More protestors flooded the streets of Syria's cities, with hundreds of thousands demonstrating daily by July 2011. When they were met with security forces that fired on them and killed hundreds of protestors, the civilians began to bring their own weapons to the protests. Rebel brigades formed and took up arms against the president's troops. Battles broke out to defend cities against government forces as the country descended into civil war. The fighting extended into the capital city of Damascus and the nation's second-largest city, Aleppo, in 2012.

This may seem like a clearly delineated conflict between groups—the dictatorial regime of Assad and the rebel forces working for democracy, much like the American Revolutionary War—but the lines are actually far blurrier, and there are a growing number of them. The majority of Syrians—as many as 89 percent—are members of the Sunni Muslim sect, while Assad is part of a small Shia sect called Alawite, or Alawi. Sunnis practice traditional Islam as set forth by the prophet Muhammad, while Alawites keep their specific beliefs within their sect, not sharing them with outsiders. This insulation of their faith creates religious barriers between the majority Sunnis and the Alawites.

The religious overlay to the conflict has attracted outside influences to ally with one side or the other: Hezbollah fighters from Lebanon and Iran and Shia militias have joined forces with Assad's army, specifically to protect their alliance with Assad against Israel. The Islamic State jihadist group (known as IS, ISIS, or ISIL), which follows a fundamentalist doctrine derived from the Sunni Muslim faith, has taken it upon itself to attack the Shia troops and their mosques, both in Syria and in its own stronghold in Iraq. ISIS took control of a large, landlocked section of Syria just over the border from Iraq, where millions of its followers have settled and militant forces defend their claim to the territory.

The Syrian civil war brings us a perspective on conflict that we have not seen before in this book: the concept of *factionalism*, in which some members of the in-group or the out-group form disagreements with the main group and its leadership. This takes place most often when the conflict goes on longer than expected, and one of the groups in the conflict can no longer envision an exclusively positive outcome. Infighting begins between members of the group, and some members may begin to rally around a new leader whom they believe will bring them to a more decisive victory that matches their personal goals.

When the differences become too severe to be sustainable within one group, the dissenters splinter away and become a faction. They may ally with one another as a matter of convenience during a violent conflict, but their ultimate vision may never be congruent with their former compatriots' goals.

This is what took place within the Free Syrian Army (FSA)—the civilian rebel forces that oppose the current Syrian government. The FSA maintains a moderate view of the country's future with the goal of removing Assad and establishing a more democratic government. This vision proved too liberal for some of its members, however, so they split from the FSA and formed their own faction to promote a more Islamist vision for the country. They became attracted to another fighting force, al-Nusra Front (now known as Jabhat Fateh al-Sham), as well as ISIS, two terrorist organizations that form a jihadist force called the Army of Conquest.

If you are confused by all of these group names, you are not alone. One of the challenges in bringing conflicts such as the Syrian civil war to some kind of conclusion is the sheer number of splinter groups, factions, and organizations operating in this part of the world. With so many ideologies at work, each with its own fiercely passionate and loyal following, Syria has been divided up into areas of conquest. The Assad government holds most of the western areas; the FSA maintains its grip in the Southwest and parts of the Northwest; ISIS defends the central and southeastern positions, and Kurdish nationalists hold a northeastern section known as the Federation of Northern Syria-Rojava (or Syrian Kurdistan). Add to this the involve-ment of Russian advisers working to support Assad, Kurdish forces backing the rebels, a limited American force on the ground specifically to battle ISIS, and the participation of Iran in ceasefire agreements, and the war becomes too complex to follow without up-to-date maps, nuanced narra-tives, and scorecards.

What if you were a mediator trying to negotiate the end of this war? You might manage to get two forces—Assad and the FSA, let us say—to the table to discuss terms, but Hezbollah, ISIS, the Kurds, and Jabhat Fateh al-Sham might have no interest at all in bringing the conflict to a close. While it may seem on the surface that these groups have taken one side or the other in the war, the fact remains that each is there to defend its own interests. Their desire for land holdings, dominance over people who follow a different Muslim sect, and protection of their own followers could easily overshadow any peace agreement between the Syrian government and the rebel forces. Even if Syria ends its own civil war, these additional factions may continue their own aggressive tactics—including fighting—because the conflict is an end in itself. As long as the militant groups keep attacking one another, they can keep their followers close and energize their base to continue to fight.

This multidimensional conflict has yet another side. The casualties of Syria's war have long since crossed its borders, causing unrest and concern on a nearly global scale as these refugees pour out of the country in search of new, peaceful homes. Turkey has opened its doors to Syrian refugees with more than 2.4 million finding shelter there, but in Europe, many have resisted offering this aid. While Germany and Sweden have admitted tens of thousands of refugees, Hungary, Denmark, the Czech Republic,

Romania, and Slovakia have worked to actively discourage Syrian refugees from attempting to enter their countries.

President Donald Trump of the United States went so far as to sign an executive order on January 27, 2017, banning anyone from Syria to enter the country indefinitely, regardless of their need, until "extreme vetting" procedures could be put in place to be certain that these refugees were not terrorists with malevolent intent toward Americans. The U.S. Court of Appeals for the Ninth Circuit rescinded this order days after it was issued, but a second, less prohibitive executive order followed it a month later—this time banning Syrian entry for 90 days. While a federal court overturned this order as well, the message to the world was clear: Syrian Muslim refugees are an out-group in their own country and an out-group on a global scale. Fear of the many terrorist organizations that align themselves with forms of Islam has made large portions of the Western world see all Muslims as potential terrorists.

CHINA VERSUS TAIWAN: A FIGHT FOR INDEPENDENCE

Back in AD 239, the government of China sent an expedition to investigate the lands and islands along its eastern border. The explorers came upon Taiwan, a sizable island on the edge of the East China Sea about 100 miles off China's shoreline, and recorded the discovery in China's detailed early history. Like any country of the time, China claimed the island for its own. This became the earliest marker in the dispute over the 245-mile-long nation, in which Taiwan maintains its right to govern itself, while China passes laws that forbid Taiwan to formally declare its independence.

Compared to the volatile conflicts in Israel and Syria, China's dispute with Taiwan may seem like a disagreement among gentlefolk to those who are unfamiliar with its history. The question of Taiwanese sovereignty affects millions of lives on the island as well as Taiwan's standing as a nation on the world stage. Late in 2016, U.S. president-elect Donald Trump attracted attention by accepting a congratulatory telephone call from Tsai Ing-wen, Taiwan's president, piquing officials in China for his acknowledgment of the island as an autonomous nation. The fact that Trump took this call out of general ignorance of the conflict between China and Taiwan softened Beijing's ire and saved the United States' relationship with China, but the incident brought the nearly century-old dispute back into the spotlight in the Western world.

To understand the issues between the two nations, we must turn back the clock to 1683, when China first formally made Taiwan part of the mainland country. Taiwan had been a shared resource between its native aboriginal people, the Chinese, and Dutch settlers, but the ruling Qing dynasty chose to claim the island for China at this point, pushing out the Dutch and other Europeans. This condition remained until 1895, when Japan invaded China in the First Sino-Japanese War and took Taiwan as a condition of China's surrender.

Taiwan remained a Japanese property until after World War II (1945), when China and its allies, the United States and the United Kingdom, won the war against Japan. The Allied forces placed Taiwan under China's temporary rule, under the Chinese Kuomintang (KMT) government of Chiang Kai-shek—the party that reunited China in 1928 after the Qing dynasty had been overthrown and warlords divided the country.

This new leadership did not suit Taiwan residents. The government under Chen Yi confiscated Japanese-owned properties, mismanaged the island's economy, and soon plunged it into a period of inflation and food shortages, leading to a black market in household goods. Postwar deficiencies on the Chinese mainland sapped Taiwanese products, leaving the island with scarce resources and outrageously high prices for rice and other commodities. Life under the KMT put islanders in a state of unemployment, poverty, hunger, and helplessness, the ultimate recipe for an uprising.

Sure enough, all of this hostility and rage came to a head on February 27, 1947, when a female cigarette vendor and a group of government agents engaged in a dispute in public in the Taiwanese capital, Taipei. An agent struck the cigarette vendor with the butt of his gun, and this drawing of first blood triggered a large-scale rebellion among the Taiwanese people. What became known as the "228 Incident"—for the largest day of demonstrations on February 28—continued in Taipei until martial law (government run by the Chinese military) was declared on March 4.

In the midst of the uprising, Taiwanese leaders emerged and formed a Settlement Committee to present demands to the KMT government. They hoped to achieve free elections of their own officials, the autonomy to run their own affairs and make decisions for the benefit of their citizens, and a halt to the unfair and disadvantageous practices that came from the corrupt Chinese government in charge of Taiwan. They demanded that at least two-thirds of the people who ran for government positions live in Taiwan for 10 years before election, and they wanted safeguards of the people's civil and property rights. They also objected to heavy tax burdens, asking that they pay only income, luxury, and inheritance taxes to the government. The Settlement Committee presented what became known as their 32 Demands on March 7, in hopes of finalizing an agreement with Chen Yi before reinforcement troops arrived from mainland China.

They did not succeed. The troops arrived and began a systematic massacre of people involved in the uprising, including students, intellectuals, and the leaders who had drafted the 32 Demands. Foreigners reported to the *New York Times* that they saw homes looted, women raped, and as many as 10,000 people murdered. Demonstrations, rioting, and looting spread to the mainland as well, with government forces killing protestors indiscriminately and at will. The exact number of deaths has never been confirmed, but the numbers released by the Chinese government put the killings at between 3,000 and 4,000. The accuracy of this figure may never be known.

With the rise of Mao Zedong (known colloquially as Chairman Mao) at the end of the Chinese civil war in 1949, the communist-led People's Republic of China came into power on the Chinese mainland. For Taiwan, this meant that the martial law that began in Taiwan after the 228 Incident remained in place until 1987. Suppression of political dissidents became an institutional practice, one Taiwanese residents referred to as the White Terror—a period in which about 140,000 Taiwanese citizens were arrested and imprisoned for expressing any sort of disagreement with the KMT, which moved its headquarters to Taipei in 1949 at the end of the civil war. The KMT justified the arrests by labeling the Taiwanese dissidents as spies for the mainland's Communist government.

Martial law finally ended in Taiwan in 1987, but the dispute over the island's sovereignty continues. In 1992, the Chinese Communist Party and the KMT came to an agreement called the 1992 Consensus, which states that there is only one China, allowing for Beijing to interpret this in its way (as the People's Republic, or Communist China), while Taiwan reserves the right to consider the Republic of China, or democratic socialism, as the one China. This document permits the two governments to agree to disagree on what their relationship is—a remarkable achievement that sealed an uncomfortable but necessary truce.

Currently the People's Republic of China governs the mainland, while the Republic of China—led by the KMT party—heads the government in Taiwan. Many governments around the globe do not acknowledge Taiwan as a separate entity, but this does not stop them from doing business with the island. The United States, for example, has sold arms to Taiwan totaling more than $46 billion since 1990. President Tsai's conversation with President Trump in 2016 was the first conversation between leaders of the two countries since 1979.

Pressure from the United Nations and allies around the globe prevent mainland China from taking any military action against Taiwan, but the island continues to maintain its commitment to becoming an independent nation, with "the future of Taiwan [to] be decided peacefully by the peoples of both sides of the Strait," as the United Kingdom's official stance on the conflict states.

So what does this teach us about conflict and its impact in the Eastern Hemisphere? China and Taiwan exist in a state of perpetual conflict, but the two entities have seen what the worst of this conflict can do. The experience of the 228 Incident and more than 40 years of aftermath remain in the region's public consciousness, with the understanding that this kind of uprising and crackdown generated no advantage for either side. Now the two maintain an uneasy economic cooperation, with the understanding that Taiwan still looks to a future of independence from China and its own fully democratic government.

The lessons here are twofold: One, uprising does not necessarily signal a permanent rift between two parties, even when that experience is particularly destructive and deadly. And two, resolution of all conflicts is not required for the entities involved to continue to function. China and Taiwan manage to move forward despite their significant differences and the tug-of-war between their values, even with the understanding that they may not enjoy the relationship or approve of one another's approach and ultimate goals.

HINDU VERSUS MUSLIM: THE PARTITION OF INDIA AND PAKISTAN

How does conflict arise where no conflict existed before? Often the issue is a new element in the relationship, a change that comes from a third party that does not take the existing situation into account. A pair of close friends may gradually become enemies when another person joins them, staking out friend "territory" and bonding with one while alienating the other. A new coach may divide a gym class into squads and deliberately create a rivalry between classmates, or a teacher may sort students into reading groups based on their ability, unwittingly pitting the students who read faster against those who read more slowly. Smart versus less so, pitchers versus hitters, blondes versus a lone brunette, or black versus white—these divisions can seem arbitrary when they are imposed upon an otherwise cohesive group by the arrival of a disruptive authority.

Centuries ago, Hindus, Sikhs, and Muslims in India lived side by side without giving their differences a second thought. They shared some traditions and language with one another and maintained their differences as well, with little concern that their uniqueness would be challenged or their beliefs disparaged. The occasional incident throughout history would certainly demonstrate that not every Hindu got along with every Muslim, but on the whole, the relationship between the two was one of comparative mutual respect and appreciation.

Granted, Muslims—or more literally, Turks—arrived as conquerors as far back as 1021, and over the next 200 years, they pillaged Hindu and Buddhist areas and established sultanates throughout much of the Indian subcontinent. Once settled, however, these sites became part of the surrounding communities, and the next several hundred years passed in relative peace and even a sharing of cultures. Some 20 percent of the region's population considered themselves Muslim by the 1800s, making them a significant part of the population of Southeast Asia.

What made these people turn against one another in the mid-twentieth century, then, until the relationship reached a breaking point? The conflict began in the middle of the nineteenth century, when the British East India Company ruled the country. The Company maintained relationships with the Hindu, Muslim, and Christian populations in India, but it favored Hindus, who resented the Company's intrusion less than people of other religions, and hired people of the Hindu faith as agents of commerce and governance. In doing this, the British made these positions unobtainable for Muslims, relegating them to lower status within the Company.

Decades after the Indian Rebellion of 1857, when the East India Company reign ended and direct British rule (called the Raj) began, the British realized that their favoritism of Hindus had given them more power than the Raj desired, so they abruptly switched their allegiance to the Muslims. The British intended to balance the power between the two religious groups, but this backfired as bitterness grew between them. Muslims felt victimized by Hindus, who enjoyed majority roles in other areas of leadership like law enforcement and government service. Britain continued to impose separation and sow the seeds of mistrust between the two ethnic groups, removing Muslims from the army to keep them from forming a dominant position there.

In 1905, seeing strong bonds form between people of one religion or the other, the British decided to partition the province of Bengal along religious lines—something that had never been done in India before this. This led to extensive protests, so the partition lasted only a short time, but it was the first demonstration of the concept of a land in which people form communities around their religious beliefs. At the same time, the British decided to create separate electorates, in which Muslims would elect Muslim representatives to Congress and Hindus would elect Hindu representatives. While this guaranteed that there would be politicians of both faiths in government, it further divided Muslims and Hindus and brought their differences on key issues to light. This "divide and rule" strategy fragmented a populace who had united to battle against the East India Company decades before and now found themselves rivals under manipulative foreign rule.

Favoring one group over another, deliberately weakening the political and military position of the less favored group, and playing up the differences between groups to broaden the divide between them—these are all tactics used by Sherif et al. (1954) in the Robbers Cave experiment described in Chapter 4. Like Sherif (who came later), the British saw results well beyond their expectations as the groups' members bonded within the group structure, chose their own leaders, and saw the others as sworn enemies whom they could no longer stand to have living next door. India became the British Raj's own social experiment, one that tore a country apart.

Out of this contentious atmosphere rose several leaders who would change the composition of the Asian subcontinent. The first of these was Mohandas (Mahatma) Gandhi, leader of the movement to end British rule in India and a decisive proponent of religious unity. Gandhi taught his followers that all of the world's great religions shared a fundamental truth and that all religions are essentially one. "The Allah of Islam is the same as the God of Christians and the Ishwara of Hindus. Even as there are numerous names of God in Hinduism, there are many names of God in Islam," he wrote. "The names do not indicate individuality but attributes, and little man has tried in his humble way to describe mighty God by giving Him attributes, though He is above all attributes, Indescribable, Immeasurable."

This inclusive perspective brought followers to him from many different religious backgrounds in the early years of his activism and leadership in India. Born a Hindu, Gandhi joined with Muslims in the subcontinent in supporting the Khilafat movement, a mobilization of Indian Muslims and Hindus to pressure the British to restore the Ottoman Sultan as the leader of Turkey after World War I. This gained him a great deal of favor with Muslims from 1920 to 1922.

By this time, Muslims in India had coalesced in the Muslim League, an organization that represented the interests of this minority. Holding itself separate from the Indian National Congress, the Muslim League was led by Mohammed Ali Jinnah, an attorney and member of Congress who disagreed with Gandhi's policies of noncooperation with the British Raj.

Gandhi's support in the Muslim community fizzled when the British suppressed the Khilafat movement, arresting its leaders and sentencing them to prison. Turkey abolished the Ottoman in 1922, putting an end to the effort.

While Gandhi continued to work toward an independent India, Muslims faced obstacles to their influence in the country's political structure under British rule. When they failed to gain ground in the 1937 elections, Jinnah chose to take a new tack to respond to the frustration of the Muslim electorate: he called for Muslims to have their own "homeland," a free and independent state, entirely separate from the British Raj and from the Hindus. When he announced this at a Muslim League meeting in Lahore in 1940, league members rallied around this idea. The gulf between Muslims and Hindus began to widen rapidly.

Over the next seven years as India moved toward liberation from Britain, Jinnah ramped up his rhetoric. He declared Gandhi to be an enemy to the Muslims in India—a fact that baffled Gandhi, who believed that the commonality of faith in a supreme being should unite all people, regardless of the name they gave their God. Throughout World War II, as famine and food shortages gripped the country, discontent spread throughout the subcontinent, and groups were quick to blame one another and assume that their neighbors of different faiths had it easier than they did. On an August day in 1946, Jinnah called for the Muslim League to carry out a Direct Action Day, with civil disruption throughout the country. This resulted in widespread violence between Muslims and Hindus and thousands of deaths, convincing the British that there could be no peaceful coexistence between the two warring religious groups.

At last in 1947, both Jinnah and Gandhi succeeded. The British government relinquished India to its own rule on August 14, at the same time forming the state of Pakistan as a home for the Muslims. It was a day to celebrate—but the Hindus, Muslims, and another religious minority, the Sikhs, chose to recognize the day and the period that followed in quite another manner. More than 10 million people packed up their belongings and moved from one side of the border to the other, with Muslims heading to the northeast (to what is now Bangladesh) and northwest to Pakistan, and Hindus making tracks for the south. Hundreds of thousands would never see their new home.

"Across the Indian subcontinent, communities that had coexisted for almost a millennium attacked each other in a terrifying outbreak of sectarian violence, with Hindus and Sikhs on one side and Muslims on the other—a mutual genocide as unexpected as it was unprecedented," wrote William Dalrymple, India historian and author of *The Last Mughal* (Bloomsbury, 2008), in the *New Yorker*. "In Punjab and Bengal—provinces abutting India's borders with West and East Pakistan, respectively—the carnage was especially intense, with massacres, arson, forced conversions, mass abductions, and savage sexual violence." At the end of 1948, when the last emigrants made their way to their new homeland or across their original one, more than 15 million people had shifted through the region, and between 1 and 2 million had died on the way.

What could drive so many people to commit acts of unspeakable and deadly violence against so many others, most of whom they had never met or even seen before? These people were not ordered to commit atrocities the way Nazi soldiers were during World War II, but their leaders had incited them to deadly force for several years. In addition to Jinnah's calls for disobedience, regional leaders of the Muslim League made speeches that encouraged bloodshed. It took little to ignite the tinderbox that was three decades of Muslim marginalization under British rule and as many years of fear and bigotry in the Hindu communities as well.

When victory becomes a release valve for decades of frustration, anger, and inflamed rhetoric, conflict has spiraled far beyond any single leader's ability to control it. India and Pakistan continue to balance on the edge of a tenuous peace, with the separation of Hindus and Muslims now understood as a necessity, one that keeps more than a century of bigotry at bay.

UNITED STATES VERSUS VENEZUELA: IDEOLOGY AND OIL

Throughout most of this book, we have discussed conflicts that affect relationships between individuals or groups of people. Some of the most visible and well-known conflicts, however, take place at the top levels of government, where the issues may be differences in ideologies—the values a country holds so central to its identity that its leaders are willing to put people at risk to maintain them.

At the same time, a battle over ideas can also mask a more practical goal: protection of natural resources like oil or precious metals, security of a political party's position and power, or defense against the loss of large sums of money. These three goals are closely entwined, of course, so just about any issue at the highest levels of national leadership may come down to which country has money, who controls the money, which nation is putting its earning power at risk, and how much it is willing to invest to protect its financial future.

Such a conflict came to the forefront of public consciousness in the early 2000s, when President George W. Bush of the United States and President Hugo Chávez of Venezuela locked horns over ideology and oil.

The United States has maintained diplomatic relations with Venezuela since 1835, becoming Venezuela's largest trading partner (the U.S. Department of State reports that trade between the two countries reached $23.9 billion in 2015, a great deal of money for a fairly small country). Venezuela is one of the world's largest exporters of oil, with 20 percent of the world's global oil reserves within its borders. When Chávez took office in 1999, he began a process of bringing the country's oil under government control, taking back its largest company, PDVSA, from private industry and raising the royalties foreign companies paid for harvesting the oil found in Venezuela. These policies made Venezuela an extremely rich country, doubling the country's gross domestic product. Chávez used the additional money to fund social programs like assuring that Venezuelans had access to clean drinking water, health care, education, and safe housing and funding government pensions and other social programs. At the same time, bringing the oil company under government control ensured that its employees could not conduct a strike or disrupt production in any other kind of protest.

Venezuela is one of the top five suppliers of crude oil to the United States, so changes in control of the South American country's oil policies had a significant impact on U.S. interests. Chávez may have seen this as a motivation for the United States to meddle in Venezuelan internal affairs. At the same time, Venezuela regularly did business with Cuba, a country with which the United States had severed ties back in the early 1960s when Fidel Castro came into power on the island and established a Communist government there. Chávez maintained a personal friendship with Castro, a fact that irked U.S. leaders.

In 2002, an attempt at a *coup d'etat* by people who opposed the government takeover of PDVSA and other communist-leaning policies removed Chávez from office for a total of 47 hours as Pedro Carmona, Venezuelan Chamber of Commerce president, declared himself president of the nation. The attempt fell apart quickly as word reached ordinary citizens that Chávez had not resigned, as they had heard from opposition leaders and the media, but that he had been forced from office. Crowds of poor people who had benefited from Chávez's social programs surrounded the presidential palace to protest the coup, demanding that Chávez be returned. Two days after he had taken office, Carmona resigned and the loyal presidential guard took back control of the palace. Chávez returned to the presidency.

Meanwhile, leaders of the U.S. government watched the coup attempt with mingled hopefulness and trepidation. Chávez had made it harder and more costly for the United States to do business with Venezuela, but the larger nation had become dependent on South American oil for use in the manufacture of all kinds of petroleum-based products, which it then exported back to Venezuela as well as to other countries. The United States declared that it had observed the coup from a distance and had played no role in it. Chávez, however, was not ready to accept this statement of non-participation from the world's leading superpower. He claimed that while he was held captive at a small island military base off the Venezuelan coast, he had seen a plane with U.S. registration numbers on it. He called this absolute proof that the United States had taken an active role in the coup and even that the country may have funded some portion of it.

President Bush scoffed at this, and investigations requested by Congress found no U.S. involvement in the coup. Chávez, however, insisted that the United States wanted him out of office and claimed that he had escaped a second coup in October 2002 and even an assassination attempt. The issue became the first reason to break positive diplomatic relations between the two countries—but not the last.

In 2008, with both Chávez and Bush still leading their respective countries, U.S. ambassador Philip Goldberg was expelled from Bolivia for playing a role in civil unrest against the country's first indigenous Indian president, Evo Morales. Goldberg was accused of "conspiring against democracy and seeking the division of Bolivia," for meeting with the governor of Santa Cruz, Bolivia's richest province. The people of Santa Cruz have voted for a series of referendums to obtain more autonomy from the government of Bolivia, actually threatening to secede from the country if Morales did not recognize their rights.

Chávez joined his ally Morales in denouncing U.S. involvement in Bolivia's internal affairs and used this opportunity to sever relations with the United States. While newly elected president Barack Obama reinstated these relations in 2009, the relationship remained rocky: in 2011, Secretary of State Hillary Clinton imposed sanctions on PDVSA for delivering components used to make gasoline to Iran, a country already sanctioned by the United States. The new sanctions prohibited PDVSA from competing for U.S. government contracts, among other things, which restricted Venezuela's ability to increase its income from its top customer. (These sanctions were lifted in 2016.)

In 2014, President Obama signed the Venezuela Defense of Human Rights and Civil Society Act. This congressional act, introduced by Senator Robert Menendez of New Jersey, may have escaped your notice if you were not following U.S.-Venezuelan relations that year, as it attracted little attention from the news media. Its purpose was to denounce a series of currency controls imposed by Venezuela's government and central bank, which were driving up inflation to the third highest point in the world—just behind South Sudan and Syria, two countries ravaged by civil war. By this time Hugo Chávez was no longer in power, passing away just after his reelection in 2012, but the new president, Nicolas Maduro, had continued Chávez's policies that put money in the pockets of the country's wealthiest citizens. Venezuela's law enforcement had expelled much of the international media from the country, imprisoned some journalists, and arrested and even opened fire on crowds of protestors, killing 41 citizens to date when the act was signed.

To express its dissatisfaction with the practices of the Venezuelan government, Obama and Congress once again hit the country where it hurt: in its wallet. The act blocks and prohibits "all transactions in all property and interests in property of a person . . . if such property and interests in property are in the United States, come within the United States, or are to come within the possession or control of a United States person." This, in essence, comes under the heading of "freezing assets," as it makes it impossible for a Venezuelan to access any money he or she may have in a U.S. bank or company. Four days later, Obama made it clear exactly which people were targeted by the sanctions when he signed an executive order, "Blocking Property and Suspending Entry of Certain Persons Contributing to the Situation in Venezuela," which specifies "persons involved in or responsible for the erosion of human rights guarantees, persecution of political opponents, curtailment of press freedoms, use of violence and human rights violations/abuses in response to antigovernment protests . . ." and so on.

This may all seem like dry dealings between government powers, but the cycles of accusations, sanctions, relaxing of rules, more accusations, and more sanctions are not so different from the arguments that take place in your own living room. The main difference, of course, is that the substance of negotiation takes place behind closed doors—as Lin-Manuel Miranda wrote in the musical *Hamilton*, "No one else is in the room where it happened"—and in the pages, on the screens, and in the websites of the news media. The structure of the conflict is essentially the same, moving from act to accusation to counteraccusation and escalation. The main difference is that the escalation becomes a matter of law and historical record, preserved for the rest of the world to reference for millennia to come.

Is this significantly different from an argument you may have on Facebook or in the comments section of a news website with a complete stranger who disagrees with your views? The stakes may be much higher and affect many more thousands (or even millions) of people, but the result is essentially the same. The angry words remain available for public view for the long term, chronicling acts and thoughts you may find wholly humiliating should you stumble across them years later. Equally important, they remain as a testament to things you felt an hour, a day, a month, or several years ago, when you may have had less understanding of a specific situation, or you felt an overriding passion about something that becomes inconsequential after time has passed.

Politicians and heads of state say and do things they are not proud of, and their words and deeds end up in presidential libraries or on Wikipedia. There is no telling today whether Hugo Chávez would see his policies as detrimental to the health and welfare of the people of Venezuela, or if he would be proud to look back at the amount of money he put into the accounts of high officials. Likewise, it is hard to know if George W. Bush and his staff did have a hand in the attempted coup d'etat in Venezuela, or if the congressional investigation truly found no connection between the U.S. government and the 2002 opposition forces. We only know that a very public conflict arose from these events, one that has landed on yet another State Department's agenda to perpetuate or bring to a close.

UNITED STATES: LAW ENFORCEMENT VERSUS AFRICAN AMERICANS IN FERGUSON, MISSOURI

In early March 2017, the city council in Ferguson, Missouri, passed an ordinance establishing a civilian review board to conduct oversight of the Ferguson Police Department. The nine-member board will investigate complaints made against members of the police department and will recommend changes to the department's policies, procedures, and training to begin to improve relations with the community of Ferguson.

Their job is far from trivial, and it has the potential to make a significant, positive difference in a community where the "Black Lives Matter" movement was born in the midst of outrage and unrest three years before.

The nation's attention landed on this suburb of St. Louis on Saturday, August 9, 2014, when Michael Brown, an unarmed black teenager, was shot and killed by Darren Wilson, a white police officer. Brown and his friend Dorian Johnson left Ferguson Market and Liquor just before noon that day, where a surveillance video showed Brown stealing a box of cigars. Minutes later, Officer Wilson—who was not aware of the robbery—met them in the middle of a street in his police sport utility vehicle. Wilson told Brown and Johnson that they were blocking traffic and to move to the curb, but they did not move immediately, and an altercation took place at Wilson's car window. Wilson fired two shots through his window, grazing Brown's thumb.

Brown ran. Wilson left his vehicle to follow him, and Brown stopped and turned to face Wilson with his hands raised, according to bystanders who saw the incident. Witnesses said later that Brown then started toward Wilson, and the officer opened fire. He shot him several times. Brown died soon after from one of two wounds to his head. Four other bullets landed in his right arm.

Some witnesses reported that Brown had punched Wilson while the officer was still in the car. They gave different testimony about whether Brown had actually leaned inside the vehicle or not, but Wilson said that Brown had reached into the vehicle and fought him for his gun. Later a medical exam would show that Wilson did have a wound on his face that could have come from Brown punching him.

Brown's death became a *catalytic event*, an occurrence that set off a firestorm of unrest in the town of Ferguson. Tensions there had been mounting for years between the police department and the largely African American community, with residents regularly reporting that police unfairly targeted and harassed black citizens. Until August 2014, these reports had fallen on deaf ears. The citizens had no access to records to prove their claims that this treatment had become an institutionalized norm, and the people in power in Ferguson showed no willingness to investigate their allegations.

The death of a recent high school graduate brought thousands of Ferguson residents together to stand against the injustice they perceived in their midst. Their outrage attracted the attention of news media in the region and soon reached a national level as demonstrations grew over the next several days. The chant, "Hands up, don't shoot," echoed by hundreds of people protesting in front of the Ferguson Police Department, became a rallying cry for people of all races in cities across the country who stood in solidarity with the citizens of Ferguson.

As the first day of this altercation passed, however, some of the protests devolved into vandalism and looting, while police in riot gear made futile attempts to get the situation under control. Those demonstrating in a peaceful fashion began to split with those who wanted to express anger. This created two separate phenomena in Ferguson, one orderly and one violent—both originating from the same catalyst and both with the same overall goal.

This split is a fairly common occurrence in social conflict, but it rarely has as positive a final conclusion as it did in Ferguson. As the nation watched on television, they saw the demonstrations as the constitutional right of the protestors to free assembly and the rioting for the outward expression of anger that it was. The nation shared this anger as well, as the shooting of Michael Brown was one in a series of incidents that had taken place across the country. Most notably, Trayvon Martin, a black teenager in Sanford, Florida, had been shot to death by neighborhood watch patroller George Zimmerman during a confrontation. Martin's death had shocked and horrified the nation, and Zimmerman's acquittal for the killing had fueled accusations of racial profiling.

Interviews with Ferguson demonstrators on national television provided detailed descriptions of the problem between police and Ferguson residents that had developed over the previous decade, in which black citizens were stopped on the street, pulled from their cars, deprived of their rights, and bullied by police officers in what appeared to be incidents of open harassment. By Monday, August 11, the FBI announced that it had opened an investigation into possible civil rights violations in Ferguson. The following day, the Reverend Al Sharpton, a nationally known civil rights advocate, arrived in Ferguson and held a news conference to ask that people stop rioting. "Some of us are making it about how mad we are, instead of how promising he was," he said. President Barack Obama issued a statement on Monday as well, asking that people "remember this young man through reflection and understanding."

The protests, however, escalated further as the Ferguson Police Department decided not to announce the name of the police officer who had shot Michael Brown or any other details of the investigation. By Tuesday night, men wearing ski masks and armed with shotguns appeared in the North St. Louis area, and shots were fired. A police officer shot and wounded a person with a gun in his hand, and a drive-by shooter struck a woman in the crowd. Other assemblies continued peacefully, with citizens marching with their hands in the air, chanting, "Hands up, don't shoot." Police met the protests in full riot gear, driving armored trucks and armed with tear gas and guns loaded with rubber bullets. In the heat of the moment, police arrested journalists Wesley Lowery of the *Washington Post* and Ryan Reilly of the *Huffington Post*, who were filling in behind the counter at a McDonald's in Ferguson when police arrived and cleared the restaurant. Reilly, who is white, asked for officers' names and badge numbers, and none answered him. "I wasn't even Mirandized," he said.

As the protests and rioting continued into Wednesday and Thursday, Missouri senator Claire McCaskill arrived in Ferguson and spoke with constituents. She released a statement saying what had become clear to people watching this drama on television across the country: "We need to demilitarize this situation. This kind of response by the police has become the problem instead of the solution."

On Thursday, Missouri governor Jay Nixon announced an "operational shift" in the way law enforcement handled the protests from that point forward. He sent the Missouri State Highway Patrol to oversee public protection, and Captain Ron Johnson of the state patrol announced that there would be no more riot gear or armored trucks. By Thursday night, as the Ferguson police stood down and state law enforcement took over, the mood in the streets of Ferguson became "almost jubilant," according to the local CBS news affiliate. "Several people stopped to shake hands with police and troopers, and some stopped to hug and chat with highway patrol Capt. Johnson. The streets were filled with music, free food and even laughter."

On Friday, August 15, the Ferguson chief of police released Darren Wilson's name and a report on the incident, and the Brown family released a statement in response. "The prolonged release of the officer's name and then the subsequent alleged information regarding a robbery is the reason why the family and the local community have such distrust for the local law enforcement agencies," the statement noted.

Protests resumed that night, with additional looting, and continued through the weekend. Governor Nixon declared a state of emergency and sent in the Missouri National Guard as school districts canceled classes. Finally, on Thursday, August 21, the unrest seemed to be at a tenuous end. Protests would continue sporadically in September and October 2014 as more details of the case came to light.

A catalytic event had provided an opportunity to bring major change to a community in systemic, institutionalized conflict, and the people had taken advantage of the chance to show the entire nation what was happening in their town. Their tenacity had brought the first concessions from people in authority: the realization that the Ferguson Police Department was violating the rights of its citizens to peaceful assembly and protest and that the people would not stop protesting until something was done.

Ferguson paid a high price to achieve this concession. More than 20 businesses were destroyed in the rioting and looting that had accompanied the protests, hundreds of people had been arrested, and several sustained serious injuries or wounds.

In November, a grand jury—made up of nine white people and three black people—decided not to indict Wilson or charge him with a crime. The county prosecutor then released forensic reports, evidence photographs, and even transcripts of the grand jury proceedings, things that usually are not shared with the media or the public. A crowd had gathered outside the Ferguson Police Department to await the grand jury's decision, and when the lack of charges was announced, they began to riot. They burned as many as a dozen buildings, looted businesses, and threw objects at police officers in riot gear. Police used smoke and tear gas in attempts to break up the crowd and clear the streets, but the rioters responded by throwing rocks and breaking police car windows. Rubber bullets replaced smoke and tear gas as demonstrations continued, and the unrest in Ferguson dragged on for weeks. Eventually, Missouri governor Jay Nixon once again dispatched the Missouri National Guard to try to stop the violence and protests.

The unrest finally dissipated as the U.S. Department of Justice (DOJ) announced that it would conduct an investigation into the criminal justice system in Ferguson. What the investigation revealed justified all of the protests: the report found that the police department harbored an institutional bias against black citizens, affecting virtually every part of its operations. It disclosed that while African Americans make up 67 percent of the population of Ferguson, they accounted for 93 percent of the arrests made from 2012 to 2014. A long list of specific incidents and denials of rights led the DOJ to the conclusion that the city's practices were shaped by revenue rather than public safety and that the disproportionate numbers of incidents involving African Americans were the result of "unlawful bias."

"The Justice Department called on Ferguson to overhaul its criminal justice system, declaring that the city had engaged in so many constitutional violations that they could be corrected only by abandoning its entire approach to policing, retaining its employees and establishing new oversight," the *New York Times* reported on the first anniversary of Michael Brown's death.

A conflict that had existed in the shadows of bureaucratic obfuscation for years came to light because of public outrage, but it took a catalytic event—the unnecessary death of a young man—to spur people treated unjustly to act as a group. Even though the group splintered into two different kinds of protest early in the process, they managed to make their message heard all the way across the country and in Washington, DC, where it could become a force for positive change.

Part II

Scenarios

Now that you have a deeper understanding of the role conflict plays in our everyday lives, you can apply this knowledge to situations that happen to you every day. The examples that follow are just a few of the many ways that conflict finds its way into relationships at home, at work, and at school. The analysis after each scenario will help you track how a conversation turned into a conflict and how the people involved can steer a discussion so it does not turn into an argument.

 ### Helping a Couple Make a Decision

Tina and Tim, a married couple, have different ideas about what to do on a Friday evening. It is March Madness season, and Tina wants to go to a local sports bar with her friends and watch her alma mater's team play a tournament game. Tim, however, wants Tina to come with him to see a classic 1960s Ford Mustang he is considering buying.

"Tim," says Tina, "I really want to see this game with my college roommate at the bar. A lot of my college friends will be there. It will be fun—and it would be great if you came, too, even though it's not your favorite team."

Tim shakes his head. "I don't want to be the only one there who's not excited about the team. We did that last year, and I looked like a jerkwad. Plus, I really want you to see this car."

"Can't we go see the car after the game?" Tina asks.

"No, the guy is only available from seven o'clock to nine o'clock tonight."

"That's exactly when we're getting together," said Tina.

Tim raises his eyebrows. "So you already told them you'd be there? Without checking with me?"

Tina's voice tightens. "So now I have to check with you before I make plans with my friends?"

"I'm checking with you before I buy this car," Tim returns. "I'm trying to do the right thing here, and you're just going off and doing what you want. I feel really disrespected right now."

"Can't you see if the guy has time over the weekend?" Tina asks.

"If I put him off until the weekend, someone else could come when he said he's available and make him an offer," Tim says. "I could miss out on this really great car."

"Well, you won't know if it's a great car until you see it," says Tina. "So you may not be missing anything at all."

"But that's exactly it! I won't know until I see it!" says Tim.

Tina throws her hands in the air. "So I have to miss seeing this game because you have to have some car you've never seen? That doesn't make any sense either."

"Some car?" Tim's eyes widen. "You know this is my dream car, and that I've been hoping for one to pop up locally since I got my driver's license. This is a chance of a lifetime for me. Why don't you care about the things I care about?"

Tina and Tim have a disagreement, one that could be worked out fairly easily through discussion and compromise. Instead, Tim escalates the discussion from making a plan for Friday evening to an indictment of the couple's entire relationship. Why does this happen? A *latent conflict* existed below the surface for Tim, one Tina did not know was there: Tim's sense that Tina does not care about the things Tim wants. Once Tim feels the pressure to bring the conflict out in the open, it becomes a *felt conflict*, and the two can deal with it and attempt to move into *conflict resolution*.

Tina can now choose one of several routes, some of which will turn this into an argument and others that will defuse the situation and bring the focus back to its original point.

Tina can say, "Of course, I care about things that are important to you. Okay, how about if we go see the car right at seven o'clock, and then I'll go watch the game afterward? If you don't want to come to the bar at that point, you can drop me off and come have drinks with us after the game." This compromise shows Tim that he is a priority with Tina; she will miss the beginning of the game but will join her friends once the game is in progress. Both get what they want from the evening, and both sacrifice a little to show the other that they respect one another's needs and interests.

Compromise is one of the most important elements in resolving conflicts. When the person on each side of the conflict proves his or her willingness to give up something for the sake of a peaceful resolution, this gesture builds trust between the parties involved. When there is no compromise, trust becomes much harder to obtain.

Or Tina can decide that this is a good time for an argument. She may say, "Well, you don't care about what's important to me, either! You knew when we got married that seeing my team in the tournament is a sacred time for me. Yet you always plan things right when I want to watch the games. Why are you trying to sabotage our relationship?" The argument now becomes a manifest conflict, one that may not end well for either of the people involved.

Tim is almost certain to respond with "When have I ever planned things during March Madness?" This invites Tina to list off infractions from previous years, pushing the argument into the realm of a full-scale battle as Tim seeks to refute the allegations.

There is yet another vector Tina and Tim can take: they can make this an opportunity to examine issues in their relationship that started to boil as soon as this discussion turned up the heat. This disagreement about how to spend a Friday evening may actually be a symptom of a much larger problem. If it is time to address the issue—and often, a small event will become the *catalyst* that reveals a much larger conflict—Tim and Tina may benefit from exposing the problem now. Keeping an ear open for opportunities to discover hidden conflicts can help guide and maintain a relationship, especially a marriage or partnership that the people involved expect to last for many years.

 ### Sorting through an Emotional Conflict

Twenty-year-old Jessica is a junior in college, and she has been seeing Ray since her freshman year. Ray has met Jessica's parents several times and came home with her for winter break earlier in her junior year. Jessica's mother and father always treat Ray as they would any of Jessica's friends, but the fact is that he is not the man they would have chosen for their daughter. When she arrives home for the summer at the end of her junior year and seems always to be texting with Ray instead of interacting with them, they feel that it is time for them to say something.

One evening, Mom has trouble getting Jessica's attention in the middle of a conversation. "Jessica, put down the phone and talk to us a minute," she says.

"Just a sec, Mom," Jessica replies, her thumbs flying as she responds to Ray's text.

Mom waits until Jessica lowers the phone. "Honey, we need to talk about something," she says.

Jessica rolls her eyes. "Okay, what now?"

"You're going to be a senior this fall—"

"Yeah, I know, Mom," Jessica interrupts.

"Don't sass your mother," Dad breaks in.

"I wasn't. She's just stating the obvious, jeez."

Mom puts up a hand to keep Dad from responding. "Yes, I am. Because I want you to see something that's not so obvious. Honey, we don't think Ray is going with you when you go to graduate school."

"What do you mean?" Jessica stares at her mother.

"We don't think he's as interested in you as you are in him," Mom says.

"What? Because you saw him for four days here in February, now you think you know everything about us? You don't know us. You don't know him!"

Now Dad adds his perspective. "Jess, you wait on him hand and foot, and he doesn't do a thing for you. He all but ignores you to watch TV and play video games. And he says he's going to be what? A philosopher?"

"He's getting a PhD in sociology, Dad, not philosophy. What difference does that make? This isn't the dark ages—I don't expect him to support me. But how can you say he's not interested in me? He loves me! You don't know what goes on between us when we're alone!"

"But what happens between you in public matters too, honey," says Mom. "And most boys would be on their best behavior in front of a girl's parents. He just didn't care. We have more experience with these things than you do—we know what a boy in love looks like."

"He's not a boy—he's a man, and you don't know everything! Like your marriage is so perfect. You don't know what it's like today!"

"Jessica, you're too young to understand what's going on here," says Dad. "I know you think you're in love—"

At this, Jessica gets up off the couch and stands over her father, who is seated across from her. "I think I'm in love? I'm not five years old—I know what love is! And you are too old to remember what that's like! How can you say something like that? Are you ever going to stop treating me like a child?"

It is easy to see what has gone wrong with this *interpersonal conflict*—one that fits the category of a *disagreement in a particular episode*. First, the parents knew they were entering into a confrontation with Jessica, although Jessica may have been completely unaware that her parents were not happy with her choice of boyfriend. The parents have attempted to confront the most central and emotional issue in their daughter's life: the validity of her boyfriend's feelings for her.

Why did this become an argument so quickly? Dad's first words in the conversation were a reprimand, putting Jessica in the position of a child instead of a woman. The parents seem to expect their daughter to accept their views without question, referring to Ray as a "boy" and Jessica as a "girl"—intimating that they see them as children. They even go so far as to suggest that Jessica is not "really" in love, denying the validity of her feelings and infantilizing her further. These choices, along with Mom's statements that imply that Ray does not really love her, put Jessica on the defensive and made a *hostile episode* inevitable.

Can the parents dig out of this conflict and turn the discussion back in their favor? Not at this moment, as they have placed Jessica in the position of defending her feelings for Ray, Ray's behavior toward her, their future together, and even Ray's major and career aspirations. Jessica, meanwhile, is too angry to revert to reasonable discourse. She feels threatened, mistreated, and undervalued, and even if she has her own doubts about her relationship with Ray, this argument can only strengthen her resolve to defend him at all costs.

How can Mom and Dad fix this? It is time for an apology and a reset.

Mom can say, "Honey, this is not what we meant to say at all. Please sit down, and let's all take a deep breath. Of course, you love Ray, and he loves you. We just want to ask you to watch out for a few things. Maybe there're even things that you and he can talk through together."

Dad may need to say, "I know you're going to have a great career of your own and that you can take care of yourself. I also know some things about the way men should treat women when they love them, and I want you to have those things from Ray. May I just tell you what I've observed?"

This may nip the argument before people say things they later wish they could take back. It is easy enough in such a situation for the fight to become an indictment of the way the parents have raised their child and the relationship the child believes she has with her parents. It is up to the parents to maintain the cooler heads in the situation and keep control of the discussion, or emotional outbursts will become the rule of the day, and the actual issue—the appropriateness of the boyfriend's behavior toward the daughter—gets lost in a much larger and more far-ranging argument.

Mediating a Workplace Conflict

Two departments of a technology corporation see themselves in competition with one another for company resources. One produces the company's hot new digital products that are generating a lot of excitement from consumers, while the other produces the traditional, "analog" products still used by most of the company's customers.

The Digital department has a new product ready to introduce called Bleen. Once it goes into production, Bleen will put the company out in front of the competition and drive lots of profit. The money to produce Bleen, however, will be diverted from the Traditional product line. Employees in the Traditional line are afraid that the Digital side of the business will eventually mean an end to their jobs.

In a staff meeting, the head of Digital talks at great length about Bleen and how it will send the company's profits soaring. Finally, the head of Traditional can take no more of this. He jumps up and says, "When you go into production with Bleen, there will be no more money for Traditional. All of my people will lose their jobs. Bleen is the end of my department. What are we supposed to do when this happens?"

"With all due respect," the head of Digital responds, "we're not going to curtail development of our new products because Traditional doesn't have any new products. By definition, Traditional is going to go out of business at some point. We are not the problem; you are."

"Well, that's just great," says the head of Traditional. "You're planning to cannibalize our side of the business so you can move forward with yours. We are people here in Traditional, and we've served this company for many years. What is our place after Bleen?"

Before Digital can say anything else to Traditional, the president of the company jumps in. "Traditional, you're right," she says. "Bleen and other digital products are the future of our company. But there will be a place for Traditional for some time."

"But the market will drop off," said Traditional.

"Yes," says the president. "And we will all have to accept that our Traditional line is going to go away eventually. But you and your employees have been the life's blood of this organization for many years. So we are not going to abandon you just because we have become successful in a different way. At the same time, we need more people on the Digital side to produce Bleen and less people in Traditional."

Digital immediately balks. "I'll need people with a completely different set of skills to produce Bleen."

"Yes, so we will need a training program to get that line started. Digital, I'm assigning you to determine what your needs will be and what that program needs to include."

She turns to Traditional. "I would like you to recommend people in your department who are best suited to start retraining to become part of Digital. I would like to hire as many people as possible from inside the company."

Both Traditional and Digital are pleased with this solution. The meeting ends with everyone satisfied with the outcome.

In this *intergroup conflict*, the president is faced with both a problem and an opportunity. Digital will indeed be the future, and Traditional will wind down over time. There is no getting around this fact, and now that Traditional has brought the conflict front and center, this is as good a time as any to begin to address it. The president can take this opportunity to set the tone for the transition that is to come and to begin to solve the problem of fear and loss of job prospects that has begun to run rampant through the Traditional department.

The president chose not to embarrass Digital publicly by reprimanding him for being arrogant with Traditional. She recognized that Digital considers itself the in-group, the company's rising star with all the advantages of new technology and nimble operation. This naturally makes Traditional the out-group, and Digital is ready to discount Traditional's value entirely. Instead of allowing this, she quickly found a way to merge the two groups over time. This gives the head of Digital the responsibility for his department's tone and manner toward the other department, making him accountable if his people do not comply.

The president perceives that Digital has become a very cohesive group, which means that they may have demonized the other group among themselves. While groups need to come together within themselves to complete tasks and function as a unit, it can be dangerous to make this kind of camaraderie a priority in a profit-making organization. The result can be one group's willingness to sabotage the other, as Digital seemed to expect to do with his words, "We are not the problem; you are."

To keep this from becoming a major rift within her company, the president established that the people in Traditional have lasting value and that the company does not intend to toss them aside. She acknowledged their fear and heard their concerns, affirmed that these concerns are valid, and put a program in place to address them. This keeps Traditional from becoming the permanent out-group, letting its members know that they have not been forgotten or discounted.

While many conflicts in the workplace are not this easily addressed— personalities, decision-making responsibility, and multiple-level reporting structures complicate each conflict and make many problems exceedingly difficult to solve—the structure of conflict resolution is there in a nutshell. People in power find themselves faced simultaneously with problems and opportunities, and the smooth functioning of business makes it critical that they find solutions that address both. When they fail to do so, the result is lackluster performance from the company as a whole and often the loss of valuable, well-trained people.

 ## Getting Control of an Escalating Conflict

The rivalry between East and West High School's football teams has gone on good-naturedly for decades, and parents and alumni turn out every year when the two teams go head to head. Fairly equally matched in their skills, they work hard on the field, and the game is always an exciting one.

This year, however, the rivalry has gotten somewhat out of hand. Two weeks before the game, East's mascot costume disappears from its locker. Making the instant assumption that West High students had swiped it, East students go to West High in the middle of the night and hoist a pirate flag on the school flagpole, smearing petroleum jelly on the pole to make it hard to take it down. West high students retaliate by burning the word West into East's football field using rock salt on the grass.

East hits West again—this time repainting the school goalposts and the fronts of the football field bleachers with East's school colors. West team members organize quickly that night and throw hundreds of eggs at the front of East High School, leaving a soggy mess for team members and the janitorial staff to clean up. Having to work with the janitors during the school day riles up the East High teammates, making them the objects of ridicule as their classmates mock their cleanup detail.

By the time the game day rolls around that weekend, both teams are agitated and ready to beat the other on the field. Coaches, while talking about team spirit before the game, tell their players to "use that anger" by playing hard that day. Parents on either side of the field yell insults and call the rival team names. Their cheers and jeers become deafening to the players on the field as the game progresses.

The teams play well and maintain a close game until the end of the third quarter, when one fullback plows into the opposing team's player harder than the play requires. He takes the player down and knocks the wind out of him, so the stunned player lies on the field for an extra minute. His teammates, thinking the fullback had done this deliberately, attack the fullback—and in seconds, other players from his team join the fight. The next thing anyone knows, the entire field erupts into a brawl as coaches and parents run out to try to stop their kids. The game is called, and both teams are forced to forfeit.

Sports team rivalries provide some of the clearest examples of intergroup conflict. These can be cheerful competitions in which players learn to master skills and work together to beat an opponent—in fact, most school teams conduct themselves in a manner considered "sportsmanlike," congratulating the other team on their win and building their skills to compete more effectively the next time.

At the same time, students are quick to bond with their teammates and form alliances that promote their own sense of belonging to something greater than themselves. The desire to win can vault above all other priorities, especially once the team has coalesced as an in-group, formed alliances and common goals, and determined that all other teams are out-groups.

We saw this phenomenon take place with surprising speed in the Robbers Cave experiment in the 1950s (see Chapter 4), and parents and coaches see it play out on the field at every game. What we do not always expect is that the conflict between teams will suddenly turn violent, as cheerful competition gives way to rage and fists at the least provocation. Team spirit can turn to anger and even temporary hatred of other teams, often with one team singled out for special, single-minded rivalry.

Why are team conflicts in schools so strong? Part of the attraction is the establishment of identity in adolescent students, whose understanding of their own place in the world has just begun to develop. The conflict outside the group establishes each team member as part of a larger whole, with an important role to play within that group. The easy assignment of team positions creates a structure that helps build this identity. When the group comes together to defeat a foe—a rival team—that identity is sealed, and there's even an opportunity to become a hero by completing a difficult play or making an interception.

At the same time, team play may serve as an allegory to other conflicts in the student's life. A tough atmosphere at home may add to the student's need to identify as a member of a group, making the regularly scheduled matches between this team and another one a release valve for the anger and frustration he or she brings from home. If this is the case, the teammate may be more prone to escalating the conflict than others on the team, making him or her quick to take the first swing at an out-group rival.

As we saw at Robbers Cave, the rift is far from permanent; rival teams can be reunited, and the people involved can drop their anger and scorn with scant encouragement. Should the coaches choose to do so, they could bring the teams together at a separate event and give them a shared goal—one that they must work together to achieve. Teammates who thought the other team's players were the scum of the earth may be pleasantly surprised to find out that these out-group members are not particularly different from themselves. Achieving a goal together makes for new pairings and more reasoned relationships, even among sworn enemies.

 ### Learning to Accept Irreconcilable Points of View

Rebekah grew up in an intermarried family, in which her father was Jewish and her mother was Lutheran. Her parents sent her to private schools run in a Christian tradition, so she formed a personal connection with Christianity. As a young adult, she met Pablo, a man from a Latino Catholic background. Eventually they married, and Rebekah found that she identified more closely with her husband's Catholic tradition than she did with either the Jewish or Protestant faiths in which she was raised.

One evening over dinner at her parents' home, in the course of conversation, Rebekah shared this view with her parents. "I've found that when it comes to religion, Catholicism is really closest to my heart," she says. "So Pablo and I will be raising our children Catholic."

Her parents stared at her, openmouthed. "You've got to be kidding," said Dad. "How can you say such a hurtful thing?"

"After all the money we spent sending you to Christian schools, this is how you repay us?" said Mom. "You just throw all of our traditions back in our faces?"

"I really thought that you'd choose Judaism in the end," said Dad.

"How could I do that, Dad? I've never even seen the inside of a temple. I don't know anything about Judaism. You didn't raise me to be a Jew. You raised me Christian, and I'm choosing to be a Christian—but in the Catholic tradition. What is the problem with that?"

"I thought I had set an example that you would want to follow," said Dad.

"Dad, I'm not saying that you aren't a good person. I'm saying I've made a different choice."

"But Catholic?" Mom said. "That's just out of the blue!"

"I would hardly say that, Mom," Rebekah said. "Pablo and I have been together for six years. I've had a lot of opportunity to experience it, and this is the religion that resonates for me. I'm sorry it's not what you want; but do I have to worry now that you won't accept your own grandchildren because they are Catholic?"

"See, that's exactly the kind of talk that frightens me," said Mom. "You know I would never do that! But now do you think less of us because you've chosen Catholicism? Are we no good to you now?"

"How on earth did this discussion get here?" Rebekah cried. "I'm just telling you that my children will be confirmed and will take Communion, and they will grow up in the Catholic Church. I don't understand why you're acting like I've joined a cult. Mom, I'm the same person I was ten minutes ago. Why are you reacting like this?"

"Because we thought we gave you a good foundation and a set of morals to live by, and you're just throwing that away," said Mom. "All for a religion that I don't even understand."

"And I really thought you would find your identity as a Jew—and now you're running in the opposite direction," said Dad.

"Mom, Dad, you're going to see that this will make almost no difference at all in your lives or your relationship with your grandchildren," said Rebekah. "But you'll have to accept that this is who I am."

Mom shakes her head. "I don't know, Rebekah, I don't know if we can do that."

Not all interpersonal conflicts can be resolved. Rebekah's choice to become something different from her parents' long-held expectations may never sit well with her mother and father. Like many parents, they may feel left in the dust by their daughter's decision to embrace the identity of her new husband's family, and their own hurt and disappointment may block their ability to see that their daughter's intention was not to reject their teachings but to find her own way.

This particular situation falls into the category of *content conflict*, as posited by Jameson (1999, discussed in Chapter 1). Content conflict involves disagreement over an ideology, whether it is a complex concept like religion or something as simple as whether towels should be folded in half or thirds. Because it often involves long-held beliefs, it can be one of the hardest to resolve.

The unfortunate thing for Rebekah and her parents is that this hostile episode probably is not the last on this topic. Because it deals with beliefs that are central to each of the characters involved, and these beliefs are in conflict with one another, there is no easy way to resolve it. Rebekah is unlikely to change her mind about the way she and her husband will raise their children, and Mom and Dad are even less likely to be happy about their grandchildren being raised in a religion in which they do not have faith. If they choose to continue to make this a point of contention, the conflict could escalate until Rebekah prevents them from seeing their grandchildren.

One of the key issues here, however, is not part of the central conflict itself. Rebekah is no longer dependent on her parents, so she is not required to resolve this conflict to their satisfaction to continue to receive support from them. This conflict, which rises to Level 3 of Braiker and Kelly's (1979, discussed in Chapter 1) levels of conflict in *interdependent relationships*, may bring this fact to light for Mom and Dad for the first time, even though Rebekah's marriage officially severed this bond of interdependence. It will be up to the parents, then, to meet Rebekah halfway and accept that she has made an informed choice as an adult. This may not be easy for them, as they have already demonstrated, but it will be necessary if they wish to look forward to a healthy relationship with their daughter's family for the long term.

Part III

Controversies and Debates

In this section, we look at some of the questions scholars and mediators grapple with in the real world of conflict and resolution. The essays collected here bring together some of the most current thinking about people and nations in conflict and the tools and techniques now in use to take on the challenge of bringing these ongoing issues to a close.

As we have seen in previous parts of this book, some of the world's most complex conflicts seem insurmountable, because they are so ingrained in the fabric of a region or a culture. Other conflicts take place on an intensely personal level, turning basic preferences into life-changing confrontations that can mean the end of friendships or marriages.

We have asked experts to address three important questions, and they have supplied disparate viewpoints for your consideration.

 Controversy #1: How Do Men and Women Differ in the Ways They Deal with Conflict?

INTRODUCTION

Few would argue that men and women do *not* deal with conflict in different ways. How this plays out in situations at home and at work, however, can affect every aspect of people's lives, from the pleasure of living in harmony to the barriers to professional advancement in the workplace.

The differences in style between men and women have been a topic of debate virtually since the study of psychology began. Psychologists, researchers, therapists, and mediators have documented the ways that women cause, handle, and resolve conflict, but the results of studies and the stacks of books written on the topic are often seen as biased, with the goal of stereotyping women's roles in society and keeping women from succeeding in business, government, and community. For example, international communications consultant Audrey Nelson, PhD, suggests in her book, *The Gender Communications Handbook: Conquering Conversational Collisions between Men and Women*, that women lean toward taking care of others rather than engaging in confrontations. Nelson observes that women are likely to hold back and not express strong opinions if they are in a dynamic group, suffering in silence or sacrificing their own comfort so that others can be comfortable. Women, she says, are people pleasers who are more willing to give up personal satisfaction and acknowledgment of their work so that others can shine. They need to be drawn into discussions and controversies and given permission to disagree with their coworkers or family members.

If you have any experience in a modern-day workplace, you may see this thinking as antiquated. In twenty-first-century America, many women do step forward, present their opinions, and fight hard for what they want in the workplace and in society. Conflict no longer serves as a male domain; women hold places in the boardrooms of many corporations and at the highest levels of government, and they offer their opinions and express their issues freely and loudly in these situations. At the same time, however, women may approach conflict with a style that produces consensus between the people involved, and they may be the facilitators and peacemakers in reaching agreement or compromise in groups.

What about men? A 2016 study at Harvard University's Human Evolutionary Biology Department found that when a conflict or competition ends, men are more likely to engage in "friendly physical contact"—handshakes, pats on the back—than are women. The study goes on to suggest that while men are more aggressive and combative than women in a conflict, they also make a point of reconnecting with their adversaries and establishing good feelings between them once the battle has concluded. The researchers concluded that women have a harder time when they compete with other women, and they feel more damaged after the battle. Men, however, are more likely to reconcile with their adversary and move on in a collegial way.

While no researcher or mediator wants to be accused of gender profiling, study after study concludes that men and women truly do deal with conflict differently. In this section, two practitioners from academia provide very different views of what happens when men and women negotiate their way through a conflict. Mike Bassow, who teaches interpersonal communication and public speaking at Central New Mexico Community College in Albuquerque, New Mexico, demonstrates the communication breakdown between man and woman in the home and provides a perspective on neutralizing the differences between the genders through a reasoned, constructive exchange of views in a nonthreatening manner.

By contrast, the second essay takes us on a tour of the studies recently completed on men and women resolving conflict in workplace situations. Juliana E. Birkhoff, PhD, is an experienced mediator, facilitation and dispute resolution trainer, and scholar who focuses her practice on complex scientific and technical problems. She has conducted extensive research on collaboration and consensus building.

RESPONSE 1: HOW MEN AND WOMEN DEAL WITH CONFLICT DIFFERENTLY

People in relationships like to argue. Why? As adults, we already know that arguments do not settle anything, especially if one of the combatants actually wins.

We know what winning is like. The winner struts around saying "I win," or "I'm right," or any number of different things. The loser, however, is lying on the couch or the bed in a fetal position. There is no way they are happy with the outcome. What is it the loser is doing there on the couch? Likely, he or she is planning revenge. Why? Because no one likes losing. It is a bad feeling. It leaves the partner wanting the other feeling—the feeling you get from winning. So the loser spends time web surfing, looking for tips on how to win. Soon, the argument begins again.

Why do so many arguments within marriages perpetuate themselves in this way? There is a fundamental disconnect. Men and women have different goals when it comes to conflict. Men want to fix things; they want to say, "Tell me what the problem is and I'll fix it." Women, on the other hand, do not want a quick solution—they want to talk it out. Men are not raised to do that. Men are raised to show very little emotion and to keep from making a lot of emotional contact. Listening is not something they like to do.

Now think about this. When women get together with their friends, they will spend a whole day just talking. When men get together with their friends, they go bowling or watch a game on TV or play a video game. They do things that are more competitive, because they started out this way on the playground when they were kids. Men do not just sit around and talk—they do things, usually in competition with each other.

How does this play out within a relationship? A husband comes in at the end of the day, and he does not know that his wife/partner has been thinking and talking about her feelings all day. He says, "Hi, honey."

She says, "I'm mad at you."

He says, "Why are you mad at me?"

She replies, "You should know."

The husband does not know. He immediately says, "All right, how can I fix it?"

His wife replies, "I don't need you to fix it. I need you to listen."

Right away, the husband is in foreign territory. He does not care about the underlying problem—he wants to find a solution as quickly as possible and put things back to normal. He thinks that if he can solve it, he wins. But his wife thinks that if she can make her husband hear her and understand why she is angry, she wins. They are approaching the conflict with completely different goals.

So what happens? Every night, one baits the other one in an attempt to move from stalemate to winning. It does not matter what the argument is about—now it is only about winning. One night the husband wins, and the second night the wife wins. And you know what happens next: this becomes a continuous cycle that may never end. The relationship becomes a game. The couple ignores most everything else as they both try to win at all costs. The result could be divorce, or the game could become the basis of their relationship.

What if this was not necessary? What if the couple could find a way to look at the problem and solve it the first time around?

Conflict Is Natural

A couple always has disagreements. Most of them are small, like if the toilet paper roll should be top-fed or bottom-fed. Then it is putting the cap on the toothpaste or leaving underwear on the floor, and it builds to the proper way to do laundry or dishes or wash the car. The problems build and focus on the kids, money, and other big issues that can end relationships. The problems grow, but the way to resolve them does not seem to change.

Conflict Is Beneficial

Two heads are better than one. But some couples seldom think about putting their heads together and coming up with solutions to problems. Let us try this:

1. **Pick a time to fight**: Fighting is not going to help—we know it never does. But if we pick a time to fight, that gives both parties the opportunity to prepare to fight. They can think about their issues and write down what they want to say.
2. **Pick a place to fight**: Home may be where the heart is, but it is a lousy place to fight. There are too many distractions. The TV is on, the kids are all over, and dinner is being prepared. All kinds of things interfere with the ability to speak to each other. Agree to discuss the issue in a different place.
3. **Pick one issue to talk about**: Most couples have a range of issues, but dealing with one rationally may help them get on the road to dealing with the others.
4. **Do not raise your voice**: You cannot fix what is wrong by yelling at each other. Talk in a normal way with no blaming or accusing.
5. **Implement the solution you choose**: You would not know if it works until you try it.
6. **Check in with each other**: Make sure things are working. If you need another "fight date," go and do it again.

Couples who commit to resolving issues this way find that home life gets better. It is not necessary to raise your voice to get what you want. If both partners are willing to try this, they will find better relationships, better home life, and better life all around.

Mike Bassow, MS

RESPONSE 2: GENDER, CONFLICT, AND CONFLICT RESOLUTION

Gender affects, and indeed permeates, conflict dynamics at the societal and individual level. Understanding the role of gender in conflict is best accomplished through an analysis of individual levels, interactional levels, and the societal level.

Within these three levels of analysis, there are also two radically different gender paradigms that direct the research agendas of social scientists working in this area.

The essentialist paradigm assumes a separate female world, one in which women are by nature different from men. In this view, women are by nature so completely different from men that we experience a different reality. This perspective focuses on women's caring, cooperative, and peaceful attributes. Some of these studies focus on women's maternal abilities as shapers of our roles as caretakers and peacemakers.

The other paradigm denies the assumptions that women and men have essential natures. As a matter of fact, it denies the essential nature of anything. Postmodern feminism focuses on the exchange between the social construction of individuals and the individuals' constitution of themselves. By focusing on language, symbols, alternative discourses, and meaning, postmodern feminism studies how social power is exercised and how social relations of gender, class, and race can be transformed. This does not rule out the specificity of women's experiences and their differences from men, since under patriarchy women have differential access to the discursive field.

At the societal level, patriarchy is characterized by historic discrimination and injustice reproduced in institutions and ideologies. Assumptions about male superiority pervade our thought processes. The life experiences on which the claims of the dominant ideologies have been founded have been the experiences of men, not women. Patriarchy, like other dictatorships, controls reality. Women and men are socialized within rigid gender expectations. Institutions such as the church, the family, and the law reproduce these biases in norms, rules, and laws. Women have historically been subjugated politically, economically, and culturally. This institutional system of oppression and injustice directly creates disputes, sustains and escalates other conflicts, and invades all other human interactions.

At the interactional level, there are a number of studies. Gender may surface in conflicts in the ways that parties interpret and give meaning to the conflict. Patricia Gwartney-Gibbs studied how gender affects the origins, processes, and outcomes of disputes in the workplace. Gwartney-Gibbs's research found differences in the origins of disputes for men and women. The social construction of the workplace conditions the way that women formulate their grievances and the ways that supervisors translate them. Although both men and women had problems in the workplace that were associated with interpersonal relations, women reported more personality conflicts than men and seemed more sensitive to them. Women also experienced more conflicts over gender role stereotypes. Gender role stereotypes cause problems if the stereotype has little to do with the requirements of the job.

Gender also affected dispute-handling mechanisms. The processes used to resolve disputes for women were less effective than for men. For example, women were more often transferred laterally instead of resolving the dispute.

The outcomes of the processes were also different for men than for women. Women's disputes seldom were framed as falling within the contract, so they received more individual responses to their disputes. Since women were more often transferred laterally, there was a direct impact on women's earnings in the workplace. This research project shows that women experience different disputes in the workplace; their disputes are handled differently from men's, and the outcomes are different for the two groups. This study is important because it directly correlates the gender differences in workplace dispute origins, processes, and outcomes to patterns in employment inequality.

Looking at the institutions of dispute handling, Terrell Northrup and Marshall Segall compared men and women's experiences with community mediation. Their study analyzed differences in women and men's feelings of vulnerability and empowerment. The researchers hypothesized that women feel vulnerable in day-to day relations, especially with men. Women's sense of vulnerability would be particularly salient in conflict situations since there is a potential for aggression and violence.

The researchers found that women more often reported feeling scared or vulnerable than did men. Women were significantly more likely to feel vulnerable in conflicts with men than in conflicts with other women. Women were more likely to talk about being afraid of normal conflict and of being the victim of aggression or violence. Women reported that concerns about children, identity, and status contributed to their vulnerability in conflicts. Lack of support from significant others and lack of trust in the other party also reinforced feelings of vulnerability.

Women and men also differed in the ways that they talked about their conflicts. Women talked in depth and at length about the context of the dispute, particularly focusing on their involvement in the relationship with the other party. Men used more rational, linear, and legalistic language to talk about their disputes. Women talked about fairness in a way that incorporated both their material interests and the network of relationships in the dispute.

Contrary to what the researchers expected, the women in the study used significantly more strategies and more kinds of strategies to resolve conflicts than did men. Also unexpectedly, women were no more concerned than were men with maintaining a positive relationship with the other party. Finally, women were as concerned with resolving the particular issue as were men.

While women felt more vulnerable, their vulnerability did not seem to interfere with their ability to actively handle their disputes. However, women talked at length about feeling disempowered and disadvantaged in attempting to deal with their conflicts. Northrup focuses on how men and women's essentially different realities may lead us to understand conflict differently and therefore to approach conflict resolution differently.

Deborah Kolb studied women as "peacemakers" in organizations. The women she studied acted as informal peacemakers within their organizations. The women got involved in people's conflicts because coworkers sought them out. They provided a sympathetic ear to their coworkers. They became involved not only because they were loyal to the organization but also because they cared how the organization treated people. They provided support for people to tell their story; they reframed people's understandings of the situation; they translated people's perceptions of each other; and they orchestrated occasions for private conflicts to be made public. Women in the study were ambivalent about their role and skills as peacemakers within the organization. They feel that the important role they fill in the organization is not understood or appreciated. Conflicts that are more systemic or structural may be individualized and depoliticized by their approach to peacemaking.

Deborah Kolb's earlier work focused on how women's ways of understanding the world based upon essential differences affected their conduct in negotiations. Kolb focused on four themes that define women's place in negotiations: a relational view of others, a contextual and related definition of self and situation, an understanding of control through empowerment, and problem solving through dialog. Women's voices are different because of early social development, and women's places in negotiation are different because of structural systems of discrimination.

Carol Watson examined whether gender or power was a better predictor of manager's negotiation behavior. She hypothesized that perceived gender differences in negotiation behavior are an artifact of status and power differences between men and women. This study provides a more realistic review of the legitimacy of such gender stereotypes by comparing the effects of power and gender on negotiation behavior.

Watson found that power was a better predictor of the feelings, behavior, and outcomes of managerial negotiations than was gender. In the study, women felt neither more cooperative nor less competitive than men. Women engaged in less subordinating behavior and more threatening behavior. Participants in the high power role, regardless of gender, felt more competitive before the negotiation, expected greater cooperation from their opponents, and felt more powerful, more in control, and more satisfied with the decision than those in the low power role. Her study demonstrates that observed gender differences in negotiations are an artifact of men and women's status and power in the United States.

However, managerial women felt significantly less confident about negoti-ating than managerial men did, and women were particularly uncomfortable when negotiating with another woman. Women did not enjoy the role-play and were very uncomfortable with whatever role was assigned to them. Women also underrated their performance compared to men.

These research studies illuminate some of the complexities of studying the role and effect of gender in conflict. Future research should focus on gender differences of parties and third-party interveners. Research should focus on how gender influences the ways that conflict is seen, felt, and understood by individuals and groups. Research on gender expands the ways that we think about conflict, justice, and social change.

Juliana E. Birkhoff, PhD

 ## Controversy #2: What Conflict Resolution Techniques Do We Need in Developing Countries?

INTRODUCTION

Why do conflicts in the Middle East and Africa seem to go on and on with-out end? The complexity of these altercations, some of which we explored in Chapter 6 of this book, makes them especially difficult to resolve. For exam-ple, the issues in Syria grow worse over time because of the sheer number of groups in the conflict—each with its own goals, making victory very difficult to achieve—and residential areas become battlegrounds that force the evacu-ation of millions of people. This creates another kind of conflict, as these people become refugees and attempt to flee their own country for sanctuary and a new life elsewhere, while other countries close their borders and refuse to allow a significant influx of refugees to become their problem to resolve.

Other countries that have largely rural land masses and little industry fall into the category of conflict over scarce resources, as we discussed in Chapter 1. In Kenya, where many people make their living raising cattle, access to water and grazing land can mean the literal difference between life and death. To get these resources, however, Kenyans have to battle cattle rustling, theft, barriers between people of different ethnicities, and government corruption. Can these issues be negotiated at a conference room table? Perhaps a different kind of conflict resolution is required, as posited by Sandra Marker, a graduate student and researcher in sociology at the University of Colorado's Conflict Resolution Consortium. Her essay in this chapter suggests a human needs approach to conflict, taking into account the complexity of human life and the insistent nature of human needs. Once people's needs are understood and met, she posits, the people involved can move on to problem-solving approaches to address fundamental sources of conflict.

Our second essay comes from Prabha Sankaranarayan, president and chief executive officer of Mediators Beyond Borders International (MBBI), and Rose-Anne Moore, a founding partner of the independent consulting firm PoleStar Partners and a strategist-turned-ethicist with an MAR degree from Yale University, who serves on the MBBI board and is board liaison to its climate change project. MBBI is an international, nongovernmental organization that builds local skills for peace and promotes mediation worldwide. Sankaranarayan and Moore advocate a conflict resolution process developed by MBBI, called Trauma-Informed Peacebuilding (TIP), which addresses the reaction of an essentially healthy community to a traumatic event (whether sudden violence or a natural disaster) and how a traumatized community, whether in a developing or developed country, will be affected. They argue that a community affected by a significant trauma, whether it is a series of suicide bombings, a major war, a tsunami, or a shared tragedy, must deal with this trauma before its people can begin to consider further conflict resolution.

RESPONSE 1: UNMET HUMAN NEEDS

Humans need a number of essentials to survive. According to the renowned psychologist Abraham Maslow and the conflict scholar John Burton, these essentials go beyond just food, water, and shelter. They include both physical and nonphysical elements needed for human growth and development as well as all those things humans are innately driven to attain.

For Maslow, needs are hierarchical in nature. That is, each need has a specific ranking or order of obtainment. Maslow's needs pyramid starts with the basic items of food, water, and shelter. These are followed by the need for safety and security; belonging or love; self-esteem; and finally, personal fulfillment. Burton and other needs theorists who have adopted Maslow's ideas to conflict theory, however, perceive human needs in a different way—as an emergent collection of human development essentials. Furthermore, they contend needs do not have a hierarchical order. Rather, needs are sought simultaneously in an intense and relentless manner. Needs theorists' list of human essentials include the following:

- **Safety/Security**: the need for structure, predictability, stability, and freedom from fear and anxiety.
- **Belongingness/Love**: the need to be accepted by others and to have strong personal ties with one's family, friends, and identity groups.

- **Self-esteem**: the need to be recognized by oneself and others as strong, competent, and capable. It also includes the need to know that one has some effect on his or her environment.
- **Personal fulfillment**: the need to reach one's potential in all areas of life.
- **Identity**: goes beyond a psychological "sense of self." Burton and other human needs theorists define identity as a sense of self in relation to the outside world. Identity becomes a problem when one's identity is not recognized as legitimate or when it is considered inferior or is threatened by others with different identifications.
- **Cultural security**: related to identity—the need for recognition of one's language, traditions, religion, cultural values, ideas, and concepts.
- **Freedom**: the condition of having no physical, political, or civil restraints; having the capacity to exercise choice in all aspects of one's life.
- **Distributive justice**: the need for the fair allocation of resources among all members of a community.
- **Participation**: the need to be able to actively partake in and influence civil society.

Why the Concept of Human Needs Matters

Human needs theorists argue that one of the primary causes of protracted or intractable conflict is people's unyielding drive to meet their unmet needs on the individual, group, and societal level. For example, the Palestinian conflict involves the unmet needs of identity and security. Countless Palestinians feel that their legitimate identity is being denied them, both personally and nationally. Numerous Israelis feel they have no security individually because of suicide bombings, nationally because their state is not recognized by many of their close neighbors, and culturally because anti-Semitism is growing worldwide. Israeli and Palestinian unmet needs directly and deeply affect all the other issues associated with this conflict. Consequently, if a resolution is to be found, the needs of Palestinian identity and Israeli security must be addressed and satisfied on all levels.

Arguments for the Human Needs Approach

Human needs theorists offer a new dimension to conflict theory. Their approach provides an important conceptual tool that connects and addresses human needs on all levels. Furthermore, it recognizes the existence of negotiable and nonnegotiable issues. That is, needs theorists understand that needs, unlike interests, cannot be traded, suppressed, or bargained for. Thus, the human needs approach makes a case for turning away from traditional negotiation models that do not take into account nonnegotiable issues. These include interest-based negotiation models that view conflict in terms of win-win or other consensus-based solutions and conventional power models (primarily used in the field of negotiation and international relations) that construct conflict and conflict management in terms of factual and zero-sum game perspectives.

The human needs approach, on the other hand, supports collaborative and multifaceted problem-solving models and related techniques, such as problem-solving workshops or an analytical problem-solving process. These models take into account the complexity of human life and the insistent nature of human needs. Problem-solving approaches also analyze the fundamental sources of conflict while maintaining a focus on fulfilling people's unmet needs. In addition, they involve the interested parties in finding and developing acceptable ways to meet the needs of all concerned.

Human needs theorists further understand that although needs cannot be compromised, they can be addressed in a generally win-win or positive-sum way. An example of this win-win or positive-sum process can be gleaned from the Kosovo conflict. When the Albanians obtained protective security, the Serbs also gained this protection, so both sides gained.

Arguments against the Human Needs Approach

However, many questions and uncertainties surround the human needs approach to solving conflicts. For instance, how can one define human needs? How can one know what needs are involved in conflict situations? How can one know what human needs are being met and unmet? Are human needs cultural or universal in nature? If they are cultural, is the analysis of human needs beneficial beyond a specific conflict? Are some needs inherently more important than others? If some needs are more important, should these be pursued first?

Other critics of the human needs approach assert that many conflicts involve both needs and interests. So conflict resolution cannot come about by just meeting human needs. For example, when looking at the Palestinian/Israeli conflict, it is understood that both needs (identity, security, freedom) and interests (i.e., resource allocation, international boundaries) are involved. Consequently, even if the needs of both parties get met, the conflict will probably not be resolved. Resolution can only come about when both needs and interests are dealt with.

Nevertheless, most scholars and practitioners agree that issues of identity, security, and recognition are critical in many or even most intractable conflicts. They may not be the *only* issue, but they are one of the important issues that must be dealt with if an intractable conflict is to be transformed. Ignoring the underlying needs and just negotiating the interests may at times lead to a short-term settlement, but it rarely will lead to long-term resolution.

Sandra Marker

RESPONSE 2: CONFLICT RESOLUTION TECHNIQUES IN DEVELOPING COUNTRIES

Pain that is not transformed is transferred.

—Richard Rohr

Do we need new conflict resolution techniques in developing countries? The short answer is "Yes." The longer answer is "That's not the right question."

The question feels patronizing: "You developing countries, you have special problems."

The key issue is not the state of economic or political development; the issue is the degree of trauma experienced and the presence of resilient features in the community.

What do "developing countries" have in common? All too often, a history of violent conquest, occupation, and colonialization. There may be overreliance on a single natural resource or, conversely, lack of any significant natural resources. Most often, there is a toxic combination of the above. These form a recipe for communal, intergenerational trauma.

There are differences between how an essentially healthy community, hit by a traumatic event (whether sudden violence or a natural disaster), will react and how a traumatized community, whether in a developing or developed country, will be affected. The good news is that resilience can be built and supported.

We recommend Trauma-Informed Peacebuilding (TIP): a curriculum designed by MBBI that combines peacebuilding work with a deep understanding of people's experiences and the effect of those experiences on behavior and relationships.

Put simply, peacebuilding and trauma can intersect in this manner: Conflict is about relationships. Trauma affects relationships. Trauma therefore affects work requiring collaboration, initiative, and follow-through.

In designing a program for a traumatized community, begin with a clear understanding of what has been experienced: What is the nature of the event? Is it man-made or a natural disaster? What are the sensory stimuli? Is it a one-time event or one among a long stream of events? Are there health issues that should be addressed before the peacebuilding work can begin? How has trauma affected the participants' ability to form and maintain relationships?

The people in a traumatized community may exhibit behaviors that could be interpreted as disruptive or negative: they may appear slow to respond, disengaged, and even stupid. Alternatively, they may seem excessively jumpy, irritable, suspicious, and cynical. These behaviors are all rooted in survival.

By being trauma sensitive, conflict resolution practitioners can prevent—or lessen the likelihood of inflicting—inadvertent mistakes.

Consider this fictitious scenario: a major flood has recently overwhelmed a small, close-knit community, and now a deadly and contagious disease threatens the survivors. You are a conflict resolution practitioner, working with health-care providers there to help start a vaccination program. The health professionals tell you that only half of the community's residents need to be vaccinated to provide "herd immunity" to the community as a whole.

Community residents who had lived on higher ground largely survived the flood unscathed, but many of those nearer the river perished. Those on the lower ground who remain now comprise about one-half of the surviving community and have been gathered together in a large camp. The doctors and nurses propose concentrating their efforts in this one camp. Do you agree?

Now consider the trauma that the whole community has experienced.

Some individuals have lost all their possessions; others, relatively little. Some have lost many family members; other families are largely intact. All have been emotionally affected.

What do you know about the community as a whole? Preflood, was the lower ground "the wrong side of the tracks"? Was there a history of flooding in the area, which could have been prevented by infrastructure investments, but the government was never convinced of the need? Or was the flood a once-in-a-thousand-years event for which no one was prepared?

Has your answer changed?

Is your answer different if you are told that this small close-knit community is located in the American South? What if it is located in southern Africa?

If you do not explain why only the lower-ground survivors are being inoculated, those residents will naturally wonder why they are being selected: Are they the only ones who are at risk of the disease? If their homes, preflood, were in the "lower-class" neighborhood, might they worry that, rather than being vaccinated against a deadly disease, they are being infected with something worse?

Conversely, the higher-ground survivors may decide that lower-ground residents are "dirty" or wonder if it is a foreign conspiracy to decimate the ranks of the "right" people.

If the traumatic events are man-made, the effects can run even deeper. Violence in a community breaks the fabric of people's connections to each other. It may therefore take much longer to take the first steps to rebuilding community. Individuals no longer know who they can work with and who they cannot.

There are many different reactions to trauma—all of them normal reactions to wildly abnormal situations. Some people manage to function through the most horrific situations, while others experience deep difficulties. Still others do more than survive: they put their own experiences to work so that no one else has to go through something similar.

Trauma affects the ability to concentrate and remember, so your job is to present one idea at a time. Remove excess stimuli. Take your time. Ask a question and expect that a "normal" response time may be 15 or 20 seconds. Break down tasks into small, manageable chunks. Give the participants the tools they need to manage their own responses.

Consider that there may be different sources of trauma: one resident of our fictional flooded community seems like a "lucky" one—she lived on the high ground with her immediate family and suffered little loss and no injuries. So why is she ignoring you when you ask her a question? She may have been deeply retraumatized because as a child, she saw her beloved grandparents swept away by an earlier flood. Do not assume.

Ask questions: not "What's wrong with you?" but simply, "What happened?" Be sensitive to the presence of historical experiences that may affect participants' ability to relate and respond.

Predictability and consistency, always critical in peacebuilding efforts, become even more important. The same is with preparation. Safety and security become essential.

Witnessing the painful experiences of others can take its toll. Prepare for this. The ABCs of self-care include Awareness, Balance, and Connection. Take care of yourself as you cannot otherwise care for others.

Facilitator traumatization is most common in situations of deep violence—if you have never seen the levels of poverty and desperation experienced by the people you hope to help, if you have never heard stories such as those you are told by the former combatants or their victims, if you have never had to face those depths, and if you are not prepared, you can be shocked into nonfunctioning. Caring has real costs: people who care can be hurt themselves. Be aware of the risks of "compassion fatigue" from vicarious trauma.

If you are prepared, you can self-regulate: you will know how to keep your executive brain function working rather than letting the furious fear-based response take control. You will still hear things that are painful, but you will be emotionally prepared.

It is helpful for the conflict resolution facilitators to work in teams of two so that each can be a support system for the other. They can debrief each other at the end of each day. It is always true that facilitators should be ready, trained, and confident, but it is especially true in an environment of trauma, because the facilitators' confidence will engender a sense of confidence in the people with whom they are working.

How can you help?

- Create a safe space for people to verbalize what they are feeling or thinking. Do not assume; ask questions. Take your time.
- Validate feelings and reactions. Delay disputing the "facts."
- Provide a daily or weekly structure that is predictable and consistent. Hold meetings at the same time, in the same place. (And do not forget regular check-ins with your staff to take the "temperature" of feelings or issues.)
- Be transparent and clear about the information that you can share. Take your time. People can accept almost anything if they understand clearly.
- Meet with dissenting groups separately to hear their concerns before bringing the two groups together. Prepare each group for what they might hear from the other (without violating confidentiality, impartiality, or trust).
- Rebuild the feeling of community by sharing meals, laughter, and celebrations.
- Acknowledge that the path to recovery is different for every individual. "Fairness" is not giving everyone the same thing but providing everyone with what they need to be successful and productive.
- Encourage self-care by modeling self-care.

Beneath the surface of the protective parts of trauma survivors, there exists an undamaged essence: a self that is confident, curious, and calm, a self that has been sheltered from destruction by the various protectors that have emerged in their efforts to ensure survival. Once those protectors sense that it is safe to separate, the self will spontaneously emerge, and the parts can be enlisted in the healing process.

—Bessel van de Kolk, *The Body Keeps the Score*

Peacebuilders have an ethical responsibility to ensure that they conduct their work in a trauma-sensitive manner. At a minimum, peacebuilding should seek to ensure that activities do not cause further traumatization or psychological harm to people already suffering the effects of conflict.

Prabha Sankaranarayan, BA, MS, and
Rose-Anne Moore, BA, MBA, MAR

 ## Controversy #3: What Are the Most Effective Methods of Conflict Resolution?

INTRODUCTION

No discussion of conflict can be complete without some exploration of the many methods of conflict resolution practiced in the United States and throughout the world. We had a look at two of these—the human needs method and the TIP method—in the two preceding essays. Different strategies are useful in different situations—for example, the two approaches noted previously may not be required for a conflict between two students who clash in a school hallway or a husband and wife bringing their marriage to an end.

If you have ever been in a situation in which you required a third party to facilitate a resolution to an ongoing conflict, you may have experienced some of the most widely used of these methods. Some mediators use facilitative mediation, for example, structuring a process that assists people in gradually arriving at the best possible solutions. The mediator asks many questions to lead the people involved on a path to finding their similarities, even as they acknowledge their differences. Another method, evaluative mediation, is used only when the parties involved are not likely to reach a peaceful, independent resolution—instead, they have chosen to take their issues to court. The mediator then examines their case in advance of a legal hearing or trial and points out the strengths and weaknesses to predict what a judge is likely to decide. (As you might imagine, this is most often used in hotly contested divorces or in child custody cases.)

Many professional conflict resolution practitioners—mediators, judges, counselors, psychologists, clergy, and others—may select a specific method and learn to apply it to a wide range of situations. They often become passionate about the type of mediation they practice, and they can see its value in a wide range of situations. Two of these people provided essays for this chapter.

Cherise D. Hairston is a conflict intervention practitioner with 21 years of professional experience and the Dayton Mediation Center's volunteer and outreach/education coordinator. She is fellow and certified transformative mediator with the Institute for the Study of Conflict Transformation Inc. and serves on the board of directors for the National Association for Community Mediation.

Malik Thompson is a youth educator with the M. K. Gandhi Institute for Nonviolence in Rochester, New York, where they work in residence at Wilson High School, supporting the school's restorative initiatives by mediating conflicts and helping students navigate personal and interpersonal conflicts.

RESPONSE 1: TRANSFORMATIVE MEDIATION

Imagine you have been living with your college dorm roommate for six months. It started out well. You both have similar interests and seem compatible. Living together runs smoothly for a few months until you begin to become mildly irritated by your roommate's cleaning habits, or lack of them. You do your best not to let this bother you, but as time goes on, it becomes harder and harder to ignore what is happening. Little things begin to irritate you, like food left out, and the frustration builds. These irritations seem small, but you start to wonder if your roommate even respects you. After all, you and she have to live in the same space together, and it is not very big. You assume that neither of you wants to have a bug issue from food left out. You try again to mention your concern to her calmly. This is the second time it has been mentioned. In response, she yells, "You're always complaining!"

This time, you are not able to stay calm and sarcastically say, "Who leaves food out like that? We'll get roaches! Who leaves their toothbrush on the floor? You're disgusting!" With that, your roommate storms out of your dorm room, slamming the door.

Several hours later, you are awakened by your roommate arguing with someone on the phone. Half asleep, you find yourself spiraling again and start yelling at her to be quiet. A heated argument ensues, and suddenly there is a loud knock at your door. The resident assistant has been called and appears at your door telling you both that you must quiet down and should consider talking it out constructively in mediation.

Many people can probably relate to this scenario. When people live together, sometimes their expectations and habits differ. These roommates are experiencing a range of emotions, including irritation, frustration, and perhaps violation, which grow as time passes and issues are unresolved. From the transformative perspective of conflict intervention, conflict is defined as a "crisis in human interaction" because the feelings of those in conflict propel them into a least effective state of being. With both roommates feeling frustrated and irritated, they naturally seek to defend themselves and view themselves as the one harmed the most. The way they interact takes on a negative and destructive tone. They become incapacitated by their experience and are unable to communicate effectively.

When they begin to discuss their situation in mediation, their negative interaction resumes. The transformative mediator begins working with the participants using a variety of interventions that help them both overcome the debilitating aspects of their conflict situation. The mediator supports both participants to help them express their perspectives. Their interaction ebbs and flows dynamically, taking on negative tones initially and becoming very heated.

Slowly both participants begin to regain their composure and become clear on what is most important to them, so they can be more effective in communicating with each other. Over the duration of the mediation, the quality of their interaction begins to shift from negative, destructive, alienating, and demonizing into a more constructive, productive, connecting, and humanizing interaction. It is from this place of greater internal strength for the participants individually, and their joint efforts to hear each other from this place of strength, that the work of making decisions on how to move forward are discussed.

Transformative mediation, created and developed by Robert Baruch Bush and Joseph Folger (1994, 2004), is based on a relational view of conflict. This proposes that conflict is best understood first and foremost as a social phenomenon that entails effort to balance an individual's own needs and concerns with an inherent desire for prosocial connection with others. Conflict is challenging and often escalates because it propels us into a less effective state of being—weak and self-absorbed—that can be a challenge to overcome. Individuals in conflict struggle to regain their sense of strength and responsiveness in the midst of the conflict interaction "Empowerment."

The roommates are challenged to interrupt this negative and destructive conflict interaction in order to even consider each other's perspective on

Destructive Conflict Cycle
Quality of Interaction

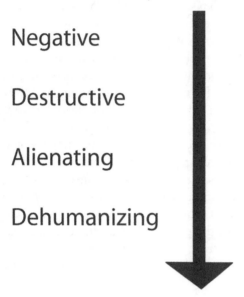

Negative

Destructive

Alienating

Dehumanizing

Destructive Conflict Cycle

their situation, hear each other out, and offer "Recognition" to each other. The roommates, as their conflict unfolds, have entered a state of weakness (i.e., unsettled, confused, fearful, disorganized) and self-absorption (i.e., self-protective, defensive, suspicious, and closed), and both are less resourceful in their attempts to engage their conflict constructively.

In transformative mediation, participants have been caught up in a disempowering experience, so the quality of their interaction degenerates quickly (see Destructive Conflict Cycle figure). The conflict interaction becomes destructive, and this is the starting place for intervention by the transformative mediator.

A transformative mediator intervenes using a variety of supportive, nondirective interventions that help people tap into their inherent capacities for strength and responsiveness. This ultimately helps transform the quality of their interaction toward more positive, constructive, connecting, and humanizing interaction.

Upon reflection, most people do not like the negative behavior they take on as a result of the conflict. Mediation participants often behave toward the other person in ways they would normally find distasteful. In the heat of the conflict, their behavior does not reflect their character. As participants work to speak to their concerns, each person has the opportunity to consider options, explore alternatives, and work effectively to make self-determined choices about their situation, exercising their "compassionate strength."

Compassionate strength is one of the greatest resources mediation participants bring to their conflict, and it is easily lost without a transformative mediator's support. Supportive, nondirective interventions (i.e., reflections, summaries, check-ins) allow individuals to hear themselves by having the transformative mediator mirror their words and emotional tone and help the individual make dynamic shifts toward greater clarity and understanding. This provides mediation participants with the opportunity to recapture their individual sense of competence and connection and reverse the negative conflict cycle. They can then begin creating a more constructive, or at least less destructive, interaction that allows them to address the issues and concerns that are most important to them, exploring with each other the possibility of working out a unique agreement to suit their needs.

In mediation, both roommates expressed frustration at not being heard by the other. Each talked about own experience, and they learned new information that helped them understand each other. When each individual expressed anger, the transformative mediator utilized the intervention that allowed the full expression of her sentiments. As the roommates shared more and more with each other and in the process felt they could take their conversation where they needed, the small shifts of Empowerment became visible and the tone of their conversation grew more constructive. These dynamic shifts, supported by the transformative mediator, allowed them to explore options for resolving their conflict on a solid foundation of increased Empowerment.

Cherise D. Hairston

RESPONSE 2: RESTORATIVE JUSTICE—AN OVERVIEW

Restorative justice is a term used to describe a framework for approaching conflict in which central focus is not placed solely upon the transgression of a law but the harm done by a person, or group, to another person, group, or community as well. Within this framework, resolution is ideally sought out by having those in conflict converse with one another to agree upon a conclusion that works for all parties involved. In theory, and when aptly practiced, restorative justice is the diametrical opposite to retributive justice, wherein punishment of those who have caused harm is prioritized while processes of reconciliation go without consideration.

Restorative justice, as a framework, is extremely malleable and utilized in contexts ranging from school discipline systems to youth justice systems. New Zealand, in particular, is renowned for its usage of restorative justice to handle adolescent cases of interpersonal harm and infringement upon the law since 1996.

Beneath the banner of restorative justice exists a polyphony of strategies to carry out the intention of the framework, collectively known as "restorative practices." Some of the most well-known, and most often used, restorative practices are community conferences, mediations, and circles.

Notably, activists across the political spectrum have been advocating for restorative justice to be adopted in public schools for years, albeit for disparate reasons. One of the most discussed deployed arguments for restorative justice is how restorative school discipline systems counteract the effects of the *school-to-prison pipeline*, a term used to describe the pattern of how harsh discipline policies push students, many of whom either have mental disabilities or come from unstable homes, out of school and, too often, their eventual entrance into the prison system.

In any discussion of the school-to-prison pipeline, one must consider the racial dynamics of the phenomena. Disproportionately, black and brown youth are on the receiving end of harsh disciplinary sentences and are disproportionately represented in the United States' prison population as well. Therefore, restorative justice is also considered necessary in advocacy for racial justice as well.

Also of importance to name, many of the practices used in restorative settings, circles especially, were originally used by the indigenous people of the lands both New Zealand and the United States were built upon for their own community building and reconciliation purposes.

The Gandhi Institute's School Climate Transformation Program

The M. K. Gandhi Institute for Nonviolence is a nonprofit that works to realize the vision of its historic namesake by helping individuals and communities create public awareness of nonviolence as knowledge critical to human thriving. The M. K. Gandhi Institute collaborates with local organizations, academic institutions, students, and committed peacemakers in the following areas: nonviolence education, sustainability and environmental conservation, and the promotion of racial justice.

As an employee of the Gandhi Institute, I work as a youth educator, predominantly working with people between the ages 12 and 24. As a part of the institute's School Climate Transformation Program, I am based at

Joseph C. Wilson Magnet High School, where I comanage a space called the Stop. Think. And. Reflect. (STAR) Room.

In the STAR Room, my colleague, Cammy Enaharo, and I meet with students to offer them emotional support as well as lead mediations between members of the school community when necessary.

Currently, the School Climate Transformation Program is being run in five Rochester City School District schools. At one location, James Monroe High School, accumulated data show that students attributed the work of the institute to higher levels of engagement at school, possessing a broader capacity to navigate arduous relationships at home and school and more supportive relationships with adults in the building.

Restorative Justice and Transformative Mediation

Given that restorative justice is a framework and transformative mediation is a practice, albeit one with its particular undergirding theory, it would be fallacious to attempt an outright comparison between the two. Rather, I am interested in sifting through the similarities, and differences, between the theory of restorative justice and that of transformative mediation.

First articulated by Robert A. Baruch Bush and Joseph P. Folger in 1994 in *The Promise of Mediation* and as described on the Transformative Mediation Institute's website, "This model of mediation practice takes an essentially social/communicative view of human conflict. According to this model, a conflict represents first and foremost a crisis in some human interaction— an interactional crisis with a somewhat common and predictable character." Along with this definition, transformative mediators encourage mediation participants to become more empowered via the process and to increase their ability to recognize the perspective of the other person(s).

While it seems a well-intentioned, perhaps quite effective, approach to conflict resolution, given this definition, transformative mediation does not seem to share the intention of reconciliation between two individuals restorative justice does. Transformative mediation also seems to lack a framework to consider how conflict may harm more people beyond those participating in the mediation as well as its theory seems to lack a consciousness of community.

Again, as pulled from the Transformative Mediation Institute's website, "In transformative mediation, success is measured not by settlement per se but by party shifts toward personal strength, interpersonal responsiveness and constructive interaction."

Given that it seems that the participants' intrapersonal relationships take precedence in this practice, I worry that those involved in the process would walk away from the process without a thorough understanding of the other person's experience.

However, in spite of this critique, I do applaud transformative mediations' intention to encourage the development of the participants' internal relationships. Rather than dispensing with the practice of transformative mediation entirely, I would rather extract what is useful from the practice and transplant these components into my own work as a restorative practitioner to bolster my abilities and effectiveness.

Malik Thompson

Directory of Resources

ORGANIZATIONS

Alliance for Conflict Transformation

www.conflicttransformation.org

ACT works with educators, youth, community, and religious leaders, and others to turn social conflicts into opportunities for peaceful change.

Alliance for Peacebuilding

www.allianceforpeacebuilding.org, @AfPeacebuilding, www.facebook .com/AfPeacebuilding

An organization geared to individuals who are interested in working and doing research in conflict zones.

American Psychological Association

www.apa.org/education/index.aspx, @APA, www.facebook.com/American PsychologicalAssociation

An organization for students who are interested in interpersonal conflict analysis and resolution.

Amnesty International

www.amnestyusa.org, @amnestyusa, www.facebook.com/amnestyusa

A global movement of people fighting injustice and promoting human rights.

Association for Conflict Resolution

www.acrnet.org, @ACRgroup, www.facebook.com/Associationfor
ConflictResolution

The most well-known professional association for conflict resolution
practitioners.

Association of Family and Conciliation Courts

www.afccnet.org, @AFCCtweets, www.facebook.com/FollowAFCC/

An international association of professionals dedicated to improving the
lives of children and families through the resolution of family court.

Center for Dispute Settlement

www.cdsadr.org, @CDSADR, www.facebook.com/CDSADR/

One of the first three dispute settlement organizations in the country back
in 1973, the CDS works to create a nonviolent, conflict-resolving community where disputes are settled peacefully and in the earliest possible
stage. The center is based in Rochester, New York, with locations
throughout western New York State.

Conflict Resolution Network

www.crnhq.org

A nonprofit professional association based in Dallas, Texas, dedicated to
the facilitation, awareness, and advancement of dispute resolution.

Foundation for Middle East Peace

fmep.org, @FMEP, www.facebook.com/Foundation-for-Middle-East-
Peace-82038934261/

Promotes a just solution to the Israel-Palestinian conflict through education and advocacy.

Fund for Peace

global.fundforpeace.org/aboutus, @fundforpeace, www.facebook.com/The-
Fund-for-Peace-184571478226160/

A global nonprofit research and educational organization that works to
prevent violent conflict and promote sustainable security.

Institute for the Study of Conflict Transformation

www.transformativemediation.org, www.facebook.com/Transformative
Mediation/

An international think tank that produces education resources, materials,
and services for professionals and the general public.

International Association for Conflict Management

negotiacm.org

Encourages scholars to develop and disseminate theory, research, and
experience that may be useful for understanding and improving conflict

management in families, organizations, society, and international settings.

Mediators Beyond Borders International

mediatorsbeyondborders.org, @MediatorsBB, www.facebook.com/MediatorsBeyondBordersInternational/

Builds local capacities for peace and promotes mediation worldwide.

M. K. Gandhi Institute for Nonviolence

http://www.gandhiinstitute.org, www.facebook.com/ROCNonviolence/

A nonprofit organization working to realize the vision of its historic name-sake, by helping individuals and communities develop the inner resources and skills needed to achieve a nonviolent world.

National Peace Foundation

www.nationalpeace.org

Committed to solving problems and preventing conflict through community peacebuilding and citizen empowerment.

Northern Virginia Mediation Services

nvms.us

Conflict resolution and education services for communities in northern Virginia.

Search for Common Ground

www.sfcg.org/what-we-do/, @SFCG, www.facebook.com/sfcg.org/

Partnering with people around the world to find shared solutions to destructive conflict.

Work It Out!

http://www.workitout.org

Education for Conflict Resolution Inc., website of the Midwest's longest operating conflict resolution and training center.

JOURNALS

Conflict Resolution Quarterly: The Association for Conflict Resolution, Wiley Periodicals Inc., onlinelibrary.wiley.com/journal/10.1002/(ISSN)1541-1508

International Journal of Conflict Management: Emerald Publishing, www.emeraldinsight.com/journal/ijcma

International Journal of Conflict and Violence (IJCV): University of Bielefeld (Germany), www.ijcv.org/index.php/ijcv/index

Journal of Conflict Management (JOCM): Sullivan University, jocm.net

Journal of Conflict Resolution: University of Maryland, SAGE
Journals, us.sagepub.com/en-us/nam/journal-of-conflict-resolution/
journal200764

Negotiation and Conflict Management Research: The International
Association for Conflict Management, Wiley Periodicals Inc.,
onlinelibrary.wiley.com/journal/10.1111/(ISSN)1750-4716

Peace and Conflict: Journal of Peace Psychology: American
Psychological Association Division 48 (Society for the Study of Peace,
Conflict and Violence: Peace Psychology Division),www.apa.org/pubs/
journals/pac/

WEBSITES

Communication and Conflict
http://www.communicationandconflict.com
Informational website of mediator Alan Sharland.

Conflict Information Consortium: The Consortium at the University of
Colorado serves as a portal to information about every aspect of conflict
and resolution. It maintains three informational websites: Beyond
Intractability (www.beyondintractability.org), CR Info (www
.beyondintractability.org/crinfo), and Moving beyond Intractability
Massive Open Online Seminar (www.beyondintractability.org/moos).

Conflict Solving at Chirchleadership.org
http://www.churchleadership.org/pages.asp?pageid=66928
A series of articles and resources that offer guidance for using Christian
    spirituality to find a way through conflict.

How to Deal with Conflict
http://managementhelp.org/interpersonal/conflict.htm
Free Management Library

Insight on Conflict
https://www.insightonconflict.org
An online resource published by Peace Direct, dedicated to local peace-
    building around the world, with blogs, articles, and conflict resolution
    resources.

Justpeace
https://justpeaceumc.org
The United Methodist Church's website with a free downloadable faith-
    based conflict transformation guide.

Mediation.com

http://www.mediate.com/index.cfm

News site for everything about mediation, from methods and practice to
ideas and effectiveness.

Public Conversations Project

http://www.whatisessential.org

A Boston-based organization devoted to providing resources for constructive dialog.

"Teens, Technology and Friendships"

http://www.pewinternet.org/2015/08/06/teens-technology-and-
friendships/

A report by Amanda Lenhart of the Pew Research Center on the integral
role technology plays in the way teens interact and the conflicts that
develop online and between individuals.

Glossary

Aftermath: The period after the conflict has been resolved, during which the parties may or may not be happy with the outcome. If they are not, it can lead to a new conflict, a continuation of the current one, or a breakup of the couple or group.

Calming: Taking control of angry feelings through meditation, positive thinking techniques, and general self-control.

Catalytic event: An event that causes a change in the status quo or that causes inaction to turn into action.

Conflict: A disagreement between individuals, an individual and a group, many people within a group, or between two or more groups.

Escalation: The process through which a conflict rises from a discomfort or disagreement to an argument and on to a battle. Each time a conflict becomes more heated, it has escalated.

Expression: Giving voice to anger, either in an assertive and forthright way to resolve the conflict or through raised voices and aggression.

Factionalization: A point in a conflict in which the previously unified group breaks into subgroups that disagree with one another's goals.

Felt conflict: The parties involved all know they are in conflict—they literally feel it.

Intergroup conflict: Two or more groups clash with one another over tasks, goals, property, ideologies, or a wide range of other issues.

Interpersonal conflict: A situation in which an individual frustrates another person's effort to reach a goal.

Interstate conflict: A demand to change the government of a specific territory by those outside of the territory.

Intragroup conflict: Two or more members of the same group or team come into conflict with one another.

Intrapersonal conflict: Conflict that arises within ourselves—the process of making a difficult decision, for example.

Intrastate conflict: A demand within a state, province, or country to change the leadership or the laws of that territory.

Latent conflict: A potential for a conflict to develop, but no conflict has come to the surface yet.

Manifest conflict: The conflict is out in the open, and the person who feels the conflict engages the other in discussion, which may well lead to argument.

Noncompromising identity: An identity that places a person at a higher rank than those around him or her—royalty, teacher versus students, government officials, or social class (as in a caste system).

Perceived conflict: The sense by some people in a group (or one person in a couple) that another member of the group may undermine the group's progress toward a goal.

Persistent identity: The perception of one ethnic group, gender group, or nationality that has been passed down through generations.

Primary identity: The elements of a person's identity that have become most important—the things a person most closely identifies with his or her beliefs and actions.

Process conflict: People who are working together disagree about assignments, responsibilities, and how to complete the work.

Relationship conflict: At least one person involved in the relationship perceives that he or she is incompatible with the others. This can result in an argument or in the end of the relationship.

Resolution: Bringing the conflict to a close, with the parties involved agreeing to a compromise or a solution.

Suppression: Changing thoughts or ignoring feelings of anger to avoid a confrontation. If the source of anger continues, suppression can become impossible as angry feelings build.

Task conflict: People involved in completing a task find that they disagree with one another's views on how to complete it.

View of the Other: The way a person perceives everything that is not part of his or her identity—members of another race, religion, task group at work, social clique, gang, political party, or any other group in which the person is not a member.

Bibliography

CHAPTER 1

Argyris, C. *Interpersonal Competence and Organizational Effectiveness.* Homewood, IL: Dorsey Press, 1962.

Baron, R. A. "Positive Effects of Conflict: A Cognitive Perspective." *Journal of Employee Responsibilities and Rights*, Vol. 4, 1991, pp. 25–36.

Braiker, H., and H. H. Kelley. "Conflict in the Development of Close Relationships." In R. L. Burgess and T. L. Huston (Eds.), *Social Exchange in Developing Relationships.* New York: Academic Press, 1979.

"Chapter 1: Introduction to the Study of Conflict Communication." Pearson High Education. Retrieved December 14, 2015. https://catalogue.pearsoned.co.uk/assets/hip/gb/hip_gb_pearsonhighered/samplechapter/0205956262.pdf.

Cupach, William R., Daniel J. Canary, and Irian H. Spitzberg. *Competencies in Interpersonal Conflict*, 2nd ed. Long Grove, IL: Waveland Press, November 6, 2009.

"Definition of Armed Conflict." Department of Peace and Conflict Research, Uppsala University. Retrieved December 16, 2015. http://www.pcr.uu.se/research/ucdp/definitions/definition_of_armed_conflict/.

Deutsch, Morton. *The Resolution of Conflict.* New Haven, CT: Yale University Press, 1973.

Evans, G. W., and C. M. Crumbaugh. "Effects of Prisoner's Dilemma Format on Cooperative Behavior." *Journal of Personality and Social Psychology*, Vol 3, No. 4, April 1966.

Fisher, Ronald R. "Intergroup Conflict." In Morton Deutsch and Peter T. Coleman (Eds.), *The Handbook of Conflict Resolution: Theory and Practice.* San Francisco: Jossey-Bass Publishers, 2000, pp. 166–184.

"Interpersonal Conflict and Effective Communication." DRB Alternatives, Inc. Retrieved December 14, 2015. http://www.drbalternatives.com/articles/cc2.html.

Jameson, Jessica K.. "Toward a Comprehensive Model for the Assessment and Management of Intraorganizational Conflict: Developing the Framework." *International Journal of Conflict Management*, Vol. 10, No. 3, 1999, pp. 268–294.

Jehn, Karen A. "A Multimethod Examination of the Benefits and Detriments of Intragroup Conflict." *Administrative Science Quarterly*, Vol. 40, No. 2, June 1995, pp. 256–282. Retrieved December 15, 2015. http://www.jstor.org/stable/2393638?seq=21#page_scan_tab_contents.

Pondy, Louis R. "Reflections on Organizational Conflict." *Journal of Organizational Behavior*, Vol. 13, No. 3, May 1992, pp. 257–261.

Sherif, Muzafer, O. J. Harvey, B. Jack White, William R. Hood, and Carolyn W. Sherif. *Intergroup Conflict and Cooperation: The Robbers Cave Experiment: 1954.* Classics in the History of Psychology. Christopher D. Green (Ed.). Norman, Oklahoma: University Book Exchange. Retrieved December 9, 2015. http://psychclassics.yorku.ca/Sherif/.

Sillars, A. L., and J. Weisberg. "Conflict as a Social Skill." In M. E. Roloff and G. R. Miller (Eds.), *Interpersonal Processes: New Directions in Communication Research.* Newbury Park, CA: Sage, 1987, pp. 140–171.

"Stages in Conflict (or) Conflict Process." AcademicLib.com. Retrieved December 12, 2015. http://academlib.com/2866/.

CHAPTER 2

Adler, Robert S., and Elliott M. Silverstein. "When David Meets Goliath: Dealing with Power Differentials in Negotiations." *Harvard Negotiation Law Review*, 2000. Retrieved May 8, 2016. http://www.hnlr.org/articles/archive/.

"The Bill of Rights: A Transcription." U.S. National Archives. Retrieved May 6, 2016. http://www.archives.gov/exhibits/charters/bill_of_rights_transcript.html.

Brooks, David. "The Creative Climate." *New York Times*, July 7, 2014. Retrieved May 5, 2016. http://www.nytimes.com/2014/07/08/opinion/david-brooks-the-creative-climate.html?_r=0.

Coleman, Peter T., and Robert Ferguson. *Making Conflict Work: Harnessing the Power of Disagreement*. Boston, MA: Houghton Mifflin Harcourt, July 1, 2014, pp. xiii–xv.

"Controlling Anger before It Controls You." American Psychological Association. Retrieved May 3, 2016. http://www.apa.org/topics/anger/control.aspx.

Czaja, Je'. "Examples of Successful Strategic Aliances." *Houston Chronicle*. Retrieved May 6, 2016. http://smallbusiness.chron.com/examples-successful-strategic-alliances-13859.html.

"The Declaration of Independence: A Transcription." U.S. National Archives. Retrieved May 8, 2016. http://www.archives.gov/exhibits/charters/declaration_transcript.html.

Gleiser, Marcelo. "Without Conflict There Is No Growth." NPR Public Broadcasting, July 23, 2014. Retrieved April 30, 2016. http://www.npr.org/sections/13.7/2014/07/23/334036507/without-conflict-there-is-no-growth.

Gottman, John. *Why Marriages Succeed or Fail*. New York: Simon & Schuster, 1995.

Kreisberg, Louis. "Identity Issues." Beyond Intractability, University of Colorado Conflict Information Consortium, July 2003. Retrieved April 30, 2016. http://www.beyondintractability.org/about/about-beyond-intractability.

Llopis, Glenn. "The 4 Most Effective Ways Leaders Solve Problems." *Forbes*, November 4, 2013. Retrieved May 1, 2016. http://www.forbes.com/sites/glennllopis/2013/11/04/the-4-most-effective-ways-leaders-solve-problems/#7e75298f2bda.

Meir Amit Intelligence and Terrorism Information Center. "The Historical Roots and Stages in the Development of ISIS." *Crethi Plethi*, Winter 2014.

Perich-Anderson, Jagoda. "Creative Conflict: Generating Innovative Ideas." *Futurist.com*, 2001.

Richards, Leigh. "How Can Conflict Be Good for an Organizations?" *Houston Chronicle*. Retrieved April 30, 2016. http://smallbusiness.chron.com/can-conflict-good-organization-741.html.

Shenkar, Oded, and Jeffrey J. Reuer. *The Handbook of Strategic Alliances*. Thousand Oaks, CA: SAGE Publications, August 30, 2005.

USDA Natural Resources Conservation Service. "Building Alliances." National Association of Conservation Districts, 1994. Retrieved

May 6, 2016. https://organizingforpower.files.wordpress.com/2009/06/
building-alliances-guidebook.pdf.

Ward, Clarissa. "The Origins of ISIS: Finding the Birthplace of Jihad."
CBS News, November 4, 2014. Retrieved May 8, 2016. http://www
.cbsnews.com/news/the-origins-of-isis-finding-the-birthplace-of-jihad/.

CHAPTER 3

Adler, Ronald B., and Russell F. Proctor II. *Looking Out, Looking In*, 13th
ed. Boston: Wadsworth Cengage Learning, 2011, pp. 398–403.

Bunashie, Joan, and Lindsay Broder. "How Leaders Can Best Manage
Conflict within Their Teams." *Entrepreneur*, June 12, 2015. Retrieved
May 16, 2016. https://www.entrepreneur.com/article/247275.

Cooley, Charles H. "Personal Competition: Its Place in the Social Order
and Effect upon Individuals; With Some Considerations on Success."
*Sociological Theory and Social Research: Being Selected Papers of Charles
Horton Cooley. Economic Studies*, Vol. 4, No. 2, 1894.

De Dreu, Carsten K. W., Bianca Beersma, Wolfgang Steinel, and Gerben
A. Van Kleef. "The Psychology of Negotiation: Principles and Basic
Processes." In Arie W. Kruglanski and E. Tory Higgins (Eds.), *Social
Psychology: Handbook of Basic Principles*. New York: Guilford Press,
December 2006, pp. 608–629.

Festinger, Leon. "A Theory of Social Comparison Processes." *Human
Relations*, Vol. 7, No. 117, 1954.

Glasl, Freidrich. *Konfliktmanagement, Ein Handbuch fur Fuhrungskrafte und
Berater*, 2nd ed. Bern/Stuttgart: Haupt, 1992, translated by the Berghof
Foundation. Retrieved May 26, 2016. http://www.friedenspaedagogik
.de/english/topics_of_the_institute_s_work/peace_education_online_
teaching_course/basic_course_4/conflict/conflict_escalation.

Gordon, Thomas. *Parent Effectiveness Training*. New York: Wyden, 1970.

Graham, Paul. "How to Disagree." March 2008. Retrieved May 24, 2016.
http://www.paulgraham.com/disagree.html.

Gugel, Gunther. "The Dynamics of Escalation in Conflicts: The Nine
Stages of Conflict according to Freidrich Glasl." Tubingen Institute for
Peace Education, Berghof Foundation, 2012. Retrieved May 26, 2016.
http://www.friedenspaedagogik.de/english/topics_of_the_institute_s_
work/peace_education_online_teaching_course/basic_course_4/
conflict/conflict_escalation.

Hadad, Marilyn, and Maureen J. Reed. *Post-Secondary Learning Experience*.
Toronto, Ontario: Nelson College Indigenous, 2007.

Kilduff, Gavin J., Hillary A. Elfenbein, and Barry M. Staw. "The Psychology of Rivalry: A Relationally Dependent Analysis of Competition." *Academy of Management Journal*, Vol. 53, No. 5, 2010, pp. 943–969.

Kreger, Randi, and Bill Eddy. "High Conflict People Drive Disputes at Home, School, Work." *Psychology Today*, May 27, 2012.

Robinson, Jerry W. "Conflict Management." October 1980, adapted from "The Conflict Approach to Community Development." In James A. Christensen (Ed.), *Community Development in America*. Ames: Iowa State University Press, 1980. Retrieved May 23, 2016. https://www.ideals.illinois.edu/bitstream/handle/2142/32656/conflictmanageme00robi.pdf?sequence=2.

Rubin, Jeffrey Z., Dean G. Pruitt, and Sung H. Kim. *Social Conflict: Escalation, Stalemate, and Settlement*, 2nd ed. McGraw Hill Series in Social Psychology. New York: McGraw Hill, 1994.

Schwartz, Michelle, and Dalia Hanna. "Group Work: Dealing with Conflicts." The Learning and Teaching Office. Retrieved May 16, 2016. http://www.ryerson.ca/content/dam/lt/resources/handouts/GroupWorkConflict.pdf.

CHAPTER 4

Brewer, Marilynn B. "Ingroup Identification and Intergroup Conflict: When Does Ingroup Love Become Outgroup Hate?" In Richard D. Ashmore, Lee Jussim, and David Wilder (Eds.), *Social Identity, Intergroup Conflict, and Conflict Resolution*. Oxford: Oxford University Press, 2001.

Brewer, Marilynn B., and N. Miller. "Beyond the Contact Hypothesis: Theoretical Perspectives on Desegregation." In N. Miller and M. B. Brewer (Eds.), *Groups in Contact: The Psychology of Desegregation*. Orlando, FL: Academic Press, 1984, pp. 281–302.

Eidelson, Roy J., and Judy I. Eidelson, "Dangerous Ideas: Five Beliefs That Propel Groups toward Conflict." *American Psychologist*, March 2003, pp. 182–192.

Forsyth, Donelson. *Group Dynamics*, 5th ed. Belmont, CA: Cengage Learning, 2009, pp. 426–429.

Hewstone, M., and R. J. Brown. "Contact Is Not Enough: An Intergroup Perspective on the Contact Hypothesis." In M. Hewstone and R. J. Brown (Eds.), *Contact and Conflict in Intergroup Encounters*. Oxford: Blackwell, 1986, pp. 34–35.

Jehn, Karen A., and Elizabeth A. Mannix. "The Dynamic Nature of Conflict: A Longitudinal Study of Intragroup Conflict and Group

Performance." *Academy of Management Journal*, Vol. 44, No. 2, April 2001, pp. 238–251.

Marx, Karl, and Frederick Engels. *The Communist Manifesto*. Moscow: Progress Publishers, 1969, first releases February 1848. Retrieved December 9, 2015. https://www.marxists.org/archive/marx/works/1848/communist-manifesto/ch01.htm.

Mills, Theodore M. *The Sociology of Small Groups*. Englewood Cliffs, NJ: Prentice-Hall, 1967, pp. 14–15.

Pruitt, Dean G. "Whither Ripeness Theory?" Working Paper #25, Institute for Conflict Analysis and Resolution, George Mason University, 2005. Retrieved December 11, 2015. http://scar.gmu.edu/wp_25_pruitt.pdf.

Rahim, M. Afzalur. "Toward a Theory of Managing Organizational Conflict." *International Journal of Conflict Management*, Vol. 13, No. 3, 2002, pp. 206–235.

Sherif, Muzafer, O. J. Harvey, B. Jack White, William R. Hood, and Carolyn W. Sherif. *Intergroup Conflict and Cooperation: The Robbers Cave Experiment: 1954*. Classics in the History of Psychology. Christopher D. Green, ed., York University, Toronto, Ontario. Retrieved December 9, 2015. http://psychclassics.yorku.ca/Sherif/.

Sumner, William G. *Folkways: A Study of the Sociological Importance of Usages, Manners, Customs, Mores, and Morals*. Boston: Ginn & Company Publishers, 1907, pp. 13–15.

Tajfel, Henri. "Experiments in Intergroup Discrimination." *Scientific American*, Vol. 223, No. 5, 1970, pp. 96–102.

Tajfel, Henri, and John C. Turner. "The Social Identity Theory of Intergroup Behavior." In S. Worchel and W. G. Austin (Eds.), *Psychology of Intergroup Relations*. Chicago: Nelson-Hall, 1986, pp. 7–24.

Volkan, Vamik D. "The Need to Have Enemies and Allies: A Developmental Approach." *Political Psychology*, Vol. 6, No. 2, Special Issue: A Notebook on the Psychology of the U.S.-Soviet Relationship, June 1985, pp. 219–247.

CHAPTER 5

Bengtson, Vern, and J. A. Kuypers. "Generational Difference and the Developmental Stake." *Aging and Human Development*, Vol. 2, No. 4, 1971, pp. 249–260.

Buck, Nancy S. "Parents and Children in Conflict." *Psychology Today*, January 7, 2011.

"Bullying Statistics." PACER's National Bullying Prevention Center. Retrieved February 16, 2017. http://www.pacer.org/bullying/resources/stats.asp.

Clarke, Edward J., Mar Preston, Jo Raksin, and Vern L. Bengston. "Types of Conflicts and Tensions between Older Parents and Adult Children." *The Gerontologist*, Vol. 39, No. 3, 1999, pp. 261–270.

Csikszentmihalyi, Mihaly, and Reed Larson. *Being Adolescent: Conflict and Growth in the Teenage Years*. New York: Basic Books, September 1, 1986.

Davis, Stan, and Charisse Nixon. "The Youth Voice Project." Pennsylvania State University, March 2010. Retrieved February 16, 2017. http://njbullying.org/documents/YVPMarch2010.pdf.

Drake, Bruce. "Number of Older Americans in the Workforce Is on the Rise." Pew Research Center, January 7, 2014. Retrieved Feruary. 23, 2017. http://www.pewresearch.org/fact-tank/2014/01/07/number-of-older-americans-in-the-workforce-is-on-the-rise/.

Dunn, Judy, and Penny Munn. "Becoming a Family Member: Family Conflict and the Development of Social Understanding in the Second Year." *Child Development*, Vol. 56, No. 2, April 1985, pp. 480–492.

Fingerman, K. L. "Sources of Tension in the Aging Mother and Adult Daughter Relationship." *Psychology of Aging*, Vol. 11, No. 4, December 1996.

Hinduja, Sameer, and Justin W. Patchin. "Cyberbullying: Identification, Prevention, and Response." Cyberbullying Research Center, 2010, p. 3. Retrieved February 23, 2017. http://cyberbullying.org/Cyberbullying-Identification-Prevention-Response.pdf.

Hinduja, Sameer, and Justin W. Patchin. "2015 Cyberbullying Data." Cyberbullying Research Center, May 1, 2015. Retrieved February 16, 2017. http://cyberbullying.org/2015-data.

Hinduja, Sameer, and Justin W. Patchin. "Summary of Our Cyberbullying Research 2004–2016." Cyberbullying Research Center, November 26, 2016. Retrieved February 16, 2017. http://cyberbullying.org/summary-of-our-cyberbullying-research.

Lingren, Herbert G. "Managing Conflict Successfully." Strongermarriage.org. Retrieved February 22, 2017. http://strongermarriage.org/married/managing-conflict-successfully.

McCallion, Gail, and Jody Feder. "Student Bullying: Overview of Research, Federal Initiatives, and Legal Issues." Congressional Research Service, October 18, 2013. Retrieved February 16, 2017. https://fas.org/sgp/crs/misc/R43254.pdf.

"Megan's Story." The Megan Meier Foundation. November 13, 2007. Retrieved February 16, 2017. http://www.meganmeierfoundation.org/megans-story.html.

Miller, Susan A., Ellen B. Church, and Carla Poole. "Ages & Stages: How Children Learn through Conflicts." *Early Childhood Today*, Scholastic.com. Retrieved February 15, 2017. https://www.scholastic.com/teachers/articles/teaching-content/ages-stages-how-children-learn-through-conflicts/.

Mislinski, Jill. "Demographic Trends for the 50-and-Older Work Force." Advisor Perspectives, February 8, 2017. Retrieved February 23, 2017. https://www.advisorperspectives.com/dshort/updates/2017/02/08/demographic-trends-for-the-50-and-older-work-force.

Pickhardt, Carl. "Five Psychological 'Engines' That Drive Adolescent Growth." *Psychology Today*, September 13, 2011.

"Ryan Halligan Loses His Life to Taunts, Rumors and Cyber Bullying." NoBullying.com, December 22, 2015. Retrieved February 16, 2017. https://nobullying.com/ryan-halligan/.

Ryff, C. D., Y. H. Lee, M. J. Essex, and P. S. Schmutte. "My Children and Me: Midlife Evaluations of Grown Children and of Self." *Psychology of Aging*, Vol. 9, No. 2, June 1994, pp. 195–205.

"Trends in the Prevalence of Behaviors That Contribute to Violence, National Youth Risk Behavior Survey 1991–2015." Centers for Disease Control, 2015. Retrieved February 16, 2017. https://www.cdc.gov/healthyyouth/data/yrbs/pdf/trends/2015_us_violence_trend_yrbs.pdf.

Whitbourne, Susan K., and Joshua R. Bringle. "Generativity, Theory Of." In Richard Schulz (Ed.), *The Encyclopedia of Aging*, 4th ed. Springer, 2006, p. 437.

CHAPTER 6

Albert, Eleanor. "China-Taiwan Relations." Council on Foreign Relations, December 7, 2016. Retrieved March 9, 2017. http://www.cfr.org/china/china-taiwan-relations/p9223.

"The Arab-Israeli War of 1948." Office of the Historian, U.S. Department of State. Retrieved October 13, 2016. https://history.state.gov/milestones/1945-1952/arab-israeli-war.

Bates, Crispin. "The Hidden Story of Partition and Its Legacies." BBC News, March 3, 2011. Retrieved March 10, 2017. http://www.bbc.co.uk/history/british/modern/partition1947_01.shtml.

Berman, Mark, and Wesley Lowery. "The 12 Key Highlights from the DOJ's Scathing Ferguson Report." *Washington Post*, March 4, 2015. Retrieved March 12, 2017. https://www.washingtonpost.com/news/post-nation/wp/2015/03/04/the-12-key-highlights-from-the-dojs-scathing-ferguson-report/?utm_term=.44aaded4b95e.

Bureau of Western Hemisphere Affairs. "U.S. Relations with Venezuela." U.S. Department of State, August 31, 2016. Retrieved March 11, 2017. https://www.state.gov/r/pa/ei/bgn/35766.htm.

"Civilian Oversight of Police Established by the City of Ferguson." City of Ferguson, March 2, 2017. Retrieved March 11, 2017. https://www.fergusoncity.com/CivicAlerts.aspx?AID=510&ARC=937.

Dalrymple, William. "The Great Divide: The Violent Legacy of Indian Partition." *New Yorker*, June 29, 2015. Retrieved March 10, 2017. http://www.newyorker.com/magazine/2015/06/29/the-great-divide-books-dalrymple.

"The Declaration of the Establishment of the State of Israel." Jewish Virtual Library. Retrieved October 13, 2016. http://www.jewishvirtuallibrary.org/jsource/History/Dec_of_Indep.html.

Durdin, Tillman. "Formosa Killings Are Put at 10,000." *New York Times*, March 29, 1947. Retrieved March 9, 2017. http://www.taiwandc.org/hst-1947.htm.

Ettinger, Shmuel. "Jewish Emigration in the 19th Century." My Jewish Learning. Retrieved October 11, 2016. http://www.myjewishlearning.com/article/jewish-emigration-in-the-19th-century/.

Forte, Maximillian. "Factionalism." Political Anthropology, Lincoln Hill, 2013, version 1.

Hassassian, Manuel. *Palestine: Factionalism in the National Movement (1919–1939)*. Jerusalem, Israel: PASSIA, 1990.

"Hindu-Muslim Antagonism." Gandhi Institutions. Retrieved March 10, 2017. http://www.mkgandhi.org/biography/hndmuslm.htm.

Lewis, Martin D. *The British in India: Imperialism or Trusteeship?* Roswell, GA: Heath and Company, 1965.

"Mahatma Gandhi's Writing, Philosophy, Audio, Video and Photographs." Gandhi Institutions. Retrieved March 10, 2017. http://www.mkgandhi.org/religionmk.htm.

McDermott, Jeremy. "Bolivia Expels US Ambassador Philip Goldberg." *Telegraph*, September 12, 2008. Retrieved March 11, 2017. http://www.telegraph.co.uk/news/worldnews/southamerica/bolivia/2801579/Bolivia-expels-US-ambassador-Philip-Goldberg.html.

"Mohammad Ali Jinnah (1876–1948)." BBC History. Retrieved March 10, 2017. http://www.bbc.co.uk/history/historic_figures/jinnah_mohammad_ali.shtml.

Office of the Press Secretary. "Executive Order Protecting the Nation from Foreign Terrorist Entry into the United States." The White House, March 6, 2017. Retrieved March 8, 2017. https://www.whitehouse.gov/the-press-office/2017/03/06/executive-order-protecting-nation-foreign-terrorist-entry-united-states.

"Official: U.S. Marines Sent into Syria for Raqqa Fight." Daily Beast, March 9, 2017. Retrieved March 9, 2017. http://www.thedailybeast.com/cheats/2017/03/09/official-couple-hundred-marines-sent-to-syria.html?via=desktop&source=copyurl.

"Our History." Jewish National Fund. Retrieved October 11, 2016. http://www.jnf.org/about-jnf/history/.

"Palestine. Disturbances in May, 1921. Reports of the Commission of Inquiry with Correspondence Relating Thereto ..." Great Britain Colonial Office, London, England. Retrieved October 12, 2016. https://archive.org/details/palestinedisturb00grearich.

"POV History of the Israeli-Palestinian Conflict." POV, Public Broadcasting Corporation, Arlington, Virginia. Retrieved October 11, 2016. http://pov-tc.pbs.org/pov/pdf/promiese/promises-timeline.pdf.

"S.2142—Venezuela Defense of Human Rights and Civil Society Act of 2014." Congress.gov, December 18, 2014. Retrieved March 11, 2017. https://www.congress.gov/bill/113th-congress/senate-bill/2142/text.

Shaw, Walter. "Report of the Commission on the Palestine Disturbances of August 1929, Command Paper 3530" (Shaw Commission report). H.M. Stationery Office, London, Great Britain, 1930.

"Sheikh Izz Al-Din Al-Qassam." Jewish Virtual Library. Retrieved October 13, 2016. http://www.jewishvirtuallibrary.org/jsource/biography/alqassam.html.

Stockwell, Sarah. *The British Empire: Themes and Perspectives.* Hoboken, NJ: Wiley-Blackwell, 2008.

"Sunnis and Shia: Islam's Ancient Schism." BBC, January 4, 2016. Retrieved March 8, 2017. http://www.bbc.com/news/world-middle-east-16047709.

"Syria's Civil War Explained." Al Jazeera, February 7, 2017. Retrieved March 8, 2017. http://www.aljazeera.com/news/2016/05/syria-civil-war-explained-160505084119966.html.

"Taiwan Profile-Timeline." BBC News, January 20, 2016. Retrieved March 9, 2017. http://www.bbc.com/news/world-asia-16178545.

"Timeline: The Death of Michael Brown and Unrest in Ferguson." CBS St. Louis, August 21, 2014. Retrieved March 12, 2017. http://stlouis.cbslocal.com/2014/08/12/timeline-the-death-of-michael-brown-and-unrest-in-ferguson/.

"What Happened in Ferguson?" *New York Times*, August 9, 2015. Retrieved March 11, 2017. https://www.nytimes.com/interactive/2014/08/13/us/ferguson-missouri-town-under-siege-after-police-shooting.html.

"What's behind the China-Taiwan Divide?" BBC News, December 3, 2016. Retrieved March 9, 2017. http://www.bbc.com/news/world-asia-34729538.

"Why Do Western Countries Not Want Refugees?" *Hans India*, February 23, 2016. Retrieved March 8, 2017. http://www.harunyahya.com/en/Articles/216822/why-do-western-countries-not.

PART III

Bush, Robert Baruch A., and Joseph P. Folger. *The Promise of Mediation*. San Francisco: Jossey-Bass, 1994.

Bush, Robert Baruch A., and Joseph P. Folger. *The Promise of Mediation: The Transformative Approach to Conflict*. Hoboken, NJ: John Wiley & Sons, 2004.

About the Author and Contributors

Randi Minetor, MA, is a writer for a number of publishers across the United States. She has authored more than 60 books, most recently *Death in Zion National Park* (Lyons Press, 2017), *Death in Glacier National Park* (Lyons, 2016), and *Hiking through History New York* (Falcon, 2016), and she has served as the ghostwriter for a number of bestselling nonfiction books. She serves as a principal copywriter for the University of Rochester Medical Center, and she writes for a number of magazines, including *Western New York Physician* and *Medical Economics*. Minetor holds a master's degree in film studies from the University of Rochester and a bachelor's degree in English and psychology from the University at Buffalo.

Mike Bassow, MS, has taught interpersonal communications and public speaking for 27 years as an adjunct professor at Central New Mexico Community College. He lives in Albuquerque, New Mexico.

Juliana E. Birkhoff, PhD, is an experienced mediator, facilitation and dispute resolution trainer, and scholar. She focuses her practice on complex scientific and technical problems about water quality and quantity; watershed planning and restoration; land use and development; pesticides and chemicals policies and community right to know issues; and other natural resources and public health issues. She has conducted extensive research on collaboration and consensus building. Her previous research includes best practices for integrating complex scientific and technical information into collaborative processes; how to integrate scientific and community knowledge in consensus building; and several evaluations of consensus-building processes.

Cherise D. Hairston is a conflict intervention practitioner with 21 years of professional experience and the Dayton Mediation Center's volunteer and outreach/education coordinator. She is fellow and certified transformative mediator with the Institute for the Study of Conflict Transformation Inc. and serves on the board of directors for the National Association for Community Mediation. Ms. Hairston provides a range of conflict intervention services, including customized conflict management training for organizations, individual and organizational conflict consultation, conflict coaching, large and small group facilitation, and integrated conflict management systems design services. She was one of the principal conflict management consultants and trainers for the state of Ohio's Employee Assistance Program's new Employee Workplace Mediation Program. She is a prolific presenter at national conferences, including, most recently, the Kennesaw State University's (Kennesaw, Georgia) International Conference on Negotiation, Association for Conflict Resolution, Antioch University Midwest, Introduction to Negotiation, and Wright State University's National Education Renewal 2014 and 2015 Conference. Ms. Hairston is a published author in two academic publications, *Mediation Quarterly* and the book, *Re-Centering: Culture and Knowledge in Conflict Resolution* (Syracuse University Press, 2008) and in 2016, "The Professional Is Personal" in *Transforming Conflict from the Inside Out: Stories and Reflections from Transformative Practitioners*. With more than 10 years of professional teaching experience at the undergraduate and graduate level (Wright State University, Miami University, and Antioch University Midwest), she is a former adjunct professor at Antioch University Midwest (Yellow Springs, Ohio) in the graduate departments of Conflict Analysis and Engagement and Management and Leading Change. Ms. Hairston completed doctoral-level studies (all but dissertation) at Nova Southeastern University, Ft. Lauderdale, Florida, in the Department of Conflict Analysis and Resolution, earning honors as an advanced practitioner in conflict analysis and resolution, an MA in conflict resolution from the Department of Conflict Resolution at Antioch University McGregor, and a BA in political science with a minor in women's studies from Miami University, Oxford, Ohio.

Sandra Marker was a sociology graduate student and a research assistant at the University of Colorado's Conflict Research Consortium when she wrote the essay included in this book. She is currently an associate professor of sociology at Black Hills State University.

Rose-Anne Moore is a founding partner of PoleStar Partners, an independent consulting firm, and serves on the board of Mediators Beyond Borders International (MBBI). She is cochair of MBBI's membership engagement committee and board liaison to the Climate Change project. A strategist-turned-ethicist, Ms. Moore is a certified mediator and an experienced executive in both corporate and not-for-profit arenas, with particular expertise in development book editing, business ethics, marketing strategy, interfaith dialog, and website usability. She holds a BA in classics from Williams College, an MBA in marketing and management policy from the Kellogg School at Northwestern University, and an MAR in ethics from Yale Divinity School. She is fluent in English and French.

Prabha Sankaranarayan is the president and CEO of Mediators Beyond Borders, an international nongovernmental organization whose mission is to build local skills for peace and promote mediation worldwide. She is a conflict transformation practitioner who has mediated, facilitated, and trained in Europe, Asia, Africa, and the United States. Her public and private sector work includes conflict analysis for public/private partnerships; consultation and assessment for industrial development zones; design and implementation of trainings for multinational corporations; interfaith dialogs; and facilitation of multistakeholder mediations. Sankaranarayan is actively involved in regional, national, and international civic activities focused on civil liberties, sexual violence prevention, conflict mitigation and mediation, and the recovery and rehabilitation of trauma survivors (Board of the American Civil Liberties Union Pittsburgh, past president of the Pennsylvania Coalition Against Rape and CONTACT Pittsburgh). She is an adjunct professor at Washington & Jefferson College. She trains and delivers presentations (nationally and internationally) on the impact of family and community violence, the intersection of trauma and peacebuilding, restorative justice, conflict resolution, mediation, and transitional justice. She speaks English, Tamil, and Hindi.

Malik Thompson hails from Washington, DC, and works at Wilson High School in Rochester, New York, on behalf of the M. K. Gandhi Institute for Nonviolence, supporting the school's restorative initiatives by mediating conflicts and helping students navigate personal/interpersonal conflicts. They also do workshops throughout the Rochester community on nonviolent communication, cultural humility, and other aspects of nonviolence for community groups of all ages. In their free time, Malik enjoys reading, writing, photography, and dance.

Index